War Bird Ace

Number Eight
C. A. Brannen Series

WAR BIRD ACE

The Great War Exploits of Capt. Field E. Kindley

Jack Stokes Ballard

Texas A&M University Press · College Station

First edition

The paper used in this book meets the minimum requirements of the American National Standard for Permanence of Paper for Printed Library Materials, Z39.48-1984.
Binding materials have been chosen for durability.

Library of Congress Cataloging-in-Publication Data

Ballard, Jack S.
War bird ace : the Great War exploits of Capt. Field E. Kindley / Jack Stokes Ballard. — 1st ed.
p. cm. — (C.A. Brannen series ; no. 8)
Includes bibliographical references and index.
ISBN-13: 978-1-58544-554-7 (cloth : alk. paper)
ISBN-10: 1-58544-554-1 (cloth : alk. paper)
1. Kindley, Field Eugene, 1896-1920. 2. United States. Army. Aero Squadron, 148th. 3. World War, 1914-1918—Aerial operations, American. 4. World War, 1914-1918—Regimental histories—United States. 5. World War, 1914-1918—Campaigns—France. 6. Fighter pilots—United States—Biography. I. Title.
D606.B36 2007
940.4'4973092—dc22
[B] 2006021612

THERE ARE ONLY TWO WAYS LEFT NOW

OF WINNING THE WAR,

AND THEY BOTH BEGIN WITH A.

ONE IS AEROPLANES

AND THE OTHER IS AMERICA.

—Winston Churchill, Munitions Ministry,
September 1917

Contents

Foreword

Jack Ballard's *War Bird Ace* chronicles the exploits of one of America's great, and relatively unknown, World War I aces. The fourth-ranking air ace of World War I, Kindley was killed in an air crash at only twenty-three years of age.

Author Jack Ballard grew up in Gravette, Arkansas, Kindley's hometown, and for many years was fascinated by the exploits of the young air ace. A former member of the history faculty at the U.S. Air Force Academy and a historian in the Office of Air Force History in Washington, D.C., Ballard found that his intensive research into Kindley's life and exploits was frequently interrupted by his own career requirements. Nonetheless, he continued his effort over the years, and it is a tribute to his perseverance that he succeeded not only in completing this biography, but in placing Kindley appropriately within the historical context of the times. There is a kind of romanticism to Kindley's brief story, for it chronicles the maturity and successes of a high-school dropout who became a leader of men. The reader will be immersed in the heroics and tragedy of the Great War and in the end left to wonder what might have become of this bright, talented young man. Jack Ballard has succeeded in bringing Capt. Field Kindley's story alive once again.

Herman S. Wolk, Senior Historian,
Office of Air Force History

Preface

New books and articles about World War I, the so-called "Great War" and the "War to End All Wars," continue to appear. To the historian, more information seems to materialize even when the subject appears to have reached a state of exhaustion. Clearly, new interpretations and insights come from renewed examination of old accounts, data, and concepts. The new publications illustrate the well-known axiom that profit can be derived from continual analysis of the past. Such is the case with this biography of the little-known Capt. Field E. Kindley, a World War I air ace. His life story, including his first published family correspondence, offers some new thoughts about World War I. Tracing the exploits of this young aerial warrior deepens our understanding of this first worldwide conflict, the heroic actions of many men, and especially the beginning of war in the air.

The term "Great War" sounds strange when placed beside other major wars later in the twentieth century, such as World War II. To the individuals living during that period, however, it was truly a global war, one that fully engulfed the United States. Through a series of events leading to the U.S. declaration of war in 1917, especially submarine attacks on U.S. ships, high emotions built up, accompanied by a patriotic fervor not seen in many years. The actions of a relatively obscure Arkansas lad who joined this fight, and the process through which he evolved into a leading air ace, provide insight as to how individual Americans responded to the war and what motivated them to do battle in distant France. Kindley's letters reveal a driving force to join in the patriotic struggle against the Germans, or "Huns," as they were frequently called. While this account is one man's reaction to a world at war, it typifies the actions of many, particularly those who volunteered to serve in the American Air Service. One can begin to grasp what prompted these young men to put their lives on the line and caused them to do some incredible deeds. In that way, Kindley serves to ably represent a generation.

John Morrow, in his book *German Air Power in World War I,* states that World War I aviation accounts fall basically into three categories:

the experiences of individuals, warplane technical works, and more general histories of ground and air operations. He goes on to find fault with each of these separate groupings. Morrow argues that some heroic individual works and more especially general military histories often left the impression "that the air war was peripheral and thus essentially unimportant" and that the air arm was relegated to the role of "providing heroes to raise the morale of soldiers and civilians."[1] Another aviation historian, John Cuneo, declared that "the personalized stories of individual experiences and feats, while furnishing exciting reading, provide little or no clue to the over-all importance of the air weapon in battle or to the overall strategy or tactics of a battle in which the air weapon played a part."[2]

Certainly this biography of Capt. Field E. Kindley falls into Morrow's first category and Cuneo's "personalized stories of individual experiences." While Kindley's wartime and immediate postwar exploits established him as the fourth-ranking American air ace and a war hero, and provided a heroic example for others, his life story also enters into the problem of balance pinpointed by Morrow's and Cuneo's remarks. Kindley's many detailed efforts in ground support operations in 1918, although agreeably small in the big picture, assist in countering, at least to some degree, the claimed peripheral and unimportant role of aviation in World War I. Throughout this biography, then, one objective has been to maintain a middle course between the general military analysts, who virtually ignore the role of airpower, and the aviation enthusiasts, who see and describe only that element of World War I.

Still considering balance, the Kindley story provides an engrossing account of the American role with the British forces, a needed correction to the heavily weighted historical coverage of Americans flying and fighting in the French sector of the Western Front. As one would expect, air and ground training, tactics and strategy, organization, and attitudes differed between the French and British. Capt. Field Kindley experienced and absorbed British ways. In addition, the two British-area American squadrons, the 148th and 17th, never received the attention that their record merited. Kindley and his colleagues in those units felt they suffered discrimination in this respect. The squadron histories complained of their relative lack of recognition. Kindley, in particular, embarked in the postwar period on a campaign to rectify what he thought were inequities in awarding decorations to pilots of the 148th and 17th. Perhaps all combat organizations feel they never receive their due, but clearly the 148th and 17th Aero Squadrons flying under Royal Air Force command deserve more exposure, and the Kindley tale provides one means to do so.

While many combatants perform heroic deeds anonymously, there seems to be some injustice when such a high-ranking American air ace as Field Kindley remains largely an unknown figure. Even in the early twenty-first century, some Americans easily recognize the name of Eddie Rickenbacker, the American ace of aces from World War I. Some can also remember individuals such as Billy Mitchell, Baron von Richthofen (the Red Baron), Raoul Lufbery, Hobey Baker, and Frank Luke, making the association with World War I flying aces, heroes, and so-called knights of the air. These names conjure up romanticized images of daring, aircraft-to-aircraft combat in flimsy-looking, open-cockpit planes. Few people nowadays, however, recognize the name of Field E. Kindley or make any meaningful association with that name. Kindley's relative obscurity may be understandable given his extremely short life; he was killed at the age of twenty-three. Yet his flying experiences and his wartime and postwar accomplishments made for action-packed years that reveal volumes of what World War I aviation and the immediate postwar aviation were like. The flying men of early aviation tended to be courageous, colorful, and notably individualistic persons bent on proving something either to themselves or to the general public. Field Kindley's experience as a flier was very much in the mode of individual self-discovery, so that he brought a unique personality to his aerial combat over the trenches in France.

Just as in the 1986 Hollywood film starring Tom Cruise, we seek explanations for *Top Gun*–style flying and Kindley parlayed a humble background into the status of a World War I "Top Gun." He stood tall with many American aerial combatants and other pilots credited with German victories. He garnered this high status through a potent combination of special character traits and acquired skills in a notably hazardous technological advance that allowed man to indeed soar through the sky. Kindley's progress to becoming an outstanding aviator and aerial warrior thus begs for analysis and study.

Kindley's life should be examined for still another important reason. His evolution from a small-town boy and high-school dropout to flight leader and squadron commander provides a lesson in leadership. How could this young man compete with his many college-educated colleagues, a considerable percentage of them Ivy Leaguers? That he did rise to command aerial squadrons brings focus on critical attributes of leaders. It is obvious that courage remained a constant when dealing with flying the early aircraft and then engaging in aerial combat, but many other skills and character traits became necessary. Kindley's time in the Air Service and his postwar air races provided examples of hard work, decisiveness, loyalty, care for colleagues and subordinates, foresight, determination, and modesty. His solid, outstanding character plus his noted accomplishments in downing German aircraft earned respect from almost everyone. Additionally, his country charm made him well liked and admired. Kindley's emergence as a leader thereby proves an interesting examination.

Due to Kindley's reputation in shooting down twelve German planes from June through October 1918, and to this top-ranking air ace's decision to remain in the Air Service after the war, he did earn a hearing for his thoughts on postwar U.S. air policy. Certainly he did not have the stature of a Gen. Billy Mitchell, nor did he achieve Mitchell's impact, but he did speak his mind in "lessons learned" reports and in testimony before a congressional committee after the war.

Interestingly, Kindley's comments seem very direct, even critical in tone, and vigorously presented, despite his being known as a modest, charming gentleman. His advocacy for a cabinet-level Department of Air that would encompass civil and military aviation and combine Army and Navy aviation may have gained him enemies that affected his postwar career. Still, he had the courage to express his opinions, and he strongly believed he was right.

Technical aspects of aircraft, flying, and World War I warfare have not been emphasized in this biography of Kindley. Still, the descriptions of the aerial combat—derived largely from family letters, flight logs, combat reports, diaries, and newspapers—provide examples of the development of important tactics and strategies. Some of these, such as the beginning of formation flying, had continuing impact on air doctrine. Also, Captain Kindley's experience in ground support aerial operations against retreating German forces gives a glimpse of significant future aircraft roles.

Kindley's participation in air races in the postwar years shows that aviation pioneers sensed that flying needed to be kept before the public if aviation progress was to be made. Both military and civilian authorities saw air races as an impetus for development of airports and air routes, and for technical advances in engines, navigation, and overall safety. This postwar activity constituted an important part of Kindley's life, and he managed to make it exciting.

The memorial statement, probably read on the evening of Kindley's fatal crash, notes that "the history of Captain Kindley can be written briefly, but in that brief history there are volumes of deeds." Certainly true! From childhood, through narrow escapes in air training accidents, to fierce dogfights against some of Germany's best pilots, and extending through postwar air race incidents, Captain Kindley's short life was replete with amazing exploits. His life story illustrates how certain individuals respond to life-or-death challenges, and not always in time of war. In more recent times, when anti-hero or non-hero attitudes seem to hold sway, a renewed examination of what makes people do what they do, in most desperate situations, proves profitable and indeed inspirational. And man will forever need inspiration.

Throughout this biography the actual words of Kindley and his family and associates speak clearly from the times, and for this reason the book includes many quotations. Also, the quoted letters tell the very human side of a war hero, allowing the character and personality of the man to emerge. Spelling in period documents, particularly in Kindley's letters, has been normalized to enhance the flow of the narrative.

Providing accurate documentation of the information given in the text has been an important goal. Obviously, the serious reader of historical material wants to know the sources, but especially in the case of Kindley's biography, it is necessary to correct a great many errors that can be found in most of the extremely brief accounts of his life. Many discrepancies originated with newspaper articles and then were frequently repeated in periodicals and essays. There continues to be a problem with World War I data, as statistical arguments arise depending on the compiler's perspective. A good example has been the ranking of Captain Kindley as an air ace. A number of sources list him as the fifth-ranking air ace when they include Lt. Raoul Lufbery. The U.S. Air Force in its official document on aces considers Kindley the fourth-ranking American air ace of World War I because Lufbery is grouped with those of the Lafayette Escadrille and its historic support of French aerial operations. There are other seeming conflicts in victory credits and other data.

Many individuals have contributed to this work, and this indebtedness can never be fully recognized appropriately. However, special thanks for their assistance go to Herman Wolk; Andy Parks and Steve Lawson of the Lafayette Foundation, Denver; Marilyn Chang, Jean Armstrong, John Bond, and Ray Casperson of the Wings Over the Rockies Museum Library; Derald Linn of the Arkansas Air Museum at Drake Field, Fayetteville; and the gracious staffs of the Denver Public Library, the University of Denver Library, the Special Collections Division of the University of Arkansas Library, and the Field Kindley Memorial High School in Coffeyville, Kansas. My wife and Robin Vidimos have provided editorial suggestions. I am glad to acknowledge that all have strengthened the research and improved the writing of Kindley's story.

Jack Ballard,
Centennial, Colorado

Chapter One

The Early Years

[A] dream of mine has come true.

I have repaid my government

for the expense of training me

and made Gravette one of the first 12 towns

in America to get a Hun airman.

Lt. Field E. Kindley,
letter to Uther Kindley,
June 28, 1918

THE UNITED STATES declared war on Kaiser Wilhelm II's Germany on April 6, 1917, becoming a "Johnny come lately" in a war that had been raging since 1914 between Great Britain, France, and Russia (the chief Allies) against Germany, Austria-Hungary, and Turkey (the principal Central Powers). By the spring of 1917, the worldwide conflict with its deadly new weapons, such as the machine gun, produced heavy casualties in mass attacks by troops on both sides. As a consequence, the war ground to a stalemate on the Western Front, the German-French boundary. From the English Channel to the Alps, trench warfare dominated. Troops endured horrible living conditions, punctuated by killing artillery barrages and gas attacks. Occasional probing advances from one trench line to another, across the barbed wire entanglements, resulted in an ever increasing malaise of depressing futility. The personnel losses and the conflict's impact on economies of the warring powers appeared to reduce the

Allies and the Central Powers to a point of near exhaustion in their respective war efforts.

America's sympathy for the Allied cause grew as the war continued. Starting with a loudly proclaimed neutrality, public opinion shifted steadily to Allied favor, helped along by German actions in Belgium and most important, German submarine attacks on Allied shipping. The highly publicized attacks on American ships, some of which were sunk, increasingly angered many in the United States. The Spring 1917 German resumption of unrestricted submarine warfare, followed by the sinking of three American vessels and the revelation of the Zimmerman Note,[1] pushed the American people, the Woodrow Wilson administration, and Congress to the point of war. Although woefully unprepared to do so, the United States entered World War I in April 1917.

American awareness of the horrors of trench warfare and tragic submarine sinkings failed to dampen patriotic fervor. When President Woodrow Wilson asked Congress to make the United States a co-belligerent with the Allies against the European Central Powers, the request ignited a general and positive national response, which one contemporary news report characterized as "exaggerated exhilaration." Throughout the country, young men rushed to volunteer for military duty. Enlistment stations became inundated with applicants.

Woodrow Wilson coupled idealistic goals with his war message to Congress. "America is privileged to spend her blood and her might for the principles that gave birth and happiness and the peace which she has treasured," he stated. "The right is more precious than peace, and we shall fight for the things which we have always carried nearest to our hearts—for democracy, for the right of those who submit to authority to have a voice in their own governments"[2] Quickly the national rallying cries became "the war to end all wars," "making the world safe for democracy," and "we won't come home till it's over, over there."[3] No doubt this idealistic touch influenced many young men to readily volunteer their services in the war effort. Even in 2005, a 103-year-old World War I veteran, Lloyd Brown, living in Charlotte Hall, Maryland, shared a Memorial Day remembrance: "Everybody was patriotic, everybody wanted to join" and "those who joined were local heroes, well-received on the public streets." Brown added it didn't hurt that men in uniform "were popular with the girls."[4]

One young man in Coffeyville, Kansas, a relatively recent transplant from Arkansas, like so many others throughout the country, responded to the call to arms. Field Eugene Kindley, age twenty-one, a part owner ("proprietor")[5] and operator of the Drexel movie theater in Coffeyville, established himself, by all reports, as a very successful entrepreneur in that city close to the border with Oklahoma. In his brief time in that community, associates and friends remembered him "as a decisive person, quick of movement and unhesitating in decision," and extremely patriotic, reported the *Coffeyville* [Kansas] *Journal*.[6] Hardly a month after the declaration of war, Field Kindley began considering military service. After weighing several options, including becoming an officer versus serving as an enlisted man, he applied for a commission as an officer in the Field Artillery Officers' Reserve Corps on May 1, 1917.[7] As part of the application requirements, he collected letters of recommendation which he solicited from friends and acquaintances in the community. One letter, from the advertising manager of Coffeyville's *Daily Earth,* read in part, "He has been in business for himself in this city for the last two years and during that time he has established an enviable reputation for honesty and success."[8] This comment and newspaper notices concerning his military service clearly indicate that Kindley had made his mark in Coffeyville life.

Kindley's application received an endorsed approval card, signed by a major in the cavalry, on the same day, May 1, 1917. The endorsement, addressed to the commanding officer of Fort Riley, Kansas, stated, "The Board is of the opinion that the applicant has the physical, moral and professional qualifications required of a candidate Infantry Officers' Reserve Corps." While Kindley's intentions for serving as an officer in the field artillery became service in the infantry, as sometimes happens in volunteering for military duty, he faced an even more daunting situation. He officially had to enlist before he could start his officer's schooling. Perhaps not at all comforting, his Enlistment Record of May 10, 1917, showed he was grade "Private," and he enlisted for six years.[9]

Several days later, "Private" Kindley, along with some other men from Coffeyville, arrived at the old Great Plains Army post of Fort Riley, Kansas, near the town of Junction City. He reported for duty to Company A of the Third Regiment of the Kansas National Guard. After the usual physical examination and a typhoid shot, he received his allotment of uniforms and army gear. After thus being appropriately equipped, Kindley trained, drilled, and marched. Before long, he decided he really didn't like infantry life.

Private Field E. Kindley, age twenty-one, outside a barracks building at Fort Riley, Kansas, 1917
Kindley family photo

A defining moment occurred while he was looking for other options. Bruce Bentley, one of Kindley's barracks buddies and later a Coffeyville businessman, recalled that "the tall, slender" Kindley read a Fort Riley bulletin board notice about the Air Service and the need for "anyone who had the desire to fly." Kindley reportedly snapped his fingers and said, "That is what I'm going to be."[10] Wasting little time, he requested a transfer to the Air Service. Approval came quickly, and by authority of a letter dated August 11, 1917, from Headquarters Central Department, Field E. Kindley was ordered to be honorably discharged from the Kansas National Guard "to enlist in the Aviation Section, Signal Enlisted Reserve Corps."[11] He first received an honorable discharge from his Officers Training Camp, 14th Provisional Training Regiment, on 14 August, and his National Guard discharge became official August 16. Kindley successfully moved from his disliked infantry duty, but he retained his enlisted status. And he would have to wait impatiently for what seemed to him an interminable period before receiving his officer's commission. At least he had in hand Special Order 119, July 6,

Field Kindley studying field map, Fort Riley, Kansas, 1917
Kindley family photo

An Air Service recruiting poster from 1917, appealing for young men to join the U.S. Air Service

Photo courtesy Littleton Historical Museum, Littleton, Colo.

1917, directing him to proceed to Champaign, Illinois, for aviation ground school training at the University of Illinois.

Before departing Kansas, Kindley spent a weekend with friends in Coffeyville. Kindley said, according to a newspaper report at the time, "that all Coffeyville men at Ft. Riley are doing fine and he believes that all will be able to 'stick' when the weeding out process is begun." The newspaper account also noted that Field E. Kindley of the Drexel Theater "had been a member of the officers reserve training camp at Ft. Riley for several weeks past and recently obtained a transfer to the aviation section, successfully passing the examination." Kindley told the reporter that after his training he could well be in France by Christmas time.[12]

While that timing proved overly optimistic, Kindley eagerly approached his aviation training and eventual deployment to the Western Front in France. Pleasantly, he left infantry training behind and embarked on his new adventure, which he fully expected would be exciting and far from the mundane routine he seemed to dread. Little did he grasp, however, what lay ahead—harrowing escapes in death-defying airplane crashes and fierce aerial combat, leading to the exalted status of an air ace.

While patriotism appears to have been the main factor in Field Kindley's volunteering for World War I military service and boredom with infantry schooling seems to have led to his decision to try the Air Service, his full motivation for stepping into the cockpit of early-day aircraft remains unclear. This young man from the Arkansas Ozarks knew little or nothing about aviation, although he indicated in his aviation application that he had made several flights as a passenger.[13] Considering his background, he could only naively guess at the demands flying would place on him physically and mentally. In addition, he lacked attributes often associated with developing flying skills, such as a strong mechanical bent or a fearless tendency to recklessness or thrill seeking. Quite the contrary, in his youthful days, he hardly appeared especially adventuresome or to have a particular drive to prove himself or to prove himself to others.

He often made his decisions with a thoughtful and calm process. One characteristic stood out, however; he always seemed open to making changes in his life. Kindley undoubtedly knew the many dangers to life and limb in flying, and thus his desire to get into the air remains a considerable mystery.

Kindley's written record, letters, logs, and action reports, provide precious little insight as to his emotions and thoughts. As historian Joseph J. Ellis comments about the young George Washington in his book *His Excellency,* Washington wrote about his actions and not about his thinking. In a similar vein, Field Kindley recorded what he did and not his reflections on what he experienced. As a consequence, one can only surmise and raise questions about a number of his life events.

Field E. Kindley was born March 13, 1896, the only child of George C. and Ella Spraker Kindley. The birth took place on a farm by Little Sugar Creek, about four miles northeast of Bentonville, Arkansas, and not far from the town of Pea Ridge, the site of a Civil War battle by that name. The Kindleys, originally from Germany, lived on a farm in Conrad Hill Township, Davidson County, North Carolina, but Field's grandfather, Cyrus Kindley, and his wife's folks, the Lambeth family, headed west in May 1851. They moved first to Searcy, Arkansas, and then on to the northwest Arkansas farm in 1854. Inexperienced in log house building, Cyrus Kindley bought a double log house with a 50-foot-long porch. The house on 500 acres of land overlooked a beautiful little valley that was the route of a stagecoach; Field's grandmother, Cyntha, served meals to stagecoach passengers.

Field's father was born June 21, 1865, in a church building in Marionville, Missouri, because the family fled the Arkansas farm when it was overrun by the opposing Civil War armies. The Kindley place served as the location of Confederate Camp Stephens in July 1861, and the battle of Pea Ridge, one of the most significant west of the Mississippi River, occurred nearby on March 7 and 8, 1862.

Area residents, like the Kindleys, at times took women and children to safer locations; the men then hid in the fields, hollows, and caves. Warring troops confiscated crops, household goods, and buildings. Besides the flying "minnie" balls, a cannon ball lodged in the Kindley roof at one time and danger lurked from raids by bushwhackers and incursions by marauding Indians from the not too distant Indian Territory. No doubt Field heard stories about how his grandfather took the family to the cellar and then ran to the barn to get a pick to dig them out in case the fireplace chimney toppled and closed the entrance. At another time, grandfather Cyrus was captured, beaten, and tied to a tree by bushwhackers but was later found alive and freed.

George C. Kindley, Field's father, at about age seventeen

Kindley family photo

Young Field Kindley looking over the shoulder of his Aunt Emma Kindley, in a photograph taken shortly after his mother's death

Kindley family photo

After the war ended in 1865, the family returned to the Pea Ridge home. Such Civil War experiences branded the Kindleys as hardy pioneers and determined settlers, and this constituted an important part of Field Kindley's heritage.

On July 5, 1894, Field's father, George Cephus Kindley, the Civil War child, married Ella Frances Spraker at Pea Ridge. Both served as schoolteachers in Indian Territory, now Oklahoma. Fate would not be kind to the couple despite momentary happiness with the birth of son Field. On November 28, 1898, at the age of twenty-nine, Ella Spraker Kindley became ill and died. Field, two and one half years old, thus barely knew his mother. This family tragedy, as might be expected, had a great impact on Field's future, and he subsequently suffered other losses of mother figures in his early life.

After the death of his mother, Cyntha Ann Lambeth Kindley, Field's paternal, widowed grandmother and an aunt, Emma Kindley, largely cared for the toddler.

They still lived on what was often known as "Kindley Hill" on Little Sugar Creek. Grandmother Kindley spent forty-five years on the Kindley farm, and she became well known in the community as a "generous and loving neighbor, devoted to her family, and possessing unusual physical and mental ability."[14] But another family blow occurred when grandmother Kindley died on July 2, 1900, and was interred in the Kindley Hill cemetery. Once again, Field Kindley suffered a close family loss but he, nevertheless, had been briefly, but strongly, influenced by a Kindley family stalwart.

The young boy soon experienced further family complications when his father received an appointment as an education supervisor in the Philippine Islands. George C. Kindley sailed to the islands, leaving Field shuttling between aunts in Bentonville–Pea Ridge and an uncle in the nearby town of Gravette. When Field was seven, his father asked that he join him in the Philippines and that he be accompanied there by his future stepmother, Mabel Hall. This surprising, long summer journey across half of the United States and then the broad Pacific must have been an eye-opening experience for young Field, not only in a geographic sense but also in getting to know his future stepmother. Immediately after their arrival, the marriage of George Kindley and Mabel Hall occurred on August 20, 1903. However, the marriage didn't last, and Mabel Hall, for reasons unknown, returned to the United States. Thus, another major interruption in stable family life developed for the young Field.[15]

A rare photograph of Field Kindley during his time with his father in the Philippines. Field went to the islands at age seven and returned to the United States at age twelve.
Kindley family photo

In a letter to his older brother "Bob" in Gravette, Field's father provided some insight as to his life in the Philippines. Noting that he had heard his brother had been ill, he had an answer:

> You folks have too many good things to eat and get dispepsia. Come to the Philippines where there is nothing to eat. Day before yesterday I went from 6 o'clock P.M. to 8 o'clock P.M. yesterday without anything at all but a cup of coffee, a potato, and a pineapple. This was 26 hours. I did not feel one bit discomfortable about it either. When I got home at 7 and got supper at 8 I then sat up and read and worked, (office work) until 2 o'clock the next morning. Got up at 5:30 feeling fine and went to work again. It is not at all unknown for me to eat only one meal a

> day. Of course I feel fine most all the time. It may have a bad effect some time, I find that if I am at all in doubt just about how I shall feel tomorrow I take an exercise of deep breathing and quinine. I take a small amount of quinine most every week. When out riding I straighten up in the saddle and take about seven deep breaths most every time I think of it. I forgot to state that the day I did not eat much I rode about 35 miles from 5:30 in the morning to 7 P.M.[16]

Field Kindley spent five years, ages seven to twelve, in the Philippines with his father. These were no doubt very important formative years, but little is known about his life there. Presumably his schoolteacher father either taught his son or ensured he received an education in the schools he served. Field may have been in the Manila area for a while, but later his father became superintendent of schools for Bukidnon Province, Malaybalay, in north-central Mindanao Island, and near the end of his father's time in the Philippines he was superintendent of an agricultural school in Pili, near Naga, in southern Luzon Island.[17] Apparently, Field learned and absorbed Philippine culture, as he indicated on one of his many military service forms that he had Tagalog language skills.[18] Whatever educational progress young Field made, however, his father decided to send him back to the United States to further his education there.

So at age twelve Field returned, accompanied by one of his father's friends, to live with his uncle, A. E. Kindley, in Gravette, Arkansas.

Uncle Amos Erastus (Bob) Kindley, the seventh child of Cyrus and Cyntha, and older brother of George, served as a justice of peace in Benton County, Arkansas (1892), and as assessor (1894). In 1898 he moved to the small and new railroad town of Gravette where he helped establish the Bank of Gravett[19] and where he served as bank cashier until his death in 1915. A. E. Kindley became a strong and noted promoter of the Bank of Gravett and a community booster.

The *Gravette News Herald* of September 5, 1919, observed the bank was "behind the earliest steps in the city's progress, in aiding many farmers and others to get financial footing—and in all this the first cashier and manager 'Bob' (as friends kindly remember him) was the moving spirit. Mr. Kindley was recognized as one of the state's leading financiers and his management of the bank was such as to ensure him a perpetual position for years hence."[20]

Uncle Amos Erastus "Bob" Kindley at about age sixteen. Bob and his wife Mollie provided a supportive family for Field during his teen years.
Kindley family photo

Respected citizen A. E. Kindley married Mary Elizabeth (Mollie) Cliburn in 1895. They had nine children and lived in an imposing brick home near the Gravette school. Field Kindley suddenly became a part of this large family and later stated that his time with Aunt Mollie was his happiest.[21] Field developed a close relationship with Uncle Bob and Aunt Mollie's son Uther and daughter Lena. Lena had married but also lived in Gravette, so Field found it convenient to visit and spend time with her. Lena remembered how Field helped her husband, Herman Chatfield, "straighten out the yard" around a new house that her husband had just built.[22] Field, however, wrote most of his letters from England and France to Uther. Also, he would likely have roomed with him at the Kindley house while in Gravette. Uther, four years older than Field, apparently was the "brother" and companion that Field missed and probably needed. Field's teenage years proved relatively uneventful and were typical of the youth at that time. He attended Gravette High School, less than a block from the Kindley house. Not an outstanding student, he achieved grades that were only slightly above average. During the years 1911 and 1912, for example, he received two grades of A–, two grades of B, and seven grades of C, with no particular strengths in any area including math or the sciences. Furthermore, his grades slipped somewhat through the year 1912.[23] As was relatively easy in a small town and a relatively small school, he made himself known by participation in stage plays (he acted in the high school play "Hearts and Diamonds" in May 1913).[24] He also played baseball and basketball, but he failed to star in any of these activities. During the years 1911–12, he played as a forward on the Gravette High School basketball team, and he pitched on the baseball team during the season of 1911.[25]

Field, by all reports, socialized easily, relating well with fellow teens and adults. One of his female friends commented that Field was always very congenial and adept at making small talk. "Conversation never lagged with him," she remarked, as he walked her home.[26] While Field apparently courted the local girls, he was not remembered as having a strong romance with any of his classmates or other girls in the community. Appropriate for the times, he did engage in the local Presbyterian church box socials and school picnics.[27] It should not be forgotten that Field had a background, and an educational experience, unlike any of his Arkansas relatives and contemporaries. He had traveled west across half the United States and then spent years in a very different land. Little wonder that he might have much to talk about and to a much interested audience.

Like most young people, the blonde (turning to brown), blue-eyed Field could not escape small-town scrutiny. He was merely average in physique, as one town resident commented: "Field Kindley was just a gangling tow-headed kid when he first came here, a very shy boy."[28] By the time he left the town of Gravette, however, he had attained a height of 5 feet, 11 inches and a weight of 145 pounds, and he had largely lost any shyness.[29] He possessed that "clean cut" appearance and townspeople considered him a "sharp dresser." Along with his generally handsome "good looks," many noted his modest, unassuming manner and consistently responsible behavior.[30]

He ably projected a country charm that played a considerable part in his subsequent business success in Coffeyville and his advancement to Air Service leadership positions. Those who knew Field Kindley during his late teen years most often remarked that "Field was just a good boy, just as good as gold" and that "everyone liked Field."[31]

Field Kindley during his teen years in Gravette, Arkansas. He was remembered as a "sharp dresser" and handsome and "clean cut" in appearance.
Kindley family photo

Because of his later prowess with aircraft and aircraft-mounted machine guns, one might have suspected that Field had a mechanical bent or had been a gun handler and marksman. He apparently did not participate in local quail, rabbit, or squirrel hunts, unlike many of the other relatively rural, youthful male residents, and townspeople did not remember him as being involved with firearms.[32] Likewise, he didn't seem to demonstrate any particular mechanical interest or aptitude. When asked if he had any technical knowledge, in his Aviation Section "Examination of Applicants," he replied, "The candidate has had experience with a car, motorcycle, and also electrical experience about a picture show." He further amplified, in response to a specific question, that he had "no theoretical knowledge of a gasoline motor," but he could make minor repairs and adjustments to a motor car and motorcycle.[33]

Toward his later teens, Field made deliveries for Joe Witty's Grocery Store on the south side of Gravette's Main Street[34] and then became the projectionist at a movie theater on the north side of Main. Here he wrestled with cranky machines, warped reels, and film breaks. His voice, heard in the darkened theater, saying "one moment please," brought him a degree of notoriety.[35] It was perhaps this job experience that led him to leave school before graduating and to later become successful with the Drexel Theater in Coffeyville. Early on, Field showed interest in commercial enterprise, taking bookkeeping in high school and securing jobs of an assorted nature. When questioned on his aviation application as to what he possessed that would stand as "the equivalent of two years' college education," he wrote, "business experience in the past five years."[36]

With likely despair and displeasure from his father in the Philippines and Gravette relatives, Field withdrew from Gravette High School and thus did not graduate. The reasons for concluding his formal education remain uncertain. As noted, he actively sought various community jobs and he obtained hands-on business experience by operating and managing a movie theater or a so-called "picture show."

It is doubtful that Field suffered notably for lack of money, with both his uncle and his father economically well positioned; therefore, personal interest in being gainfully employed seems more likely a factor in his job seeking. At this same time, Field's reaching manhood while living with his uncle's large and also maturing family may have told him it was time to be on his own. Additionally, Field through his youthful experience of moving about, even halfway across the world, demonstrated very early that he was not reticent in trying new things and undertaking new endeavors. After dropping out of high school, even though he was near to finishing, Field left Gravette to search for a job. Field and one of his pals, Charles Kenney, went to Kansas City together seeking employment. Mr. Kenney recalled how they both made applications at one large bank, Fidelity Trust Company, and Field's application was rejected on the grounds that "you write too good a hand and you wouldn't stay with us for the money we could pay you."[37] Subsequent to the try at bank work, no doubt influenced by Uncle Bob's banking involvement, Field spent some months as a traveling salesman working out of Kansas City.[38] He soon tired of this occupation and before long ended up in Coffeyville with his own business, the Drexel Theater. The choice of Coffeyville occurred because a Kindley cousin, E. E. Kindley, located in that area and Field seized an opportunity to put his Gravette movie theater skills to immediate use.[39]

Little in Field Kindley's early years provided clear indicators that he would emerge as an aviation leader and consummate aerial combat tactician. In fact, he seemed to have strikes against him. His turbulent early life of losing, in relatively rapid succession, the key caregivers—his mother, grandmother, father, stepmother, and father again—would have doomed many individuals. He received an education but failed to graduate from high school. He had a small-town identity but failed to demonstrate any particular excellence. He wasn't lazy, but he did not show any outstanding initiative. He displayed business acumen but left that behind to enter military service and volunteer for aviation, something for which he outwardly seemed to lack aptitude.

At the same time character traits surfaced that were to be Field Kindley's future strengths. His travel to and from the Philippines provided a worldly, cosmopolitan background and outlook unlike most of his contemporaries and thereby fortified a courage to face unknown challenges. Despite his key early development years with his grandmother, later with his father in the Philippines, and with crucial support from his uncle's family in his teens, Field never seemed anchored to one location or one family unit; indeed, he felt neither reluctance nor fear to move to another adventure. This trait undoubtedly served him well in his numerous military assignments. Throughout, he possessed a learning curiosity that propelled him through unusual times and events. Congenial and talkative, after perhaps some initial shyness, he communicated an easygoing, genuine, modest, unassuming persona that charmed his acquaintances and friends.

Beneath this likeable, even gentlemanly aura, however, was an unusual toughness and determination that was once evident in the Civil War Kindleys. Such resolve could and did lead to an unassuming, methodical fighter pilot who would doggedly pursue an enemy aircraft, ensuring one victory after another.

Even though our knowledge of Kindley's early years is limited, his experiences growing up provide a key to understanding his later heroics and his World War I and postwar reputation as a great flyer. So with Kindley's youthful period established, his maturation to pilot and aviation leader begins.

Chapter Two

Training for the Big Show

"I'm feeling pretty much at home in the air now. But after doing very many vertical banks I feel rather sick and dizzy. If to-morrow is a good day, I am going up to ten thousand and shut off and spin down and see what happens. I am quite good at spinning but it makes me a little sick. I guess I'll get over that, tho, and I think a lot of it is due to the castor oil from the motor."

John MacGavock Grider,
American flying cadet in England, diary entry, from Grider,
War Birds: Diary of an Unknown Aviator, 66–67

THE EXACT DATE when Cadet Field Kindley arrived at the campus of the University of Illinois at Champaign-Urbana cannot be determined, although it was probably in early July 1917. It no doubt was the first time he had visited a major university, and certainly he must have been impressed and perhaps eager to explore this new environment. His time there, however, was not to be a relaxed introduction to academia. The School of Military Aeronautics, established to provide ground training for World War I pilots, required long hours and concentrated study.

The School of Military Aeronautics at the University of Illinois was one of eight such schools located at major universities. Others were located at the Massachusetts Institute of Technology, Cornell University, Ohio State University, University of Texas, University of

California, Princeton University, and Georgia Institute of Technology. The Air Service chose these universities for aviation ground schools because the scattered flying bases were overwhelmed and incapable of accommodating the quick bolstering of the pilot ranks. The Air Service rightly considered that the very few existing bases at the start of the war had their hands full with flying and crew training as the war build-up continued.[1]

Field, like other cadets, found that the eight weeks of ground school, with intensive instruction in a wide range of subjects from aeronautical engines to telegraphy, began with practical, hands-on training, including machine guns and other weapons. For the first time, he learned something about aerial combat: bombing, aerial observation, map-reading, combat patrol and reconnaissance, meteorology, photography, and flying instruments. Not to be left out were officer's customs and behaviors, army regulations, military law, and cooperation with infantry and artillery units.[2]

To master such an array of subjects, Field, as a cadet, began his day at 5:30 A.M. and usually kept busy until 7:30 P.M. Physical fitness would be maintained by calisthenics and drilling. Cadets at the ground school

Air Service cadets in training checking aircraft controls at the University of Illinois School of Military Aeronautics, 1917–18
Wings Over the Rockies Museum Library, Scamehorn Photo Collection

were paid the rate of a first-class private, or approximately a dollar a day, with about an additional dollar a day for rations with quarters (housing) provided. Upon completion of the ground courses, the students were sent to aviation school squadrons for primary flying training.[3]

The Army Signal Corps and members of the university faculty managed and directed the University of Illinois aviation ground school. During its eighteen months or so of existence (most of the centers closed by February 1, 1919), it trained 3,453 students, and 2,644 of its graduates continued to flight schools.[4] At the same time, the Air Service expanded from 75 flying officers to 11,425 and over 5,000 of these pilots and observers eventually went to France.[5]

Field graduated from the University of Illinois School of Military Aeronautics on September 1, 1917.[6] He still carried the rank of cadet in the Signal Enlisted Reserve, but he had moved a significant step closer to the coveted officer's commission. That was to come belatedly after months of flying training with the British Royal Flying Corps and then the satisfactory completion of the Reserve Military Aviator test.

Field Kindley departed the United States on September 16, 1917, en route to Great Britain.[7] It seems likely that he traveled from New York aboard R.M.S. *Carmania,* which sailed through submarine-infested waters in a convoy that formed at Halifax, Nova Scotia, about September 20, 1917.[8] His assignment to primary flying training in Great Britain rather than at U.S. bases occurred because the expansion of the American flight training program and the bases to accommodate it had not kept pace with the growth of the ground school. Consequently, Field became part of a relatively early group detailed to train with the British. An initial contingent of 53 American cadets arrived at Oxford, England, in early September, and by the beginning of October more than 200 aviation cadets, Field included, started their training in the old English university town.[9] Field began his training at Oxford ground school on September 30, 1917.[10] Early on, the British had turned to their universities to house their ground training and thus provided an example for the United States.

Much to the chagrin of the Americans, once at Oxford they found they had to undergo British aviation ground school. One man in the American group groaned, "We've got to go to Ground School all over again. . . . And we hear that everything we were taught at home is all wrong."[11] No doubt the British, with their years of flying combat, be-

Air Service cadet Field E. Kindley at the University of Illinois, 1917

Kindley family photo

lieved in their own way of doing things, but part of the delay in getting the Americans into the cockpit was caused by a shortage of planes and equipment. Field, for example, did not start his primary flight training until mid-November 1917.[12]

The disappointment of another stint of ground school was eased considerably by the rich and ancient surroundings. Some cadets lived at Christ Church College, for example, and had a mess hall in a chapel-like building "with stained glass windows and the most wonderful paintings all around the wall." One cadet observed that his barracks must be a million years old "because it took that long to cool off to this temperature." A very accurate observation was that "the whole place is very ancient and has all that charm and dignity that only antiquity can give."[13]

There were other amenities, however. The resplendent English green fields could be enjoyed with bicycle rides, and afterward wayside pubs or inns provided most welcome ale, Scotch whiskey, cheese, and bread. "I never saw such quaint places or quaint people," remarked a cadet.[14] One minor, almost humorous problem was the British comprehension of spoken American English and vice versa, and, of course, the British drove on the "wrong side" of the road.

The British ground school, also called the School of Military Aeronautics, would last six weeks and, in contrast to that of the University of Illinois, would emphasize the Vickers machine gun and rotary motors, both much in use by the Royal Flying Corps. Most of the Americans went to the Machine Gun Training Centre at Grantham, Lincolnshire, some 100 miles north of London, and Field Kindley proceeded there on November 3, 1917, for a thirteen-day course. Field received an introduction to both the Vickers and Lewis machine guns, and his high marks in ground gunnery (85–95 percent) foretold future aerial gunnery success. This was not the last time Field would receive gunnery training and practice; his training record indicated "passed" remarks as late as January 1918. Later on, as noted in March 1918, Field recorded a 72 percent and 100 percent in aerial gunnery at Turnberry, on the east coast of Scotland.[15]

Meanwhile, American cadets groused while absorbing British lessons. "Aren't we ever going to fly?" and "Aren't we ever going to receive our officer's commission?" they complained. Statements like "I hope I never see another machine gun, I came over here to fight—not to sit around and talk about it forever" reflected a general American feeling.[16]

Cadet Field Kindley left the ground school at Oxford and gun training at Grantham and finally was ordered to begin his flying training at Northolt, outside London, on 19 November. Other Americans completing ground school were sent to other airfields. In his initial assignment to Training Squadron No. 4 of the Royal Flying Corps, Field began his flying in the Maurice Farman "Shorthorn" trainer, sometimes called a Rumpty.[17] This flimsy, French-built aircraft powered with a 100-horsepower Renault engine must have given Field pause, as it did others.

One American cadet remarked at the time, "These old short-horn Farmans are awful looking buses." He claimed there were stories that they tested the rigging by putting a bird between the two wings—if the bird got out, a wire was missing. "I am surprised they fly at all," he concluded. The Americans made another disturbing observation about their instructors: they were "wilder and younger" than those in the ground school. One cadet described his instructor as a "mere kid." "He's about nineteen and is trying hard to grow a mustache," he observed. The explanation for the instructor's youth was not comforting. "I was told that they kill off more instructors in the R. F. C. than pupils and from what I've seen, I can well believe it."[18]

The British system of training pilots, called the Gosport method, made use of a communication tube between the student and instructor.

A Maurice Farman "Shorthorn" Trainer, the aircraft in which Kindley first learned to fly

Photo courtesy Lafayette Foundation

This proved important and valuable in speeding pilot training, for the British emphasized rapid pilot advancement from aircraft to aircraft. Some critics maintained the fast method resulted in higher pilot casualties. In contrast, the French used a more gradual approach, even starting out with Penquins, clipped-wing planes, used to practice taxiing aircraft. A slow progression, depending on the student's absorption, followed from large-wing aircraft to faster, more powerful planes. The French system took longer to produce an accomplished pilot, but they argued it saved lives. Both the British and French utilized veteran instructors, sometimes newly arrived from combat, who had a profound impact on the American trainees.

Kindley recorded his first flight on November 24, 1917, a fifteen-minute circling of the airfield, or "circuit." During these initial flying minutes with his instructor, the flight logbook's remarks noted, "Hold of controls." Two days later, after thirty-five minutes in the air, the remarks read, "one bad landing–took off heavy on controls."[19] Field's flying had begun inauspiciously, but this was not in any way unusual. Any fear and thrill of being in the air must have been tempered with a feeling of relief that at last he was actually flying.

More training flights occurred during the following week with gaps in days that surely must have been due to the approaching winter weather. By December 3, Field had accumulated two hours and fifteen minutes of dual flying time. The instructor comments were not encouraging. They noted: "made few turns very bumpy" and "seems to be very slow in learning." On December 5, however, the log remarks said, "Doing better made two good landings—took off." A momentous day came three days later, December 8, when Field Kindley flew "solo" for the first time. After only five minutes' solo flying, he recorded a "bad landing"; this was followed by another twenty minutes of air time, but the landing this time was noted as "crashed under carriage."[20]

Field Kindley progressed in his flying training, and after completion of fifty minutes of solo time, on December 18, 1917, he was assigned to "Number 40" Reserve Squadron at Croydon, outside London. Up to this point he had totaled three hours and fifty minutes of dual and four hours, five minutes of solo time, with seventeen landings. He had even experienced half an hour of formation flying.[21] A new thrill awaited, however, as he now began training in a more advanced aircraft, an Avro Trainer. Although all the Americans rejoiced at leaving the Rumptys, the Avro posed a new challenge. One cadet remarked,

"They are entirely different and I have to learn to fly all over again."[22] The two-seater Avro 504B biplane had been adopted as the "Standard Training Machine" by the British because of the aircraft's "simplicity, strength, and controllability." It had a maximum ground-level speed of 95 mph when variously powered by a Gnome, Le Rhone, or Clerget engine. For the fledgling pilots, the Avro provided the appropriate training machine for the cadets who were practicing flying cross-country before graduating to higher powered war aircraft.[23] Field took his first flight with an instructor in the Avro on Christmas Eve, making turns and flying the "district" course for forty-five minutes. With the instructor in the rear seat and Field in the front, additional dual flights provided practice of more turns (some termed "bumpy"), with gradual progression to takeoffs and landings. By January 14, 1918, he had accumulated ten hours and twenty-five minutes of dual time in the Avro and had gone cross-country and done "stunts and spins."[24]

Field took time during the Christmas season of 1917 to send a greeting card to his Aunt Mollie and his cousins in Gravette. The card was inscribed, "A Merry Xmas from Northolt" and contained a New Year's saying:

May the New Year be a
Happy one to you, Happy to
Many more whose happiness
Depends on you, so may each
Year be happier than the last.

The card was signed "Field," followed by "Royal Flying Corps, Northolt Aerodrome, Ruislip, Middlesex, Xmas, 1917."[25] Despite the busy flying training, Field, like so many Americans overseas, no doubt felt sadness at being separated from family during big holiday celebrations.

Cadet Field Kindley's advancement in the Avro Trainer reached a milestone on January 14, 1918. This was the date of his first solo in this aircraft, and it included the usual turns and spins during a thirty-five-minute period.

More noteworthy, however, was the experience of having the "engine cutout." He met the test of bringing the plane down in a dead-stick landing, as it was frequently called, but he must have considered himself rather lucky.[26] Aircraft accidents during flying training occurred all too frequently. "A horrible thing happened today," wrote one cadet. "We

An Avro Trainer, which Kindley flew as his second aircraft, a significant step up from the Farman "Shorthorn"
Photo courtesy Lafayette Foundation

were all out on the tarmac having our pictures taken for posterity when somebody yelled and pointed up. Two Avros collided right over the aerodrome at about three thousand feet. God, it was a horrible sight. . . . They came down in a slow spin with their wings locked together and both in flames. . . . I kept trying to imagine what those poor devils were thinking about as they went spinning down into hell. It made me sick at my stomach to watch. We all went up later and felt better after a little flying."[27] Of the approximately five hundred Americans who received training by the British, thirty-four were killed in training accidents, and the number seemed to be especially high for the first contingent.[28]

As Field's flying training continued, he became more comfortable at the controls of an aircraft. "I am getting more accustomed to the air and don't mind dropping three or four thousand feet," he wrote. His flying solo, however, was not without thrills. "The first time I was up I did some stunts, the loop, spin, and Immelmann drop. I made sure I was high enough, about three thousand feet, and then started." After thirty minutes, Field said, "I felt my engine go dead. I was two thousand feet up and so had plenty of time to glide into the airdrome." After that success of a dead-stick landing, Field commented: "When I came in the English officer seemed to think I had done quite well to bring in a dead engine, to say nothing of my stunts. The major says he wishes they had more American nerve over here. I cannot say it takes much nerve, as you are as safe up three thousand feet as at home in bed." He may soon have begun to wonder about a comparison with "safe as home in bed," because he again wrote, "The second time I was up three thousand feet I started a spin over a town and my engine went dead. I came down to three hundred feet over a house before I got it again." Not only did Field have the engine, the altitude, and the town to be concerned about, but "I was afraid of the church steeple that stuck up like a mountain, and when I got my engine going again I was the happiest man on earth, or rather in the air."[29]

Despite these narrow escapes, Field claimed he loved flying: "One has not lived until he has been in the air. I like it very much and have done as high as two and three hours a day lately. Tomorrow I go into a fast machine. It is harder to fly, but I would rather have it. We used to think sixty miles an hour was fast, but now we want 130 or 150 miles."[30] During the next series of flights, he successfully dealt with other engine problems. His flight logbook contained entries such as "two cylinders out," "one cylinder out" (four different times), and "switch cut out."[31] These nerve-tensing challenges were interspersed in the increasingly difficult maneuvers of spins, loops, and rolls.

While flying dominated the interest and time of the American cadets, other training continued. Field learned "buzzing," a wireless communicating and signaling with artillery units. He had to pass a three-minute test of sending and receiving eight words per minute. Also, training time was devoted to photography, wherein Field was certified as passed by taking "six successful photographs of given pin points."[32] And then there was more machine gun instruction. Field, for example, was sent to machine gun school at Turnberry, Scotland, in February. One American cadet probably expressed a growing consensus when he stated, "Machine gun class is awfully boring."[33]

Kindley experienced another training advancement on January 27, 1918, when he had his first solo flight in a Sopwith Pup.[34] Field did not record how he viewed this transition from the Avro Trainer to the Pup, but probably his reaction was much like that of another American cadet: "Today I saw my first scout machine, a Sopwith Pup. It's the prettiest little thing I ever laid eyes on. I am going to fly one if I live long enough. They aren't as big as a minute and are as pretty and slick as a thoroughbred horse. Tiny little things, just big enough for one man and a machine gun."[35]

The Sopwith Pup had an early war reputation of being "one of the most delightful machines to fly," and with high performance, too, considering a low-powered 80-hp Le Rhone engine. It could climb to 5,000 feet in 7 minutes, 40 seconds, and had a speed at 10,000 feet of 99 mph.[36] By the time of Kindley's training in early 1918, however, the Pup had been relegated to advanced flying training by the development of more powerful combat aircraft, such as the Sopwith Camel.

Field Kindley's first flight in the Pup lasted 60 minutes at 3,000 feet. The next day he managed two flights with loops and rolls. During the week ending February 5, 1918, Kindley had one occasion of a cylinder being out and had incorporated ground strafing into his flying maneuvers with a total of over six hours of flight time.[37]

It would be a serious mistake to conclude that the American cadets undergoing flying training with the British did nothing but train, fly, and train some more. There was time to relax, drink, and court the available girls. Although Field seemed quite circumspect in any reporting of his "off-duty time," comments by other American cadets left little doubt they held their own in drinking bouts with their British counterparts and in socializing with the women—from barmaids to "ladies of the night." One American noted, for example: "With good pay, good clothes, no responsibility and no place to spend my money except girls, life was sweet. Girls weren't expensive, all of them trying to do their bit for King and Country. What more could a fellow ask?"[38] One cadet reported problems with the food. "We did not have any meat for about three months," he asserted. "The English imported jackrabbits from Australia and they smelled so bad we couldn't eat any. We would go into London on weekends and eat at the Savoy Hotel. They had good food."[39]

The British rail system allowed the cadets to make excursions to London and other cities. "We have been posted to London Colney, which is the greatest place yet. It is only twenty miles from London and they have Pups and Spads and Avros. . . . We go to London when we please," reported one American cadet.[40] And what did they do when they got to London? "We met Jim in London and had a wild party. . . . After the show we had Beatrice Lillie and the entire cast of *Cheap* up in our suite at the Court."[41]

A British Sopwith "Pup," once a scout fighter but relegated to a trainer by development of better aircraft like the Sopwith Camel

Photo courtesy Lafayette Foundation

While the flying uniforms might have helped attract the women, the Americans were not happy when they compared their "duds" with those of the British. Some of the British fliers seemed to sport tailor-made uniforms, while the Americans complained: "I'm an American and I'm proud of it but I'm damned if I can take any pride in the boobs that are running the flying corps. For instance how can we fly when our necks are being choked off by these 1865 model collars? The staff must think they are still in Mexico wearing O.D. [olive drab] shirts."[42]

Another continuing complaint was the slowness of the officer-commissioning process. In March 1918 a cadet noted, "There's a bunch of Americans up here (Turnberry, Scotland) and a few of them have gotten their commissions. I wonder what's happened to ours."[43] Some of the Americans had completed their aerial fighting school but had their posting to France held up to await their commissions. A major worry was a circulating rumor that General Pershing "recommended that pilots be sergeants and not officers and that flying pay be abolished."[44]

Fortunately for the Americans, the rumor was only a rumor. Field Kindley, however, must have been one of the latest ones of the initial cadet contingent to Great Britain to receive his commission. It was mid-April when he became First Lieutenant Kindley.[45]

Still a cadet, Kindley entered into the final phase of his flying training with the Royal Flying Corps. He received a Royal Flying Corps "Graduation Certificate," dated January 29, 1918, stating that he had "completed a course in the military wing, and is qualified for service in the Royal Flying Corps."[46] In early February, nevertheless, he continued flying the Sopwith Pup with more attention given to cross-country flights. On February 13 he recorded a cross-country flight with a "forced landing due to darkness & mist at Sidcup" and later cross-country flights to Brooklands, Brooklands to Croydon, and in an Avro Northolt to Croydon.[47]

On February 19, Field went to the "Fighting School" at Ayr, Scotland, a town of about twenty-five thousand on the southeast shore of the Firth of Clyde, where he learned formation flying, ground strafing, and more stunts. On his first day, in three successive flights of approximately fifteen minutes' duration each, he noted "one plug gone," "another plug gone," and "another plug gone." He reached a milestone on February 23 when he recorded his "first Camel solo." He had taken controls of a first-line combat aircraft.[48]

The British-built Sopwith Camel was an enlarged and modified Pup with several distinctive features–a great dihedral on the bottom wing combined with a flat top "plane" or wing and the noticeable hump over its two Vickers machine guns. The modifications were designed to provide higher performance with a 130-hp Clerget engine and better maneuverability. This "Fighting Scout" tractor biplane had a speed at 10,000 feet of 113 mph and climb time to 5,000 feet of 5 minutes.[49]

A better appreciation of what Field Kindley faced when he made the transition to this higher performance aircraft can be gained by noting a few flying characteristics of the Sopwith Camel. The large rotary engine—the whole engine went round with the propeller—rotated clockwise as viewed from the cockpit and gave added right-turn capability. For pilots like Field, who had just finished flying the Pup, this came as a disconcerting surprise. During a steep right turn, the Camel's nose tended to drop and in left climbing turns it rose. The pilot had to use left rudder in these maneuvers to counter the effects of the clockwise rotating engine. Also, Camel pilots had to keep the engine at full power to fly through a loop using full rudder rather than pulling back on the stick, as with other aircraft, and waiting for the

A British Sopwith Camel, one of the most successful aircraft in World War I. Kindley trained and fought his aerial battles in this aircraft.
Photo courtesy Lafayette Foundation

machine to complete the circle.[50] Because of these characteristics, the Camel developed a nasty reputation in many quarters as one of the most difficult airplanes to handle; even worse, it became known as a pilot killer. V. M. Yeates in his true-to-life novel *Winged Victory* colorfully described the Camel: "unlike ordinary airplanes, being quite unstable, immoderately tail heavy, so light on the controls that the slightest jerk or inaccuracy would hurl them all over the sky, difficult to land, deadly to crash: a list of vices to emasculate the stoutest courage. . . . The first flight of a Camel was always a terrible ordeal."[51]

Elliott White Springs, who would later join Kindley in the 148th Aero Squadron, declared, "Camels deserved their reputation." He complained, "They stall at 15,000 feet and lose 1,000 feet on a turn. You had to climb or glide."[52] Another American claimed they were "very bad shooting platforms."[53] Still others considered them too slow, especially when compared with the German Fokker D.VIIs. Pilot Yeates, referring to the Camel, said, "If only it had been fifty per cent faster." "A Camel could neither catch anything except by surprise, nor hurry away from an awkward situation, and seldom had the option of accepting or declining combat," he said.[54] All these criticisms clearly indicated that pilots must be well trained in the Camel aircraft before combat, with the pilots fully grasping the idiosyncrasies, deficiencies, and strengths of the aircraft.

The Camel's big advantage, a truly major one, rested in its agility. Elliott Springs, for example, declared it "could fly upside down and turn inside a stair well."[55] Capitalizing on this strength, this single-seater fighter proved very successful in combat with an "immense amount of work in 1917." By the end of the war, the Sopwith Camel had recorded more aerial victories, some 1,294 enemy aircraft, than any other Allied airplane.[56]

Although the Sopwith Camel excelled in maneuverability, it had a vexing problem in its performance at high altitude. V. M. Yeates in his *Winged Victory,* for example, commented at one point about flying his Camel and "reaching the chilly height of eighteen thousand feet," which proved "too high for a Camel to fly properly."[57] As a consequence, the RAF's S.E. 5, the other principal British scout aircraft in 1917–18, with its in-line Hispano-Suiza engine, flew faster, landed more easily, provided a more steady gun platform, reached higher altitude, and performed better at higher altitude. Therefore, the S.E. 5 more often assumed responsibility for top cover in layered tactics of pursuit aircraft and in bomber escort.[58] Yet Yeates argued that the "Huns preferred fighting SE-s which were stationary engined scouts more like themselves, for the Germans were not using rotary engines, except for their exotic triplanes, and the standard Hun scout was the very orthodox Albatros." Accordingly, Yeates said, the Germans "knew where they were with SE-s, which obeyed the laws of flight and did as properly stabilized aeroplanes ought to do. If you shot at one, allowing correctly for its speed, you would hit it; it would be going the way it looked as if it were going following its nose. But not so a Camel. A Camel might be going side-ways or flat spinning, or going in any direction except straight backwards."[59]

The Camel tended to stay and fight at or below 15,000 feet, where it proved most successful. Elliott Springs, like Kindley, believed, "The Camel could make a monkey out of a Fokker at tree-top level." However, you had to "suck the Fokkers down," he said. Yeates concluded that "Camels were wonderful fliers when you got used to them, which took about three months of hard flying. At the end of that time you were either dead, a nervous wreck, or a hell of a pilot and a terror to Huns, who were more unwilling to attack Camels than any other sort of machine except Bristol Fighters."[60]

One American pilot, Lt. Thomas L. Moore, a comrade of Kindley and a pilot who became known for his Camel flying, openly expressed his affection for the aircraft. "It was a great little plane. It could turn on a dime," he declared. Nevertheless, he noted that it did have troubling idiosyncrasies. "On takeoff, we had to use full left rudder"; "most students had trouble with the Camel." A particular problem, according to Lieutenant Moore, was the Camel's "tendency to go into right-hand spins. When that happened we were instructed to use full left rudder, pop the stick forward and ease her out of it. A lot of students did spin in."[61]

Field Kindley remained strangely silent on the many challenges of flying the Sopwith Camel. His correspondence and logs contain little information on his thoughts and experiences with the aircraft, unlike the comments of pilots previously mentioned. Nevertheless, his successes in downing German aircraft, eventually reaching twelve in a few months of combat flying, fully demonstrated his mastery of this difficult aircraft.

Field clearly did not miss a beat in moving to the Camel. For several days after his first solo in this aircraft, he recorded "spins & rolls," turns, and ground strafing. On February 27, 1918, he did a cross-country with "firing." Flights in late March included remarks of "Dual fighting," "Camel fighting," and "Formation & maneuver." By March 25, 1918, Field's record showed a dual time of 12 hours and 5 minutes, and solo time of 56 hours and 5 minutes.[62]

Not all the American cadets made the transition to the Sopwith Camel, as Field Kindley did. Some advanced instead into the French Spad. One American stated on February 15, 1918, "Flew a Spad to-day. Easy to fly but dangerous as hell . . . and it has the gliding angle of a brick." Others flew the British S.E. 5a. "Heard to-day that Ludwig was killed flying an S.E. He got into a spin close to the ground."[63] Whatever the aircraft, many of the Americans concluded their flying training at the School of Aerial Fighting at Ayr, Scotland, on the west coast south of Glasgow. Also at Ayr was a holding pilot's pool where the trained pilots waited for their combat assignments to France. Since the British expected the Americans to be commissioned as officers before being assigned to combat squadrons, some delay was due to tardy commissions.

The Americans voiced few complaints about their British instructors. Yes, they noticed they were "young and wild," but they seemed to have a true appreciation for their instructors' knowledge and skill. After all, many were experienced in battle, and if they survived both training and combat, that in itself was worthy of respect. Lt. Raymond Watts, a flying friend of Field, reported that a training squadron often had "three flight-commanders who acted as instructors and who were, for the most part, fellows who had put in five or six months in France and were then given a stretch of about three months of H. E. (Home Establishment)."[64]

Also, there was an understanding about the shortage of equipment in the training squadrons. "Rather than having 16 planes, they'd have 12; one truck instead of three," Lieutenant Watts commented.[65] Another American flying cadet observed, "There are only two Avros for about thirty of us so we will be here for some time."[66] Periodically, the American trainees wondered about British operational efficiency, but increasingly they realized the training squadrons were being run more like the combat squadrons in France. The lack of a confining, strict discipline in their life at the training squadron was momentarily enjoyed and later appreciated as hastening their adaptation to the combat squadron way.

The Americans were also absorbing some of the British traditions with regard to flying, drinking, and partying, and they listened dutifully to British experience. "An English general made us a talk and said this was no great adventure: you were either scared to death or bored to death all the time."[67] One Yankee, now a lieutenant, declared, "Everybody here wants to get out of the U.S. Army and join the R.F.C. where they'll get a square deal. . . . We owe the British a lot and have a lot to get even with our own army for."[68]

Although the Americans, including Field Kindley, believed they were ready, finally, to get into aerial warfare, they waited at the pilot's pool or at other British bases for the assignment to France. Their eagerness to get to the front was perhaps tempered by the sobering realization that many friends and acquaintances had already been lost in the many training accidents. But ground training and flying training were now behind them, and they were anxious for the "big show."

Chapter Three

Ferrying Aircraft

For a few minutes I lost my thoughts but when I came to I found I was pinned in the wreckage and had to wait till some men who heard the crash and commenced to look for me in the fog, found me and pulled the wreckage off of me . . . I am just a lucky boy who should feel lucky he is yet on earth.

Lt. Field E. Kindley,
letter to Uther Kindley,
May 12, 1918

ON DECEMBER 28, 1917, Field Kindley's father on Mindanao Island wrote "Dear Mollie" in Gravette, Arkansas, expressing concern that he had not "heard from Field for so long." "It is indeed queer that he neglects me so much when he knows that I am anxious about him," he complained. The father presumed that Field had gone to France and with some resignation to that thought added strong patriotic comments. "The bloody Kaiser has forced death to so many. . . . If Field could only be the one of thousands who may be fortunate to cast a ton of explosives on the head of the tyrant I shall be satisfied and die believing that my life has been well spent." In conclusion, however, he returned to worry about his son. "I shall never be happy until I hear Field has been successful and returned."[1]

Field, during the time of his father's letter of concern, was busy with his training with the Royal Flying Corps and was still many months away from going to France. Even though by February he had begun flying in higher performance fighter aircraft, the Sopwith Camel, he waited first for his officer's commission and then for the American leaders to make up their minds as to the disposition of the trained pilots. There were rumors that they might be sent back to the United States to serve as instructors or that they might be held in England until American squadrons could be formed. Lt. Raymond Watts, a colleague of Field, declared, "We . . . were very irritated being held around this way."[2] During this waiting time from March to May 1918, Field and other Americans were assigned to ferrying aircraft about the British Isles and across the Channel to France. In this interregnum at least they could further hone their flying skills.

As part of the aircraft ferrying system, Field Kindley and a group of other Americans reported every morning to the ferry pool, which was being directed from some rooms at the Baker Street Hotel in London—across from 221 Baker Street, the address made famous as the home of the fictional detective Sherlock Holmes. A pilot would be assigned a plane to be delivered from some factory or depot to a designated airfield. When the pilot arrived at the factory, he was to carefully inspect and pre-flight the plane and, like a test pilot, not accept the machine unless it was in good shape. After accepting the aircraft, they "would take it up, throw it around a bit, and take-off by map and deliver it." After arrival at the airfield, they would often then board a train for the return to London.[3]

Delivery of an aircraft to a training squadron was special and required a show: "You would come down in a roaring dive, slice across in front of the hangars, pull up in a big zoom, and throw the plane around . . . showing them that this was a hot-stuff plane. Then you would land and ask the nearest person, 'Is this the 40 T. S. and is there someone to sign a ticket for this new bus? Quite a nice, new Camel.' They'd take you in the office, sign the paper, and get you transportation to the nearest railway station."[4] The best laid plans and the best shows didn't always work out, however. "A ferry pilot brought over my new machine day before yesterday and smashed it all to pieces landing," reported one American. Whereupon, he decided to go get his own "service machine" by having a fellow pilot fly him in an Avro to the Brooklands depot, and he then proceeded to fly back in his new aircraft.[5]

Delivering planes across the Channel to France usually involved a somewhat routine procedure. The aircraft would be flown to a small airfield at Lympne, close to the English coastal city of Folkstone, where the pilot would "check in" before the Channel crossing. Lympne officials would notify the appropriate anti-aircraft personnel of the flight path, type of plane, time, and destination. After proper clearance, the pilot would then fly over Folkstone using the pier as a heading for Cap Gris Nez in France.[6]

Field Kindley had a number of such ferry flights. On March 29, 1918, his flight logbook reported he ferried a Camel (No. 6524) from Norwich to Lympne and thence to the French town of St. Omer. The remarks section read, "Delivered Camel." Two days later, he again flew a Camel from Norwich to Lympne and the next day from Lympne to Marquise, on the French Channel coast. This time he recorded trouble with a "dead mag." On April 1 and 2 he ferried an aircraft back from France, and on the leg from Croydon to the RFC depot at Brooklands he simply noted, "Lost." During a flight from Lincoln to Wye on April 20 he encountered some notorious English fog and reported, "Soft wheat field crashed." On May 1, in a departure from entries of trouble, he noted, "Nice trip" on a ferry flight from Lincoln to Marquise, France, and two days later he ferried his first S.E. 5a aircraft from Brooklands across the Channel.[7]

Field's experiences ferrying aircraft reached a frightening climax on May 6 when he was flying a Camel out of Norwich to be delivered to France. Because of an extremely low ceiling, Field had landed at Lympne. In addition, there was very bad weather over the Channel. Lt. Raymond Watts, Field's ferrying colleague, flying low following a railroad, landed at Lympne shortly after Field and told his friend that he had enough of the bad weather and was spending the night at Lympne. After lunch the two pilots got a report that the weather was improving a bit at Marquise. Field decided to try the flight across the Channel. Watts believed Field was interested in getting to France because he had made an acquaintance with "a very charming French girl" at Boulogne, where they often caught a boat back to England. Watts later remarked, "It was the only time I ever saw him show much interest in French or English girls, he was a very shy fellow." They cleared Field Kindley for take-off and up he went. Less than an hour later it was reported the weather was bad again.[8]

Flying in his Camel, Field not only experienced the horrible weather but also began having engine problems. "It was like this," he wrote Cousin Uther, "my engine started to fail that is vibrate so badly I knew soon it would be absolutely dead if I did not throttle down so I did throttle down to reserve what little engine I had left for landing. This let me down into a very thick fog so that I could not see 25ft in any direction." Upon checking his instruments, he was uncertain whether he was over land or sea, but he quickly discovered he was still over the Channel. "I opened up my engine and started west, soon I saw the beach and at the same time I saw a high cliff 25 ft away."

Field was headed straight for the white cliffs of Dover. "It was too late to turn so I just pulled back my 'joystick' in an attempt to lose flying speed and did not have to wait long for the crash."[9]

In the next few seconds Field saw pieces of his machine "flying here and there." The wreckage fell on top of him, pinning him in the debris. "Being belted into my machine I fell over backwards in it and hit a something about 75 feet below off of which I bounced and hit about 50 ft further below." Field momentarily lost consciousness with the shock, and when he came to, he still had to wait for some men who heard the crash to find him in the fog and then pull the wreckage off of him. "However, after examining myself I found I had no broken bones but a few black and blue spots, a gash on the forehead and my shoulder seemed to hurt very badly."[10]

Meanwhile, Lieutenant Watts and others at Lympne had retired to the officers' mess, which was in a "beautiful old country house, situated on the cliffs, with a garden overlooking the Channel." A stairway had been built on the cliffs to provide access to the beach. "Presently . . . up this stairway came Field! He was a mess! A cut across his face, his trousers torn, and his clothes were soaked. We all asked, 'Field . . . for heaven's sake . . . where have you come from?'"[11]

Field's response to the question summed up the situation: "Well, I don't know! I got over the Channel and it was terrible! I couldn't find my way, so I decided to come back. I made what I thought was a 180 turn, had to stay right down over the water to see anything. When I thought I was nearing the cliffs, I pulled up into the fog, but I stalled out and hit the cliffs." The next morning the group went to look at the plane. "There it was, laying in the surf, a complete loss. You could see the mark, about eight-to-ten feet from the top, where the plane had hit."[12]

Field revealed to Cousin Uther in Gravette, Arkansas, that he had spent time in a hospital as a result of the crash. "For my first time I was in a hospital a few days ago after having hit the Dover cliffs. . . . But a few days in the hospital found me O. K. and I have been flying since so guess I am just a lucky boy who should feel lucky he is yet on earth."[13]

Field was lucky in another respect. Lieutenant Watts reported that "The Adjutant" had prepared an accident report that "gave the impression that Field had made a mistake in trying to cross the Channel at this time and other words to that effect." Lieutenant Watts stated that the commanding officer read the report and then tore it up. Furthermore, the commanding officer dictated the report he wanted. It stated: "Lieutenant Kindley had taken-off in extremely bad weather to deliver a plane badly needed at the Front. The weather proved much worse than expected, and only by skillful flying was he able to return. Apparently his altimeter was at fault and he failed to clear cliffs."[14] According to Lieutenant Watts, the commanding officer exclaimed, "That's the kind of report to write!" The rationale for a favorable accident report was clear. "If you had been to the front as I have, you would know that this is the kind of pilot we need. One who will try to do a job; a person willing to take a chance."[15]

Despite flirting with death, Field reported pleasure with living in London. In his May 12 letter to his relatives in Gravette he wrote, "I am sitting here waiting for it to stop raining so I can hop on a street car, run out to my machine just outside London and take it to France." When on the return, he indicated, "It is nice to fly right into London . . . come into the little room of mine, have supper, see a show at night, go to bed and enjoy a good night's rest and then be able to take a street car out to your machine in the morning and have dinner in France."[16]

In a personal aside, Field expressed his disappointment at not receiving letters from Cousin Uther, but noted that he had received "three of the nicest letters from father." He provided some insight into the father-son relationship when he wrote, "It is the same old story though, thinks he will stay in the P. I. regardless of whether he leaves the government service or no. It makes me mad because when should a man of his age throw away his life in such a country." Field took comfort, however, in the knowledge that his father "thinks I did right by joining the army so I feel better. I knew he would though for a real father would want his son to go but of course hopes for the best. He is like you, imagines the worst."[17]

Although Field indicated that he thought his father wanted to stay in the Philippines, there must have been some ambivalence in the father's attitude toward remaining there. In a letter to Mollie on December 28, 1917, he shared some very negative opinions about the islands. He had "so much work and such disagreeable work," he said. "Considering political relations between the American and the Filipino that it adds to drudgery and makes it almost insurmountable at times." He continued, "There is no friendship in the world across the water; no friendship as we know it in America, although it is often times at fever heat outwardly it is only for a reason, an ax to grind."[18]

Field's father wrote on July 7, 1918, acknowledging receipt of a letter of April 28 from Field. Besides expressing his relief at hearing from his son, he was glad to know he had received a promotion.[19] Apparently what he referred to was Field's long-awaited officer's commission as a first lieutenant. Indeed, Field was honorably discharged from the U.S. Army "by reason of accepting commission 1st Lt.—Sig. RCAS complied with active duty orders April 15, 1918." The official form stated Field E. Kindley was "21 5/12 years of age."[20]

Field continued some ferry flights after receiving his first lieutenant rank, but with his commission in hand he was soon destined for the war front. He recorded his last aircraft ferry, another Camel, from Norwich to Lympne on May 18, 1918. It happened to be noted as a "fine trip."[21] Four days later, May 22, his orders attached him to No. 65 Squadron, Royal Air Force, for war duty.[22]

Lt. Field E. Kindley, weighing his training and ferrying experience, probably believed he was surely ready for combat. From March 27 to May 18, despite near-fatal crashes, terrible British weather, and other problems, he had succeeded in accumulating 29 hours and 10 minutes of solo time in the Camel and even 1 hour and 35 minutes solo in an S.E. 5a. Adding training time, Field had slightly over forty hours in the Camel, the aircraft in which he was to fight. Up to May 22, 1918, when he was assigned to the 65th Squadron in France, Field's record indicated he had a "total time in the air," dual and solo, of slightly more than 102 hours.[23]

All his time in the air and all his training would now be put to the test against the Germans. Field, like the other Americans then flying across the trenches in France, would be learning something new every day. Besides the idiosyncrasies of the aircraft, and the usual mechanical problems, there now was a life-and-death contest between airmen—an all-out effort to knock each other out of the sky.

Chapter Four

First Combat

Well old man you are missing half your life by not being out here and especially in the air. It is great to be flying along in formation gazing down upon the trenches below watching artillery fire & etc and then all of a sudden our leader throws a fit (that is a few rolls etc) and we have to "fit" after him. Of course a little archie and the popping of machine guns behind makes you wish you could do 210 m.p.h. instead of 110 but yet 110 m.p.h. soon turns the tables on Fritz and he has the pleasure of cak cak cak sounds. The sound of machine gun fire at you is different than from you I assure you.

Lt. Field E. Kindley,
letter to Uther Kindley,
June 4, 1918

With their training completed, the American pilots trained by the British, including Lt. Field E. Kindley, were assigned to Royal Air Force units or to two American squadrons in the British combat area. Although the 148th and 17th American pursuit squadrons were eventually organized by the new American pilots, they had been totally equipped by the British as well as completely trained by the RAF. In typical action, Lieutenant Kindley received orders first to the 65th Squadron of the Royal Air Force in France and later moved to the 148th American pursuit squadron at the northern British front.

The preponderance of the U.S. air effort in the war occurred in the French rather than the British sector of the Western Front. The U.S. Air Service located its headquarters there. American commanders planned the U.S. aerial buildup in France in basically two ways. Some squadrons, formed after initial training at U.S. air bases, would deploy as units or partial units to the European continent. Other squadrons would be organized after individuals reached France and were then trained by French flying schools and ground crew training centers. In the French sector, since the planes, engines, and equipment were French-made, training at French bases became critical to getting the Americans combat-ready as soon as possible. Americans already flying with French squadrons and under French command, such as the Lafayette Escadrille, would provide seasoned leaders for some of the new American flying units. Raoul Lufbery became one of the most noted fliers to make the move from French to American control. Many American pilots graduated from French flying training and then were assigned to the French front for combat. These pilots, similar to those in the British situation, would work in a French squadron or eventually make the transition to a newly created American one. The three top U.S. aces in World War I, Eddie Rickenbacker, Frank Luke, and Raoul Lufbery, trained with the French and fought in the French portion of the Western Front. They represented by far the greater number of American pilots fighting in World War I.

As the United States continued its build-up to support the war effort, it formed Aviation Instruction Centers in Europe to train more American crews with American instructors. A large Aviation Instruction Center at Issoudun, France, sixty-five miles south of Orléans, for example, conducted training in French Nieuport planes. Lt. Edward V. Rickenbacker was an engineering officer and instructor at Issoudun. Other Aviation Instruction Centers offered specialized training of some kind, such as preparing officers for observation and bombardment, although there was some duplication in various centers' efforts. These Aviation Instruction Centers proved extremely important to the formation and preparation of American flight crews.

While most attention understandably focused on collaboration with the French, some Americans received training in Italy, mainly at an Aviation Instruction Center at Foggia, and most of them went into combat with Italian squadrons. Capt. Fiorello H. LaGuardia, former congressional representative from New York and later mayor of New York City, was one of the notables there.[1]

Whether the pilots came from British, French, or American training, there was a sense of urgency in getting the greatest number to the Western Front as soon as possible. The collapse of tsarist Russia and the ensuing Bolshevik revolution freed veteran German soldiers for transfer to the West. The British and French were aware of trains arriving with these eastern troops. This indicated a German massing of men for a probable spring offensive. In turn, the Germans apprehensively watched the arrival of American soldiers in ever increasing numbers. To the Germans, it was important to strike a decisive blow at the earliest posssible moment. The big question for the Allies was where the offensive would begin.

German Gen. Erich von Ludendorff, now the lead commander on the Western Front, decided that the 1918 offensive would begin on the British Somme River sector with an operations plan code-named "Michael." The German attack, including sixty-seven German divisions, would take place on a forty- to fifty-mile front stretching roughly from the town of Arras on the north southward to the Oise River. If he could achieve a breakthrough in this area, Ludendorff reasoned, he might drive a wedge between the British and French forces, wheel about into the Allied rear areas, roll back British armies against the Channel ports, and bring about the disintegration of the Allied front, eventually leading to victory in the war.

Ludendorff, appreciating the growing importance of air support for ground operations and for such an ambitious offensive, believed a larger German air force would be needed, and that a major effort in this regard was especially necessary before the United States became a greater participant. He, therefore, strongly urged the War Ministry as early as June 25, 1917, to increase aircraft and engine production to equip a minimum of forty new fighter groups and seventeen new flight units. "America's entry into the war compels a considerable strengthening of the air force by 1 March 1918," Ludendorff and the High Command declared. The goal was "to be somewhat equal to the combined English-French-American air fleet." This expansion initiative became known in German circles as the American Program.[2] However, when the spring of 1918 actually came, the Germans faced growing Allied numerical superiority, and the German aircraft industry was beset with all kinds of shortages and increasingly disgruntled workers.

Toward the end of February, the British War Cabinet in its London deliberations still had doubts about a major German offensive on the Western Front. Ironically, one of the bits of intelligence providing more positive information about German intentions came from a Royal Flying Corps report that troop concentrations seemed pointed toward a push in the vicinity of St. Quentin.[3] Meanwhile, the French captured German papers that appeared to confirm a German offensive planned for early March.[4] British commanders in the area concluded that an attack was imminent and, with some uncertainty, that it could strike the British Third and Fifth Armies deployed in the old Somme battle area.

On March 21, 1918, the big German offensive began. With the careful and detailed planning and preparation by Germany's artillery genius, Col. Georg Bruchmüller, the most massive artillery barrage of the war and in history to that time commenced at 4:40 A.M.[5] Some six thousand guns, with over twenty-five hundred of them heavy caliber, bombarded a nearly fifty-mile stretch of the British front.[6] For several hours the German artillery concentrated on British counter-batteries, command posts, and communications centers, and then turned to attack the front lines. The Germans fired 3.2 million rounds on that first day.[7] Shells containing deadly gas were interspersed with high-explosive ones, with the intent to paralyze British response and to create confusion. Lt. Herbert Sulzbach, a seasoned German artilleryman, reported that the sound was "as if the world were coming to an end."[8] "Machine gun posts were blown sky-high—along with human limbs," recalled one British soldier in the hard-hit British Fifth Army. "Men were coughing and vomiting from the effects of gas, and men were blinded. The whole earth around us turned into an inferno."[9] After the intense shelling and behind a creeping barrage, German infantry, led by storm trooper groups, poured out of their trenches in a charge across no man's land. "Heavy fog until late that morning favored the attackers and tended to prolong the effects of the German gas."[10] "The German tactics of that morning were well suited to the foggy conditions: Infiltrate. Avoid the defended positions. Push on fast."[11] Dazed by the initial shock wave, the British troops left their trenches, where they could, scrambling over each other, but leaving behind piles of dead bodies.[12] Many were captured. The initial results of the offensive exceeded German High Command expectations.

The heavy fog during the early hours of the assault prevented Allied planes from getting airborne and providing desperately needed reconnaissance. Therefore, the disciplined German soldiers, led by groups of seven to ten storm troopers, advanced over British trenches and took full advantage of the bad weather to increase battlefield confusion. The British lines became fractured, putting the whole sector of the front in serious danger of collapsing.

The weather improved later that first day, and British air squadrons began the attack on the advancing Germans. Flying low, they tried strafing and bombing, inflicting heavy casualties on men and horses pulling artillery forward, but in the fluid condition of the enemy offensive, pilots at times held their fire for uncertainty where Allied troops were with respect to the advancing Germans and the withdrawing British. The Royal Flying Corps, with as many as thirty-six squadrons seeing action, flew to the "limit of their ability" the first day of the German offensive.[13] The next day again began foggy, but the weather cleared so that aircraft could resume their attack. They tried in vain to stop the German penetration of British defensive positions. While unable to do much more than harass the German ground assault, the Royal Flying Corps performed well in denying heavy German air attacks on the British troops and equipment retreating westward. Up and down the front, British pursuit pilots engaged the German squadrons. At one point, the RFC had downed forty-two enemy planes, while losing eleven. Even Richthofen's famed circus had trouble against the inspired British pilots, now desperately protecting endangered British ground units.[14]

The German air force, in support of the offensive, had constructed new airdromes close to the front lines, but had orders that it was "absolutely necessary to screen the concentration of our flying units" so as not to betray the forthcoming attack. Squadrons were moved forward at the last minute, and every effort was made to deny Allied reconnaissance machines from the region. German aircraft then were concentrated under the command of von Richthofen, and they outnumbered Allied planes 730 to 579.[15] Richthofen's airdrome (at Cappy) "was always so far forward as to be within range of the enemy's artillery, and the great success with which he met is to be attributed to the fact that he always sought to keep on the heels of the enemy," recorded one

German airman.[16] The weather (fog), along with the plan to support the infantry, led to low-flying German air sorties at first, but as the fog lifted, furious air battles ensued between German aircraft and British planes trying to protect observation planes and balloons, seeking to scout the movement of the German troops and supply columns. The battle in the air almost matched the fury of the ground conflict.[17]

Five days into the German offensive, on March 26, the weather turned cold and clear, and air activity increased. Major General Salmond, commander of the Royal Flying Corps in France, issued orders: "Bomb and shoot up everything that can be seen. Very low flying necessary, all risks to be taken. Urgent."[18] The RFC, despite its all-out effort, had a mixed record. On the one hand, its bombing and strafing caused German casualties, had an impact on enemy timetables, and largely blocked German air attacks on the British forces. However, it failed to stop the enemy's advance, lost coordination with the artillery, and sustained major losses from both ground fire and German aircraft pouncing on the RFC's low-flying aircraft. Author Martin Middlebrook, in his book-length account of the offensive's first day, March 21, succinctly described the pilot's difficult work: "Imagine these young men sitting in their cold, open cockpits in the slip-stream of a noisy engine, the ever-present danger of German fighters which might drop down on them out of the sun without warning, the danger of the low-flying work over the battlefield with perhaps hundreds of rifles and dozens of machine-guns firing at one plane, the fear of engine failure at low level, and the worst fear of all: fire and no parachute. And, when the flight is over, there were damaged planes to be landed back at airfields that were perhaps half obscured in mist."[19] Ludendorff decided to exploit the near-breakthrough of one of his armies and directed it more southwest toward Amiens. The British had been more successful in holding their lines in the north around Arras. Ultimately, the Germans drove some forty miles into the British sector, but the advance began to stall partly because the French finally responded with reserves, helping to plug the gaping hole in the Allied lines, and the Germans began to outrun their logistical support. By April 4, the front began to stabilize. General Ludendorff now believed he needed to switch his offensive farther north, still against the British. He erroneously calculated that he could yet break the British. The second offensive was launched April 9 on both sides of the valley of the Lys River, centered near the town of Armentières. Following the pattern with the German near-breakthrough in the initial March offensive, another massive artillery barrage began at 4:15 A.M. Gas and high-explosive shells pounded three British divisions defending an eleven-mile segment of the front. After the bombardment shifted to the trenches and machine gun strongpoints, the troops advanced. Once again, the Germans experienced early success, but as a heavy mist lifted, the British began relentless air attacks. Every squadron went into action, and never had more bombs been dropped or more sortie hours flown in a single day.[20] But the Germans broke through the lines, taking towns, and penetrating more than seven miles by April 12. Heavy air attacks on that day helped slow the German advance, and the senior French and British commanders, General Foch and General Haig, respectively, were able to move reserve divisions into place to shore up the new front. By April 29 Ludendorff's offensive had again made a significant dent in the Allied front but had not achieved the sought breakthrough.

General Ludendorff continued to hold that his strategy of knocking the British out of the war was correct, but he and the High Command considered how, in the preceding two offensives, there was the rescuing movement of French troops to the British front. He decided, therefore, to launch his next offensive against the French, perhaps convincing them to stay on their lines, and then he could return to concentrating on the British forces. With carefully planned deception, he chose an attack along the Aisne River to hit weak French and British divisions known to be in that region of difficult terrain.

The usual opening bombardment began early in the morning of May 27, but unlike the previous artillery barrages, this one made use of gas ammunition in guns and mortars for the first ten minutes, in the hope of breaking morale and creating confusion.[21] The Germans then succeeded in advancing thirteen miles in one day and came within two miles of the ancient city of Rheims and approximately eighty miles of Paris.

Despite the success of this German offensive in reaching the Marne River on June 4 and threatening Paris, this advance, like the others, started to grind to a halt. The Germans again outran their logistical support, and at this point of the war the troops were fatigued and exhausted with another major push deep into Allied lines. Also, the French recovered from the initial shock, and the Germans encountered fresh American troops around Château-Thierry. Some U.S. soldiers had already seen action before this when they were assigned to the Somme front to help stop the first Ludendorff offensive. Now the American Expeditionary Force (AEF) became a factor in the war. The Germans, however, made three major dents in the Western Front, and the Allies badly needed to regroup and consider counter-offensives.[22]

Aerial operations intensified, keeping pace with the rising demands of the German advances. Losses became heavy, with the concentration of German aircraft matched by everything the British and French could muster. During the first ten days of April, for example, the RAF suffered the loss of 478 airplanes along the entire front; by the end of April the total was 1,302 aircraft.[23] The air war had become a major struggle for aerial superiority, particularly over the battlefield. Like the struggles of ground forces engaged below, the aerial battles developed into a war of attrition. Could the British and French counter the Germans in number of airframes, engines, and pilots? The Germans, realizing their gradually growing inferiority in numbers, sought to respond by fielding technologically better aircraft—the Fokker D.VII—and by tactically massing greater numbers of aircraft at points of their choosing. In their plan four *Jastas,* or squadrons, amounting to fifty or sixty pursuit aircraft, would stagger in altitude with the commander's squadron in front at the lowest altitude, two others higher and to the right and left, and a fourth flying top cover. The lead squadron directed the attack on enemy planes, hoping to shatter any formation into individual prey for those at higher altitude.[24] The Allies, in counter, would ultimately develop their own aircraft concentrations, carry out aggressive offensive operations over German lines to destroy German aircraft, and similarly employ layered formations.

Lt. Field Kindley was thrust into this period of extreme Allied difficulty and evolving tactical operations. He was ordered to France, according to Special Orders No. 67, and assigned for duty to the 65th Royal Air Force Squadron near Amiens on the Somme River front.[25] At last, Kindley's eagerly awaited day came. On May 22, 1918, at 7:00 A.M., he bade farewell to two friends at a railway station in London. After a long day Kindley, with about eight other pilots, arrived at what was called a pilot's pool. The time was 1:30 A.M., and the new men soon found themselves sleeping "on various things somewhere in France." At daybreak, they reported to the officer in command. Here they found pilots of all types, that is to say, pilots flying every type of machine. Some had been there for weeks, others were as new as themselves. Ignorant of where they had moved, and how long they would remain, they fixed themselves as comfortably as possible. In the afternoon, while exploring this new area, Field Kindley discovered his name posted on a bulletin board—the second time a life-changing event had happened through reading a bulletin board. The notice confirmed his assignment to the RAF's 65th Squadron, and it was not long until a vehicle from that organization pulled up outside, loaded Kindley and baggage, and roared off to the new squadron area.[26]

The vehicle wound its way up the long, straight roads, with tall, old trees on either side. Young Kindley soon realized that these were typical of the northeastern section of France, and he heard it said that they were a heritage of Napoleon's time. The sun was setting, and shortly cars began dodging each other in the moonlight, for lights were not used except when absolutely necessary. As they passed through moonlit villages, small bodies of men could be seen forming. Kindley thought perhaps they were Americans, then, perhaps French, or British. They were dressed for inspection, as in days of training. The flashes from the artillery told him the battle lines were near and the soldiers probably destined to go there. This was all new to the young man, and indeed exciting and perplexing.

As Kindley continued to travel to the 65th Squadron area, he could see trenches for miles on both sides of the road. He also saw aircraft flying with navigation lights, which added to his fascination. His curiosity could be restrained no more, and as he bent forward to offer the driver a smoke, he whispered the questions, "Where are we and where are we going?" He was somewhat surprised to hear that he was about twenty-five miles from the front lines. Soon flashes were more visible and the sound more noticeable. His thoughts were suddenly jarred when the driver said, "Here is the 65th Squadron, sir." Only later did Kindley discover that he was near Amiens, France.

Kindley reported to the designated English officer and then had something to eat. Squadron personnel were not surprised at a new face, but an American officer was more of an exception. After a night's rest, he reported to the commanding officer and found that he was assigned to B Flight. He next officially presented himself to RAF Capt. A. A. Leitch, the flight commander. Kindley liked his immediate superior from the beginning, and respect deepened into real admiration as time passed. It did not take Field Kindley long to get into the air once he had taken care of the preliminaries. He had already developed a love of flying, and like so many pilots everywhere, he gloried in the telling and retelling of flying experiences. In addition, he was a determined young man with a strong ambition to be a success in this, his first combat organization. As he remarked at the time, "I was determined, either to break my neck, or make a good showing." As it turned out, it was to be very much the latter.

The 65th Squadron was assigned the Sopwith Camel, and it was this familiar aircraft that Kindley boarded for his first flights near the battle front. He had been genuinely thrilled when he climbed into the cockpit of this first-line fighter plane on February 23, 1918, during the last phase of his flying training, and he felt a new surge of excitement to now man the controls near the edge of battle. He had been tutored by veteran RFC pilots just back from the dogfights over the front, and he was anxious to put his training to use, but squadron procedures first required that he familiarize himself with the area. Therefore, he had to be content for three or four flights roaming the Allied side of the front. The squadron was now positioned not far from Albert, France, near the western edge of the battle line. The German Somme offensive in late March had brought plenty of action to this area.

Kindley recorded his first flight for the 65th Squadron on May 25, 1918, a twenty-five minute "district" sortie at 3,000 feet. Other short flights followed, labeled "practice," including a "firing practice" for over an hour on May 26. Two days later, Kindley was placed on "Aerial Sentry," flying at 12,000 feet near Albert. On that same day he noted that he led a for mation on a cross-country. The next day, however, he "started on patrol" but "broke tail skid." May 30 marked his "first patrol," followed by another one the succeeding day where he remarked "nothing seen."[27]

Kindley began serious practicing of formation flying during this combat orientation time. He often flew right rear, keeping the formation tight. It had been pounded into his head that he must do so or suffer the consequences. On June 3 he reported that he had seen five enemy aircraft while on "offensive patrol." Although no hostile engagement had taken place during this time, Kindley reported that during one patrol they had been fired upon, by mistake, by a group of Allied machines. It was rather ironic, and a bit distressing, that the first shots to be fired at Kindley came from friendly aircraft.[28]

Also, at this time, Kindley observed that it was not always easy to know when you were behind enemy lines. "At our height you cannot see the men in the trenches. Furthermore, there are so many trenches and shell-holes you do not know which are which. Of course, the best way of telling when you are over Hunland, is when "Archie" commences to burst about you. This is not what you might call a pleasant teacher." On June 3 and 4, Field noted in his log that his flying was to "learn the lines." He also wrote about old trouble on June 1, when he noted in the log comments, "Engine cutout."[29]

As Kindley's combat zone familiarization progressed and he accumulated more offensive patrols, he learned operational skills that later proved crucial to his success. One thing that he noted, and readily absorbed, was the importance of the leader of the patrol. "The leader decided when to attack and of course, as he cannot blow a bugle to charge, all he does is to stick his nose down and go for them. You follow sometimes not even seeing the enemy, for the leader is supposed to see more than a new man or even one behind him. . . . He must not only decide when to attack but he must recognize Allied machines as friendly and Huns as enemy machines at a great distance by their build and outline. If you should wait to see the markings, then it is too late for the scrap would have started."[30] Kindley was pragmatically studying his lessons.

Life on the air front was typically punctuated with periods of boredom followed by periods of feverish activity and excitement. The patrols did not come regularly. Some were at 3:30 A.M. and some at 7:30 or 9:30 P.M. The early patrol was most dreaded, Kindley complained, because it cut short his rest time and because the sun was in the east and the enemy cunningly concealed himself in it to surprise you. The German sorties over or near the airdrome were also worthy of complaint. "The noise we hate more than the buzzing overhead," he said, "for we can sleep under the buzzing but the guns firing nearby cheats us out of our night's rest. The early 4 o'clock 'show' (show means offensive aerial patrol) comes very early and with so little sleep it is not enjoyed so much especially if no Huns are to be found." There was an answer for sleeplessness, however. "In order to waken us up we usually go over the lines at a low altitude and let Archie (Archie is the Hun anti-aircraft shells) burst around us for a while."[31]

Although Kindley did not record the typical sequence of beginning a Camel sortie, other pilots graphically reported the lift-off from the airdrome. V. M. Yeates in *Winged Victory,* for example, described what happened after the Camel pilot climbed into the cockpit. As the pilot settled into his seat, he reported, "a mechanic called out 'Switch off, petrol on.'" The pilot "answered with the same words, and pumped up pressure, fastened his safety belt, waggled the joystick, kicked the rudder bar, and pulled up the CC gear piston handle, while they turned the engine backwards to suck in gas." The mechanic shouted, "Contact!" and the pilot replied, "Contact." "The engine started at first swing." The pilot "eased the throttle back and adjusted the petrol flow until it was ticking over." With the engine roar, he "looked at the rev counter, throttled down, and waved his hand. The mechanic pulled away the chocks from the wheels of the undercarriage, and ran round to the rear of the plane to hold the rear struts in order to help him turn." The pilot then held the "Camel's nose down to gain speed, and then pushed the stick over to the left as he let it zoom."[32] As the weeks rolled by, this takeoff procedure became second nature but always got the adrenalin going. The patrols varied in nature. Sometimes they were eighteen planes strong and at other times included only six machines. There were offensive patrols and occasionally there were bomber escort assignments. If there was any action with enemy aircraft, it nearly always had to be over enemy lines and then, as Kindley with keen disappointment wrote, "sometimes we do a whole two hours patrol without seeing a one." Kindley observed that it was difficult to get the German aircraft into a fight unless they outnumbered the Allied planes by about three to one. "If we get a fight out of an even number we have to circle around them and head them off from getting home," he moaned.[33]

As Kindley observed, the Germans increasingly became more defensive, remaining over their side of the battle lines in order to husband their resources. The British, at the same time, pressed offensive operations. By this time in the aerial war, tactics had evolved from single-plane encounters to far more sophisticated formation flying. Indeed, the German circus of massing flights and squadrons of aircraft led to similar Allied counter-measures. As early as January 1916, the RFC ordered formation flying to combat the new German aircraft.[34] In addition, the attacks from above led to layering of formations with the top flight responsible for lookout and protection of aircraft below.

Observation planes on both sides, often two-seaters with a gunner in the rear, still endured precarious single missions, but they increasingly required protective cover of the pursuit flights. The usual combat effort of getting on an enemy's tail needed modification when pursuing an observation plane with a rear gunner able to fire in a wide arc. One tactic that was developed involved one pursuit aircraft trying to fly a feint from the side while another tried to close underneath.

The image of aerial warfare presented to the general public clung stubbornly to the myth of aerial knights fighting one on one, embodying chivalrous gestures. The pilots, however, knew the brutal truth that this was deadly, unforgiving warfare. In reality, it meant kill or be killed, often at close range, and as the sky became filled with more and more airplanes the deadly peril to life increased greatly with no time for or thought of chivalry.[35] Most pilots viewed with disdain the heroic tales reported in various publications.

The action Field Kindley seemed to crave came soon. In a letter to his cousin Uther, dated June 4, 1918, he described what must have been some of his first combat experience: "Yesterday we had a nice interesting scrap over the lines at about 10,000 ft. Three of us happened to be firing at one poor Fritz and now we can not decide who got him but never the less we know he won't fly on this earth again. We all returned safe and sound. One of our machines had a few holes in it but holes can quickly be patched up but Fritz can not. I have been lucky for I have not received any holes in my bus yet. Knocking wood!!!"[36] In the same letter Kindley showed some maturing reactions to the sights and sounds of warfare: "Once in a while flying low the Hun Infantry opens up with rifles & machine guns but we have the advantage and gain in the long run for they only waste their ammunition. Of course I have seen the time when I wish I was fighting a school day fight rather than the Huns for by the 4 years war plus the 30 years preparation they should be able to shoot straight."

On June 26 Lieutenant Kindley gained his first aerial victory on an offensive patrol. It was a great day in the life of this young aviator, and as he commented, "It is useless to say that the day I got my first Hun was the most interesting one of my life." While it was a day for celebration, it was also a sobering time, as one of his best friends, Lieutenant Eaton, a Canadian, was shot down at the beginning of the action. At 8:30 in the evening Captain Leitch was leading the patrol of six Camels at 11,000 feet and climbing to meet eight or nine enemy aircraft, when Kindley noticed below and to his right, at about 8,000 feet, a Pfalz close on a Camel's tail. The Camel was Lieutenant Eaton who had left the formation a short distance to Kindley's right. At once, Kindley turned and dove upon the Pfalz. His attack was too late to save his friend, as he saw the Camel in a steep righthand turn with smoke coming from it. The Pfalz immediately turned east, but Kindley closed within 100 yards where he fired a long burst and saw the enemy half-roll and then go down in a flat spin on his back.

Black smoke began issuing from the Pfalz's fuselage, but Kindley had to turn away as he noticed the approach of three enemy aircraft. The kill was confirmed by Captain Leitch, the flight commander. "Later the infantry confirmed him and now I am officially credited with a Hun," wrote Kindley to his Arkansas relatives.[37]

Remarkably, Kindley had scored his first aerial victory against Lt. Wilhelm Lehmann, who had downed four Allied aircraft and had recently taken command of one of Germany's outstanding fighter squadrons, Jagdstaffel 5. At the end of the war, Jagdstaffel 5 ranked third among all German squadrons with over three hundred confirmed victories.[38] The Germans took note that it was Lt. Field E. Kindley who had killed Lehmann.

Kindley's first downing of a German fighter aircraft did not bring an end to this combat engagement. He rejoined his formation to open an attack on a German plane on which Captain Leitch had been firing. The machine went down, with the flight commander following to

A German Pfalz D.III aircraft, of the type that Kindley downed in his first aerial victory
Photo courtesy Steve Lawson, Denver, Colo.

confirm the kill. Kindley "stayed above to fight the two Huns remaining above." "Soon they got too hot for me and I had to fight my way back over our lines," wrote Kindley. More trouble developed, however. "I was shaking hands with myself when out of a cloud came one of the Hun's best machines, a Fokker Triplane. He and I went around and around trying to bring our guns into action but he was too much for me and I evidently enough for him for neither of us got a shot into one another."[39]

While Kindley's Fokker triplane adversary "got tired and went east," he again joined his formation. This time Kindley and his colleagues were surprised by three German Albatros Scouts. "They had the height on us so of course all they did was dive, fire and zoom up again. We had to zoom and fire from below." Kindley reported that his guns then stopped and he had "to retire because my engine was also playing out." The day's action pleased Lieutenant Kindley; he had been thoroughly battle-tested and thereby had gained a new sense of confidence. He had met in the air three different German aircraft, among their best, and he had held his own. "The results of the combat for the day was two Huns, one by my flight commander and one by your Hon Coz, Ha! Ha!"[40]

Kindley continued his combat with the 65th Squadron, not always experiencing success.

> Yesterday however the tables turned because three Huns got me in a corner and I had a hard time to get out. Three dove on me with guns firing to beat the band. I fly as I never fly before. Well do you blame me with 6 machine guns firing at you. You remember how popcorn used to pop over those hot winter fires, well multiply that by five and you have the sound I heard but not in the same comfort as I was around those nice winter fires at Aunt Mollie's place in the winters of 08, 09, 10, 11, & 12. Soon they must have run out of ammunition for they soon turned east and then I became brave and turned to fire on them. Why should a person not be braver when the guns are pointed the other way.[41]

Perhaps Kindley's mortality loomed larger in his mind than it ever had before as a result of his combat. In the same letter in which he celebrated his first victory, he gave some specific instructions for his

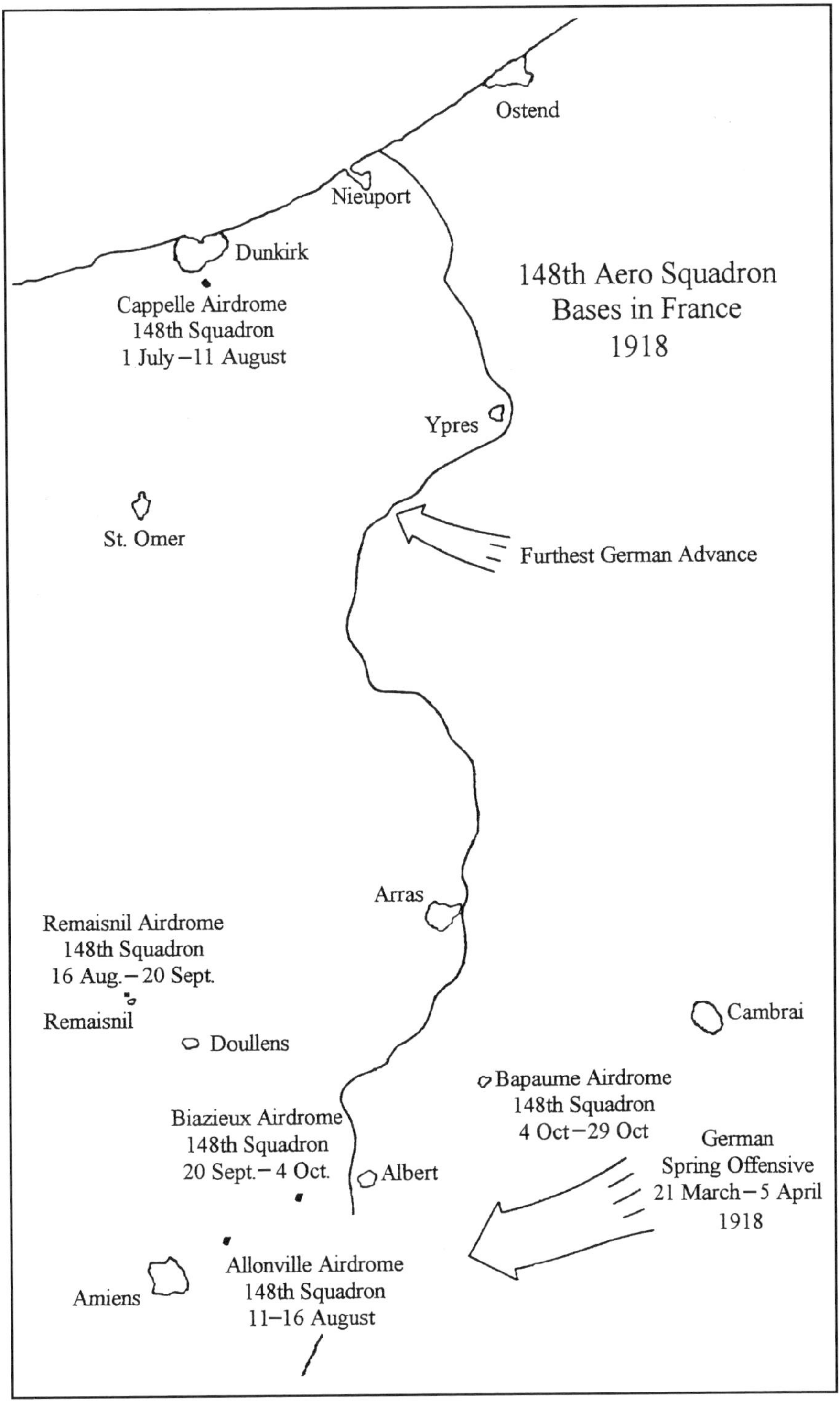
Ostend
Nieuport
Dunkirk
Cappelle Airdrome
148th Squadron
1 July – 11 August
148th Aero Squadron
Bases in France
1918
Ypres
St. Omer
Furthest German Advance
Arras
Remaisnil Airdrome
148th Squadron
16 Aug. – 20 Sept.
Remaisnil
Doullens
Cambrai
Bapaume Airdrome
148th Squadron
4 Oct – 29 Oct
Biazieux Airdrome
148th Squadron
20 Sept. – 4 Oct.
Albert
German
Spring Offensive
21 March – 5 April
1918
Allonville Airdrome
148th Squadron
11–16 August
Amiens

cousin Uther "if you get notice from the War Department of my being missing." He identified his "War Risk Policy" (No. 103, 968), whom to notify, and the location of some of his belongings at the American Express Co., London. "I am leaving a letter in my tent to tell friends what to do in the case I am missing. I am also leaving a letter for the American Express Co. It is to be hoped they will never have to open them," he wrote. But then Kindley's thoughts turned more positive as he ended his June 28 letter saying, "Shall close hoping to hear from you often and that I get a few more Hun's soon."[42]

Kindley was to score again shortly, but for a different organization. On July 1 at 10:00 A.M. he received orders to report to the American 148th Aero Squadron some distance away. Field felt a genuine regret at leaving the RAF squadron. He had enjoyed the good-natured British and Canadian officers he had fought beside and had grown to greatly respect their skill and valor. Thus, it was with a heaviness of spirit that he threw his belongings into a truck and boarded the vehicle for the journey to his new squadron. It was one o'clock in the afternoon.[43]

Chapter Five

Four Victories

> *I don't think I am making a mistake in saying our squadron has demanded respect from the British and thus gained a name among the British that the Yankee is a good airman. It is true we have lost some men in doing it but very few considering our work. A squadron that gets 60 Huns in 2 mo demands respect even from the Hun. We did it. I am talking for the boys here not myself. When you see and fight with them you are proud to be from the country from which they came: "USA."*

Lt. Field E. Kindley,
letter to Uther Kindley,
September 30, 1918

ON JULY 1, 1918, after a dusty trip, Kindley arrived at the American 148th Aero Squadron airdrome near Dunkirk on the English Channel. It was nearly 10:30 P.M. as he pulled his baggage off the truck. He had just turned to shake hands with one of his "old Yankee friends" when he heard a whizzing and then a large explosion. A faint hum of an engine could be heard, and it was obvious that "Fritz" was overhead. It sounded as if he was headed their way, so the two friends fell to the ground waiting for another explosion to follow. Something must have happened for none came. All lights at the airdrome were now out and none were allowed to be illuminated. Kindley, with his lack of familiarity with this airfield, felt around in the darkness and made a little place to rest for the night.[1]

The 148th Aero Squadron had been formed on November 11, 1917, at Kelly Field, San Antonio, Texas.[2] The enlisted men who were to maintain the squadron planes and support all phases of the air operations were dispatched almost immediately to flying fields (sometimes referred to as Taliaferro Fields) at Fort Worth to get technical training in airplane engines and rigging, administered by the British Royal Flying Corps. By January 1918 the squadron was located at Hicks Field, north of Fort Worth, and under the command of Maj. Cushman A. Rice. Some flying cadets, training on JN-4 Jenny aircraft, had been attached to the unit, so there was some semblance of an operational aero organization.[3]

The 148th personnel received orders to Europe on February 12, 1918, and two days later departed Hicks Field for the East Coast. After a cross-country train trip to New York, the men embarked on the unescorted fast ocean liner *Olympic* to Liverpool, England, arriving March 5. Shortly after arrival, pilots were withdrawn and sent to British flying schools, and the rest of the unit moved across the Channel to France where they continued training with several of the British combat squadrons. Although the squadron's Flight "A" initially trained and worked on S.E. 5 aircraft of an RAF squadron, the 148th, when reconstituted with fliers, was expected to receive Sopwith Camels, so support personnel were mainly assigned to Camel-equipped British squadrons in the northern British sector of the front in France.[4]

To make sure the squadron would have technically informed personnel, ten ground support men/mechanics, sometimes called "fitters," were sent to the RAF Engine Repair Base at Pont d' l'Arche, near Rouen, for special instruction in the Clerget rotary engine. This proved important as the squadron could get more "revs" from the engines and the unit reportedly had "no casualties resulting from fitting or rigging failures."[5]

During the time the three scattered squadron flights were assigned to the British units, they got a quick taste of war. The big German spring offensive, beginning March 21, put the British front in a desperate battle to stem German advances. The Americans experienced heavy artillery shelling, bombing, and hastily ordered moves from airfields. The 148th headquarters element and "A" Flight suffered the loss of ten men killed and others injured when three German bombs struck their encampment near Chaulnes Station. But at the same time the 148th men were rapidly learning combat aircraft maintenance by supporting their British counterparts in the hangars and on the flight lines. They avidly watched, along with the British, as the scout aircraft lined up on the field by flights and then roared airborne in formation flying to do battle near the front lines. They too soon waited expectantly for the first sign of returning aircraft and then listened intently as the "pilots told in matter-of-fact tones how their flight had come out or how that Hun had got away and so on."[6] Members of the 148th's "C" Flight, training with the RAF 43rd Squadron, were allowed to take complete control of the aircraft flown by American officers, thereby providing true operational experience, to the great benefit of the 148th later.[7]

For the most part, American pilots repeatedly flew an assigned aircraft unless it was disabled. In addition, usually they kept the same flight line crew normally consisting of a sergeant first class, assisted by a corporal, and a private first class or private mechanic. The permanent crew had responsibility for the service and repair of the aircraft, and the crew chief checked off on completed work before declaring the plane flight-ready.[8]

The ground crews were considered sufficiently trained by the end of June 1918, and the dispersed 148th elements were reunited at Cappelle airdrome close to Dunkirk. It was the first time in four months that the squadron had been together. The last to arrive at the airdrome were the flying officers, but only one, William J. Cogan, of the original Texas group of pilots ever returned to the unit. Lieutenant (soon to be Captain) Morton L. Newhall assumed command of the Squadron. The twenty-one pilots assigned were all RAF flying school–trained, and eight, including Kindley, had been with the "War Bird" September 1917 group. Some were already combat-experienced: Lt. Elliott White Springs, Lt. Bennett Oliver, Lt. Erroll Zistel, and Kindley.[9] As all the parts came together, there was great exchanging of stories about the different organizations to which they had been assigned and anxious discussions about the war and the flying to come.[10]

At Cappelle airdrome the squadron received from the British nineteen secondhand Sopwith Camels with the 130-hp Clerget engines. The ground crews immediately set about painting the 148th's solid white triangle insignia on the sides of the aircraft.[11] As soon as the machines were ready, the pilots began daily practice flights, some in formation, diving and firing on a silhouetted plane in a nearby St. Pol marsh.[12]

Kindley reported to his new squadron commander, Lieutenant (soon to be Captain) Newhall, who was a native of Philadelphia, Pennsylvania, and a one-time Harvard quarterback. He was ordered to assist in getting the inexperienced pilots ready for combat flying. The core of the squadron was eight battle-tested pilots who had been over enemy lines and had thirteen enemy aircraft to their credit. Kindley and the other flying "veterans" worked with the new machines and the pilot and support crew novices. Training progressed well, and within seven days the first patrols were over the lines.[13]

In typical standard organization fashion, the 148th Squadron was divided into three flights with combat-experienced pilot leaders for each flight. 1st Lt. Bennett ("Bim") Oliver of Pittsburgh, Pennsylvania, was named "A" Flight commander; 1st Lt. Elliott W. Springs of Lancaster, South Carolina, "B" Flight commander; and 1st Lt. Henry R. Clay of Fort Worth, Texas, was given command of "C" Flight. Lieutenants Kindley, G. C. Whiting, E. H. Zistel, Lawrence Callahan, Lawrence Wyly, and Harry Jenkinson, Jr., completed the RAF-experienced core group, crucial for success of the new organization.[14] Like Kindley, these officers had gone through Oxford, machine gun schooling, and flying training at various British bases. Like the flight commanders, Captain Newhall was a several-month veteran of RAF combat at the time he assumed command.[15] Most of these Americans had become a close-knit group as a result of their shared training, and later they were frequently referred to as the "War Birds," a name made all the more notable in time by a published diary kept by Lt. John M. Grider and edited by Elliott Springs. Some American officers, likewise British-trained, remained individually assigned to RAF squadrons.

Also contributing to the unit's cohesion was a college-type camaraderie, as a surprising number of the pilots were Ivy League college graduates or former students. For example, Elliott White Springs, twenty-two, the son of a South Carolina textile manufacturer, had a reputation from his college days at Princeton for hard drinking and partying. The reputation carried over into his flying experience, and he had diary-recorded drinking bouts with fellow Princetonians on a number of occasions.[16] Lt. Bennett Oliver was a 1917 graduate of Yale and the son of a senator from Pennsylvania. Lt. Larry Callahan had graduated from Cornell. A half-dozen Ivy Leaguers in the new 148th Aero Squadron could have been selected as flight leaders.[17] This situation undoubtedly proved interesting and likely intimidating for Lieutenant Kindley, the Arkansas high school dropout. Although these Americans, with varying backgrounds, had already interacted in the preceding months in the course of learning to fly, Kindley was now thrust into a solely American unit of many college-educated companions. Unlike Lt. Frank Luke, Jr., who was reportedly disliked and who kept to himself, or Lt. Eddie Rickenbacker, the eventual top U.S. air ace, who was also a school dropout and considered an "older" loner, Kindley seemed to have adjusted well to the new personnel and they to him.[18] Apparently his unassuming and Arkansas-friendly personality overcame any educational stigma. Of course, it certainly helped that he had already recorded an aerial victory. Proof of his acceptance in the squadron came soon, when Lt. "Bim" Oliver became ill and Kindley was given command of "A" Flight in his place.

Long after the war, one of Field Kindley's pilot colleagues was asked to compare the three flight commanders. In his assessment, "Kindley was a born leader. I don't believe he had a nerve in his body." As for Lieutenant Springs, "The best way to describe him is to use a term which is common now. He was a 'real swinger' and 'a good pilot.'" The Flight "C" Commander, Lieutenant Clay, "was outstanding. None better."[19]

Living conditions at the 148th airdromes were certainly below the standards encountered at British training centers. Kindley wrote, however, that "many people still think that we live in trenches and dug-outs, and at all times have a gas mask, tin hat and revolver buckled to you, but such is not the case." He observed that they were out of artillery range and "were it not for the occasional bombing-raids, we would hardly know there is a war on." "Our huts are quite comfortable, with sand-bags piled about them. Of course, wallpaper, rugs, etc. are not expected but most of us have honest to God sheets, feather pillows, and wash pans."[20]

The pilot's "anti-room [*sic*] is far above par," said Kindley, "with plenty of magazines, papers, steamer chairs, a Victrola and piano." He considered his dining hall the "best one in France." The dining hall, or "mess," had white ceiling and walls, decorated with black and with the flags of each Ally prominently displayed. The white oilcloth on the table and the chairs made things "look clean indeed." But the best feature, concluded Kindley, was "that which decorates the table at meal times." He dared not list a menu, he said, for fear of an investigation. Nevertheless, "white bread is not a stranger" and "nice fish and roast are common; salad, tomatoes, sugar, butter and jam are getting old." Then there were the special occasions. "Ice cream is served each pilot's birthday, upon each victory, and when the staff is to dinner." Humorously, he added, "Outside of these bad points the mess is fairly good."[21]

In addition to the 148th's white triangle insignia, large white letters *B, N,* and *S* were placed in front of the triangle to designate the flight commander. In some RAF squadrons a colorful streamer identified a flight leader and deputy flight leader. Lieutenant Kindley's Camel, E 1537, had a large *B* as "A" Flight commander. The large British bull's-eye, or roundel, was placed in the middle between these two markings. In contrast, the U.S. 17th Aero Squadron carried a white dumbbell instead of the white triangle.[22] The assignment of Camels to the 148th meant Kindley would not face a problem in having to make the transition to a new aircraft. He was comfortable and skilled in the Camel, as forthcoming events would surely indicate.

Identification of a Camel flight commander by the large letters proved to be an important element in combat operations. Inexperienced pilots, in particular, would anxiously look for that marking after getting lost during a bombing raid or a dogfight. Seeing that designation go flashing past would allow the pilot to "tack on" behind the flight leader—a man he could trust to lead him back safely. "Confidence and trust in a good flight-leader" was almost a "religion with not only the new man but those who have 'followed' for months."[23]

Lieutenant Kindley believed the morale of the Americans was excellent. Contributing to it was the leadership. "An asset a squadron can have is having a good commanding officer, so therefore, we claim we have the greatest asset." This was high praise, indeed, from one who had before admired his British superiors. Also, he sensed the combat eagerness that pervaded the unit and no doubt fueled his own feelings. He remarked, "If there is a scrap and some of the pilots happen not to be in it, they have the 'blues' the rest of the day." Always positive in outlook, Kindley declared, "Our future is limited by the length of the war."[24]

At the time of the deployment and reconstitution of the 148th Aero

Squadron in early July 1918, the war had started taking a new turn. Ludendorff's spring offensives had driven significant dents into Allied lines, but each one in turn had stalled. In the first German offensive on March 21, 1918, Ludendorff massed his planes against the British, providing for numerical superiority over an advancing front. Manfred von Richthofen, the remarkable Red Baron, and his "Flying Circus" and other Jastas pressed the air attack to support the German advances and on one day flew 118 sorties, destroying 13 Allied aircraft without loss. Richthofen himself increased his victories to 73. The Allied air squadrons, particularly the British, were hard pressed. But even Richthofen sensed gloomy days ahead. He remarked that the war had "become awfully serious" and in his opinion "there is nothing left of the 'lively, merry war,' as our deeds were called in the beginning. Now we must fight off despair and arm ourselves so the enemy will not penetrate our country."[25] Indeed, the Allies, strengthened with fresh American manpower, now planned to take the offensive, and by midsummer they felt strong enough to attack the German salients and roll back the German lines.

By July 18, 1918, the last German offensive drive was collapsing, and the Allies, including the Americans, began their first counter-attacks on the Soissons front. Ludendorff had to abandon any thoughts about a future Flanders offensive to the north in order to strengthen his forces at the Soissons bulge. The Germans were now on the defensive. Lt. Col. Harold Hartney, commander of the U.S. 1st Pursuit Group (based in the French sector), flying high over the opening Allied artillery barrage, was duly impressed with the smoke and dust emanating from the many shell bursts. "No man ever saw a more magnificent or, rather, a more significant sight. Here was the tide of a world war involving twenty million men actually turning before my very eyes," Hartney declared.[26]

The Allied counter-offensive against the Amiens salient was most important to the 148th Aero Squadron because of its geographic proximity to the squadron's airdrome. The attack would be a joint British-French affair, with the British providing 17 infantry divisions, 600 tanks, 2,000 guns, and 800 aircraft. The French would supply 10 infantry divisions and 1,100 aircraft. Against this force the Germans could counter only 20 divisions, few tanks, and fewer than 400 aircraft.[27] Clearly, the balance of power on this sector, as on others, had tipped in the Allies' favor.

After careful preparation and planning, a major Allied counter-offensive began on August 8, and although fog delayed air observation and ground strafing, the Allies succeeded in advancing nine miles into and through German trenches. Thousands of German soldiers surrendered and others pulled back hastily. Ludendorff called this date "the black day" for the German forces. The Germans momentarily formed new defensive lines, but by August 26 Ludendorff had ordered a general withdrawal in the Amiens area to a depth of nearly twenty miles.[28]

During the month preceding the Allied counter-attack against the Amiens salient, the American 148th Aero Squadron continued its battle-front orientation and the combat training of the pilots and crews. In keeping with the British policy of easing into combat operations with area familiarization wherever possible, the squadron had been based in the north of the British front, which was relatively quiet.[29] As a consequence, early offensive patrols did not involve aerial combat. For the first few days in July while at Cappelle airdrome, Lieutenant Kindley was bringing new machines to the squadron, and on July 4 he tested the new machines and chose one for himself. Over the next several days Kindley noted "shooting practice" and "formation flying." The first "line patrol" occurred on July 11 with one enemy aircraft reported as seen.[30]

The first "real war-work" involved escorting British De Haviland Nine (D.H. 9) bombers as they attacked the Belgian coastal cities of Zeebrugge, Ostend, and Bruges. The bomber escort tactics were best described in a letter by American Capt. Bogart Rogers, flying with the RAF: "The bombers always leave long before we do and climb and climb to get their height. Then we take off, get up to them in a few minutes, and take them across. It's the same coming home. We trail them over the line, and when they are well out of danger we pass them and are all washed up by the time they land." In another letter Rogers reported on a particularly successful escort mission. "Thirty bombers went over on a little raid, and two scout squadrons escorted them. The bombers were below at about 12,000, one bunch of scouts slightly above them, and we sat on top at about 16,000. The bombers came across the line in three groups at about ten minute intervals. We would meet the first bunch at the line, take them over while they laid their eggs, bring them back to the line, and take the next over. Everything went off without a hitch and woe to any Huns who might have come snooping around. The sky was full of our machines just like a big flock of sparrows."[31]

Although not particularly bothered by enemy aircraft, the 148th escort planes experienced almost continuous anti-aircraft "Archie" fire. One of the German "Archie-batteries" became identified as one of the best and most accurate in all they faced during their war flying. But thankfully, "not a plane or man was lost while on this work."[32]

The cold proved an important factor in escorting bombers, particularly as the war moved into the fall months. The S.E. 5 pilots, usually flying top cover, taking advantage of the S.E. 5's better high-altitude performance, bore the brunt of the uncomfortable cold. Capt. Bogart Rogers, an S.E. 5 pilot, reported, "Today I wore a pair of silk gloves, a pair of chamois gloves, and a heavy pair of flying gloves over the lot, and my hands nearly dropped off. The winds are getting cold, the nights are getting cold."[33] Even the Camel pilots, however, experienced the cold conditions. Lt. Elliott Springs noted that he smeared his face with ill-smelling whale oil to offer some protection. Others used a facial cold cream. Springs reportedly refused to wear goggles in combat and complained his eyelids were red and raw from the wind.[34] German pilots also took note of the effects of the cold, in addition to the other strains on the flying men. "Among other things they had to endure the appalling cold, which at the height of 15,000 feet was often as low as –50 degrees Centigrade even in summer, and owing to the long periods during which they had to remain at these altitudes they suffered from the lack of oxygen," wrote one German pilot.[35]

Kindley's experience with the British 65th Squadron proved invaluable as he worked with the rookie pilots of the 148th, particularly developing formation skills. He described formation flying:

> What I mean by keeping pilots in formation is to keep one on each side and twenty-five yards to your rear and two more to their rear. . . . To do this you must know your pilots and place them where they fly better. If possible, it is best to have the two best observers to the rear, so you will not be surprised from the rear. The other two, if possible should be the stoutest men and who you can depend upon in a good fight, or who are always ready to attack. Of course, the deputy leader generally flies immediately to your right. In every formation you must know where your poorest machine is, so that you can regulate your speed, etc. Never let a man struggle.[36]

Flying the Camel in formation was no easy matter. A British pilot, Arthur Gould Lee, recalled, "I found it tiring to fly in formation for a long period. She's so sensitive you can't relax for a second, and you have the constant pressure on the joystick, which in two hours' flying makes your right arm ache."[37] In *Winged Victory,* Camel pilot Yeates declared, "It would not fly straight for more than a second at a time."[38] The 148th's German opponents also held strong views about the need for formation flying. Richthofen, for example, wrote, "Surprises can be avoided only when flying in close order," and "No machine should be allowed to advance or keep back."[39]

In mid-July, when Lieutenant Oliver became ill, Kindley became acting "A" Flight commander and then permanent commander later.[40] A major responsibility of the flight commander was the watch for enemy aircraft. "Recognizing E. A. is indeed something to study . . . if you wait until you see the black cross, maybe you or some one in your formation will have been shot down. So you must learn the build of machines, in order to tell they are Huns by the outline of them," Kindley wrote. He added, "Watching for E. A. will take most of your time, for every machine has its dead angles, that is to say, on some

Flight "A" of the 148th Aero Squadron, (*from left*) Lt. Lawrence T. Wyly, Lt. Louis Rabe, Lt. Field Kindley (with Fokker), Lt. Walter B. Knox, and Lt. Jesse Creech

Photo courtesy Lafayette Foundation

148th Aero Squadron "B" Flight pilots, commanded by Lt. Elliott White Springs (*third from left*)

Photo courtesy Lafayette Foundation

machines you cannot see directly above you. This calls upon you to continually keep turning your machine up, so as to be able to see above." In checking for the enemy, a major difficulty was always the sun. "Then the enemy, as well as ourselves, know that it is impossible to see a machine, while setting up in the sun." As a consequence, all pilots had to be on the "look-out for a surprise attack in the mornings from out of the sun."[41] Because the Germans had the morning advantage on their eastern side of the battle front, this constituted a major lesson that had to be learned. The importance of "seeing in the air" could not be overemphasized, added another pilot writer—"inexperienced pilots were shot down easily because they did not see approaching danger; the first weeks over the lines were quite the most dangerous."[42]

Kindley quickly made clear that there was more to do as a leader than just to watch for enemy aircraft and keep from being surprised by the enemy. The flight commander had to be attentive to ensuring that his pilots kept "in formation, watching for E. A. maneuvering for position, dodging Archie, and retreating." Very often a retreat is necessary, he noted. "In some cases the leader has made the mistake of retreating too fast and leaving one man behind who is not likely

148th Aero Squadron "C" Flight pilots, commanded by Lt. Henry R. Clay (*fourth from left*). Lt. Clayton Bissell (*second from left*) played an important part in Kindley's story.

Photo courtesy Lafayette Foundation

to return. In retreat a close formation in my mind is very necessary for occasionally you can turn and fight them off. In most cases, when they think you are going to make a stand, they happen to think of the black bread and one ounce of salted bacon waiting for them, and at once they go to it."[43] Once you are confronted or you see the enemy aircraft, a host of questions come to mind, Kindley concluded:

> After seeing the enemy and you are not in a position to attack, then it is best to maneuver for the position, such as getting in between the E. A. and sun or getting height on them. Much must be considered before attacking. Are there more E. A. above you, in or above the clouds, or concealed in the sun? Is this type of E. A. fast to climb, maneuver or get away? Are they two-seaters with guns that can be fired from the rear? If so, a different method in attacking must be resorted to. Is the wind strong, if so, will it carry you over Hunland or back home? How far are you over Hunland at present? If the enemy has not seen you, try to make a surprise attack. Surprise attacks won many a great battle in historic days, and it holds good in the air.[44]

Ground fire, of course, always remained a problem for the pursuit aircraft, particularly when engaged in ground strafing missions. The pilot could ignore it only at his peril. Controversy, for example, continues to this day over whether Richthofen was shot down by ground fire or by Capt. A. Roy Brown, a Canadian pilot.[45] The anti-aircraft fire complicated aerial maneuvers, and since most offensive patrols were over or beyond German lines, the pilot had to be wary of ground fire as well as enemy planes. Kindley had some thoughts on this concern:

> Most every time you cross the lines anti-aircraft shells, or better known as Archie, are put up at you. When they burst, they look like black balls or spots in mid-air, but very soon it forms a small black cloud. If you see the cloud and nothing has happened, you are O. K. as far as that goes, but the question in mind is, where will the next one go? If he has your correct elevation, it is more wholesome to change it. At other times changing your course from time to time by making flat 30 degree or forty degrees turns, is best. The time to change is when you think the next volley is about to burst. They say that one burst in 10,000 hits you. Very well, but some of us have had 9,999 fired at us. Very cheerful, eh![46]

A British Camel pilot wrote of his experience with rifle and machine gun fire. "We ran into mist and low cloud as soon as we took off, and

Drawing of Lt. Field E. Kindley's Sopwith Camel with his "B" designation while leading Flight "A" of the 148th Aero Squadron. The 148th used the solid white triangle insignia shown to the right of the British roundel.
From Frank, Aces: 52 Sopwith Camel Aces of WWI, *by permission of Osprey Publishing, Ltd.*

as we were flying at 50 ft, we were much too occupied in keeping the compass steady to check our route on the map. Suddenly, there was a tremendous racket of gun fire from below, and bullets cracked past our ears."[47] Like the British pilot, Kindley had to check his compass and read his map while flying in an open cockpit and remaining on the continuous watch for enemy activity below as well as in the air.

The official history reported that the 148th's "first flight . . . over the lines from the Cappelle airdrome near Dunkirk" was on July 20.[48] Lt. Kindley, however, got into combat a week before that. At 8:57 A.M., July 13, while on patrol between Poperinge and Ypres, and flying about 12,000 feet, Field saw six enemy aircraft below him. While he was contemplating an attack, a German Albatros plane came out of the clouds at Field in his Sopwith Camel. "After climbing head-on over him, I half-rolled and shot two bursts of one hundred rounds into him at point blank range," Kindley reported. "Soon he and another E. A. were on my tail, diving vertically at me." Field then observed that the aircraft he had fired at tried to come out of its dive but his "tail came loose and he went down in a vertical dive with the tailplane hanging to his fuselage." The Albatros continued its vertical plunge through the clouds, and Field believed he "must have crashed not far from the lines South East of Ypres." Then Lieutenant Kindley put into practice his thinking about a tactical retreat. "By this time three E. A. were firing upon me and I maneuvered my way through the clouds back to the lines and rejoined my formation."[49] Field Kindley's second aerial victory was subsequently confirmed, and he marked his flight log with a German cross and a large lettered "Second Hun" in the remarks column.[50]

There was a big celebration by the squadron that evening. Congratulations were received from all around. Brig. Gen. E. R. Ludlow-Hewitt, commanding officer of the RAF 10th Brigade, telegraphed the joyous group: "Please convey my congratulations to the 148th Squadron and Lieut. Kindley for marking up the first points scored against the enemy by the American Air Service."[51] Other messages were received of the same tone.

An element of friendly competition began developing between the 148th and the other British-sector American Squadron, the 17th, formed about a week before the 148th. Kindley delighted in noting that they "had to take the count when we beat them in getting one

Lt. Field E. Kindley in full flight gear next to his Sopwith Camel
Signal Corps Photo 111-SC-24232

of Fritz's beautifully colored machines."[52] The 148th's first bragging rights didn't last long, however, as the 17th Squadron recorded a Fokker shot down on July 20. It was now the "dumbbell" insignia squadron's chance to collect bets and toasts.[53]

The last days of July remained relatively quiet for Lieutenant Kindley and the 148th Aero Squadron. Kindley's flight log during this period reported "tests" of aircraft and offensive patrols (O. P.) with remarks of "nothing seen" or "uneventful." On July 28 he did write, "Practice bomb dropping." Action picked up on August 3, however, when Lieutenant Kindley's 9:30 A.M. flight on a scouting mission at 11,000 feet over Ostend was attacked by four German Fokkers. In the ensuing aerial battle, other squadron flights got into the melee, and Field Kindley succeeded in "firing 75 rounds at 80 yards" at a Fokker biplane. This comment provided clear evidence of Kindley's typical tactic of closing on an enemy to point-blank range before firing a burst. Kindley observed that the enemy plane started to turn, "his nose went down and he fell on his back for a few seconds and then into a slow spin." Kindley continued to fire until the Fokker went into clouds. "Later I went down under the clouds over Ostend and saw S. E. of Ostend what appeared to be an aeroplane burning on ground underneath scene of engagement," Kindley reported. 2nd Lt. Lawrence T. Wyly also indicated he got a "short burst into him."[54] Field Kindley was credited with his third German aircraft and Lt. Elliott Springs, "B" Flight commander, recorded his fourth victory.[55] Five days later, August 8, Kindley dove firing on a German two-seater aircraft while on offensive patrol, but without a victory this time. Up to this point on the war front, from July 1 to August 9, he totaled 13 hours and 45 minutes of "practice" flying and 35 hours and 20 minutes of "war flying."[56]

On August 10 "A" Flight Commander Kindley inspected a "new airdrome," and the following day he reported his aircraft "all landed O. K." at the new airfield.[57] One of the problems that the American squadrons had been experiencing was that their bases were too far from the front lines, reducing the amount of time they had over German territory because of fuel requirements. Also, as part of the big Allied offensive against the Amiens salient, the 148th and 17th Squadrons needed to move closer to support the battle area. As a result, the 148th moved to Allonville airdrome, or Horseshoe Woods, a few miles northeast of Amiens. The site was known as Horseshoe Woods because of the shape of the nearby forest as viewed from the air, always an important geographic feature to recognize for returning pilots. The airdrome at Horseshoe Woods was also very near the grave of Germany's Baron von Richthofen. The squadron now became attached to the Fourth British Army, which began attacking on a twenty-five-mile front from Albert to Roye.[58]

The pilots could fly to the new airdrome quickly, but the ground crews had to move some seventy-five miles south in a truck convoy. They were not to arrive until the next day, August 12. Nevertheless, the redeployment of the 148th progressed with remarkable speed, and flight operations began with little delay.[59]

The 148th now faced a far more challenging battle environment. First, there was a major Allied offensive under way, which meant that determination of enemy and friendly trench lines and identification of advancing and retreating units was far more difficult. Second, the squadron was much closer to the action, with more available time over enemy emplacements. Third, squadron aircraft would likely be called upon to support the ground advance with reconnaissance, strafing, and bombing missions. Fourth, the Germans massed their aerial forces to counter those of the British, French, and Americans. Fifth, although the German aircraft were outnumbered, they were now employing the new faster, higher altitude–capable, and more highly maneuverable Fokker D.VII biplane, which according to many observers may have been the best pursuit aircraft of the war.[60]

Only two days after transferring to Allonville airdrome on August 13, Lieutenant Kindley got into a major air battle while on another line patrol north of Roye. At a height of 6,000 feet, Field spotted six enemy aircraft some distance away. Believing the Germans had not detected his flight, he devised a tactic of turning and then, with a projected intercept out of some clouds, to try to gain surprise. Coming out of the cloud cover, engaging immediately four Halberstadt two-seaters and two Fokker biplanes with the surprise hoped for, Kindley fired a "burst of 125 rounds into a two-seater." "Those in the rear of the Hun formation were doomed. Three machines fell out of control, and the pilots either killed or wounded."[61] Field observed that his victim "went down with left wing low and upon landing ran into a shell hole turning up on his left wing and nose." Kindley proceeded to attack another enemy aircraft at 50 yards range when both guns jammed. When he was unable to clear them, he beat a tactical retreat.[62] An RAF communiqué credited Lieutenants Kindley and Lawrence T. Wyly with one victory each. The destruction of another was shared by Lieutenants George C. Whiting and George V. Seibold.[63] The other German aircraft fled to the east.

Celebration of these three victories was severely tempered by Lieutenant Wyly's failure to return after being credited with his victory over a Halberstadt. The next day, however, a telegram informed the squadron

148th Aero Squadron flight line at airdrome in France

Photo courtesy Lafayette Foundation

that Wyly was safe. After following his victim down, his engine had quit and he made a dead-stick landing just inside Allied lines. Lieutenant Kindley drove a touring car to the site to pick up his fallen comrade.[64] He found Lieutenant Wyly having a great time firing a machine gun at enemy aircraft overhead as he had befriended an anti-aircraft machine gun company. Lieutenant Kindley reportedly said he preferred "to restrict his attention to viewing the Front Line from the air after that."[65] Only a few days later, Wyly in another engagement received a hit in his arm and made another landing inside friendly lines.

Lt. Field E. Kindley, in somewhat of a surprise, went on leave on August 15 and did not return to the war front and combat action until September 1. The reason for this break is not known. Perhaps there was some evidence of combat tension and fatigue, or perhaps it was merely a part of a British practice of periodically giving the fliers a respite from combat. In Kindley's flight log there was a remark on August 14 of an "explosion."[66] What this meant cannot be determined, and whether this had any impact on the leave is uncertain. Whatever the explanation, Kindley welcomed this two-week relaxing interlude, particularly since it was in London.

The 148th Aero Squadron history graphically described what Field Kindley and others must have felt about an impending leave from battle:

> It wasn't a bad life either when the regular British leave came around to each man within three months of his first war-flying at the Front. How he would look forward to that leave, dream about it nights, and even on patrol when his mind should have been on those little, black dots in the East, he could see himself taking that leave-boat to England. Then, as the day drew near, he would become more nervous than ever. Every patrol he could see himself whirling down in flames, crashing in Hunland, or any other dire happening which could blot out that precious two-week leave. Always the "day before" was a sort of sanctuary, and [the] lucky pilot was not asked to go on patrol that day. The next morning, very early, the touring-car would be waiting. After a hurried breakfast, off they went on the long ride to Boulogne; there to catch the leave-boat in the early afternoon. Then that leave, with all travel paid to anywhere in the United Kingdom, Scotland or Ireland or London, that Mecca for the

A German Albatros aircraft, of the type involved in Lieutenant Kindley's second aerial victory
Photo courtesy Lafayette Foundation

> officers and men on leave. All too soon the two weeks of dances, theatres, and entertainment slipped by, and then back to work again, "dawn shows" and all the rest. Every pilot will vouch for the fact that he feels much more like going after the Hun when he returns from that leave than he did before. Just why they cannot seem to explain.[67]

In a September 30 letter to Cousin Uther Kindley, Field said, "To say the least the two weeks I spent on leave in London were the sweetest of my life." There were multiple reasons for this. "First I high toned those who I once used to have to say 'Sir' to, next was because I had been away from civilization so long, third because I felt like I had deserved the leave and now could face the people and say 'I have been there,' fourth because I knew the next two weeks were safe and that my mind and nerves were at absolute ease." In a personal note, Field added, "Then too I meet a mighty nice black haired, dark eyed Spanish lady. So all in all I enjoyed myself as never before."[68]

Chapter Six

Becoming an Air Ace

The head lines you are reading from day to day tell you where I am for I have been in the thick of it. Sometimes I think it is too thick but after once into it it does not matter. It is the waiting for it that gets your nerves.

Lt. Field E. Kindley,
letter to Uther Kindley,
September 30, 1918

LIKE ALL SOLDIERS AND SAILORS a long way from home, Field Kindley looked forward to hearing from his father and cousins, and he kept them informed by letters as best he could. The correspondence flow from the Philippines to France and vice versa must have taken a long time indeed. George C. Kindley, Field's father, writing on August 19, 1918, from Malaybalay, acknowledged Field's letter of June 4. "You don't know dear boy how proud I am of you at this time," he wrote. "I am so pleased to know you are doing so well and hope that you may take care that no Hun gets you in the fights."[1] In a previous letter, on July 14, he had told his son, "I am very lonely to-day and wish I could spend the time with you but it is impossible." He added, "Be careful Field and shoot hell out of them but don't let them get you. Write often for I look for your letters each mail."[2] The father's anxiety was no doubt heightened by Field's letter of May 10, when he informed him of his survival in the crash on the cliffs of Dover. On August 4, George Kindley wrote, "Field I was sorry to know you had such narrow escape with your life in the accident with your machine but hope you are all right now and trust that you will not be so unfortunate as to get into another bad fog with a broken wagon." He then scolded his son for not having told him about the incident in an earlier letter.[3] Field in his letters to his Arkansas relatives provided some colorful descriptions of his experiences, punctuated by personal requests. In a June 4, 1918, 1etter to his cousin Uther he asked for a pair of house slippers (size 9), BVDs (undershorts), some Prince Albert (tobacco), and a few envelopes. He wanted Herman and Lena Chatfield to send him some Kodak film. As important as the other items, he wondered if Edna, Uther's wife, "can not practice on making fudge and send me a little of the results."[4] Getting letters and packages from home ranked close to leave, even in London, for Field Kindley.

Only a few days after Field started his leave, the 148th Aero Squadron was ordered to make another move. On August 18, the unit was assigned to Remaisnil, near Doullens, to be still closer to the developing Allied offensive. The 148th was now under the RAF 13th Wing and the British Third Army. In August the RAF overall assembled fourteen fighter squadrons and massed more than sixteen hundred planes to support the British drive for Cambrai.[5] The 148th Aero Squadron would be an important part of this aerial force.

When Lieutenant Kindley returned from leave, he not only found a new airdrome and base of operations but also greatly increased air activity. For example, on the very day that he returned from leave to duty, 1 September, he had an 8:30 A.M. bombing mission where he reported he had dropped four bombs from 2,000 feet on "transport" and horses at Morchy. Then at 3:20 P.M., he had another assigned bombing mission in which four bombs were released from 2,000 feet on "transport on road N. of Beaumetz." In the afternoon sortie he told how he engaged two two-seaters over Morchy and fired 150 rounds but was immediately attacked by nine enemy aircraft. Since no further description of an aerial battle was recorded, it seems likely that this was a time for a quick, and successful, tactical retreat for Kindley.[6]

"After coming back from leave I found the war in the air had changed. For we were where the battle was raging," Kindley wrote. "The Huns' best pilots and machines were just across the line from us and every day we engaged them in the air." While the British, French, and Americans managed to gain air superiority, there were some difficult days for the air units. "However the only fight in which we got the worst end was a few days after my return from leave. Nine of us engaged 25 Fokkers. Three of our men have not been heard of because we attacked them on their side of the lines. One died of wounds while we only got two of them."[7]

Field continued his description of this big air battle: "Three got on my tail and indeed I had a hard time. Finally I managed to get one but by then I was too badly shot up to fight any longer so I worked my way back across the lines. Upon landing I found 36 holes in my bus. Ten had burst on the butt of my guns and the splinters sprinkled my face, while one bullet went through goggles missing my temple by 1/4 inch. My machine could not be flown again, however I had another small scrap that afternoon."[8] Kindley later identified his attackers as a Fokker and a Hanoveranner, "who were very stout," he commented. "The Fokker left, but the Hanoveranner continued to riddle me with bullets." Kindley added he could "get only one burst into him."[9] Finally at the airdrome, Kindley told how he leaned to one side while a stream of bullets passed so close the sound almost deafened him.[10]

The action on September 2, 1918, had resulted from the assignment of the 148th's "A" Flight, under the command of Kindley, and "B" Flight, commanded by Lt. Elliott Springs, to a bombing and strafing mission on German forces retreating along a highway from Albert to Cambrai. These ground support missions were dreaded by the pursuit squadrons because of the danger of anti-aircraft fire and the low-altitude attacks that made a German aerial ambush more likely. Such was the case at 11:50 A.M. on that early September day when about twelve German Fokker D.VIIs came out of a low cloud on Lieutenant Springs's "B" Flight, which at that moment had been flying cover for some British artillery observation planes below them. Kindley above "B" Flight barely caught a glimpse of the attack and subsequent dogfight; moving into protective cover of a cloud, he wheeled his flight down to assist Springs and his pilots, now in extreme danger.[11] More Fokker aircraft joined the battle from clouds above, and the sky became full of twisting, diving, and turning aircraft. Kindley at a height of 3,000 feet dove on a Fokker biplane that was close on the tail of a Camel. After firing only a short burst, the enemy aircraft went over on its back "with a stream of black smoke issuing from his fuselage." "The smoke cleared away before he crashed," Kindley noted in filing his combat report.[12]

Although Lieutenant Kindley had claimed his fifth victim and thereby attained status as an air ace,[13] the September 2 aerial battle

A German Fokker D.VII airplane, considered one of the best pursuit aircraft of the war. Kindley shot down nine of these planes.
Photo courtesy Lafayette Foundation

had resulted in costly losses for the 148th Squadron. Two pilots had been killed, two taken prisoner when forced down behind German lines, and one, Lt. Jesse Creech, from Washington, D.C., had landed safely behind Allied lines. As indicated by Lieutenant Kindley, many aircraft had to be patched up. These losses came on top of an August 24 casualty when Chicago native Lt. George Seibold and Lieutenant Creech were surprised while on a bombing-strafing sortie. Seibold was shot down in flames and killed, while Creech made it back to base at Remaisnil. Lieutenant Seibold had three enemy planes to his credit at the time of his death. Lt. Marvin K. Curtiss, from Cleveland, Ohio, on a later strafing mission, was forced down and became a prisoner.

Because of the Camel's maneuverability, it proved to be one of the best aircraft for attacking ground targets, particularly strafing. It could easily dive on a trench, gun emplacement, or vehicle, and then just as quickly turn and zoom back to altitude. As a consequence, Camel-equipped squadrons received most of these very dangerous missions. Typically, a flight would fly at an assigned altitude across the front, and then the flight leader would waggle his wings or use a point-down gesture to signal the dive to some ground target. The flight leader would lead the dive, followed by the other flight aircraft. If the sortie involved strafing, the pull-out altitude might be extremely low. The aircraft were then most vulnerable to all kinds of enemy ground fire.

The American 17th Aero Squadron, which was likewise involved in the British offensive, sustained heavy losses. Lt. Lloyd Hamilton, a flight commander who was credited with nine victories, had been shot down by ground fire on August 24. Two days later, nine Camel pilots and planes of the 17th fought for their lives against superior German numbers. Six of the 17th pilots were shot down, three of them killed and three taken prisoner. The British withheld the 17th from further action until replacement pilots and planes could arrive.[14] As an American pilot flying in a British squadron observed, "The new Fokkers are giving us hell."[15]

In addition to pilot talk about the new German aircraft, there was much discussion about their combat adversaries. Particular attention went to German Jastas that had "blue tail" aircraft. The blue-tail pilots were considered among the very best, perhaps even better than Richthofen's Circus, and many an Allied pilot dreaded seeing them drop out of a cloud onto an Allied formation.

The blue-tail aircraft came from the elite Jagdgeschwader II, a German group designation consisting of four Jagdstaffeln (Jasta), or squadrons, numbered 12, 13, 15, and 19, and commanded by a Kommandeur. Each Jasta had approximately fourteen aircraft and pilots. The German High Command's "Amerika" program created Jagdgeschwader II and III, patterned after the success of Richthofen's organization, as part of the preparation for Ludendorff's spring 1918 offensive. It became a most formidable fighting unit, particularly when led by Hauptmann Rudolf Berthold (Kommandeur, March 12–August 13, 1918), who began the painting of the group's aircraft rear fuselage and tail a colorful blue. Each squadron sported a different nose color, and individuals added their distinctive fuselage insignias. The legendary Berthold, called the "Iron Knight," flew and fought, usually in a Fokker D.VII, "despite unhealed bullet wounds of the right arm and crippled right hand," which gave him great pain. Berthold's aggressive spirit, unerring marksmanship—mostly at extremely close range — patriotism, and strong sense of duty enabled him to survive his disability and to achieve forty-four personal victories and receive the Pour le Mérite.[16] The commanders of the four Jastas, including Ltn. Josef Veltjens, Ltn. Hans Pippart, Ltn. Hermann Becker, and Ltn. Franz Buchner, likewise recorded impressive personal victory totals, as did each Jasta.

At the end of the war, Jagdgeschwader II reported an amazing 352 victories against 38 losses.[17] Little wonder that the Allies, and especially the relatively inexperienced American pilots, took special note of the German blue-tail squadrons.

The blue-tails had been observed mostly on the British front as they supported the German offensives and aimed to counter the Royal Air Force. Later, during the American campaign against the St. Mihiel salient, American pilots reported them active on that front.[18] Indeed, the Jastas of Jagdgeschwader II reported many victories over American pilots. A notable one was the downing of 1st Lt. David E. Putnam, 139th Aero Squadron, one of the few American aces, by Ltn. Georg von Hantelmann of Jasta 15.[19]

A further concern for the American and Allied pilots was that the German tactics and strategies continued to change, and Allied pilots had to adjust accordingly. The German air leaders recognized that the "air force could be readily concentrated and employed with maximum force at the decisive time and place." This meant that the so-called "barrage patrols" created "dispersed strength without any compensating results" and needed to be abandoned. At least three-machine patrols replaced single ones, and more protective flights were required to accompany observation and artillery-spotting aircraft. In addition, airdromes were moved as close to the lines as Allied artillery fire permitted. These changes were intended to thwart Allied air attacks over German lines.[20] As the war continued, however, and attrition of pilots and machines, plus fuel shortages, became more of a problem, the German command had to conserve its strength, and the Germans sought to restrict their air concentrations over their own lines when they could tactically exploit a numerical advantage. Ever larger German formations would be massed on a certain sector to try to achieve local air superiority as a counter to overall increasing Allied numbers along the entire Western Front. As the German air effort tended to become more defensive by the late summer of 1918, the Germans also chose to stress quality of the aircraft—the Fokker D.VII design—over total numbers of machines. Thus, the British and American pilots engaging the German air force on their front sectors found their missions were as difficult, stressful, and dangerous as ever.

Although this was a period of hard times for the 17th and 148th Aero Squadrons on the British front, the action continued unabated. Only days after the big air battle of September 2, Lieutenant Kindley's formation on an offensive patrol at 9,000 feet over St. Quentin Lake experienced an attack by two Fokker biplanes. They dove out of an enemy formation of nine machines overhead. Kindley turned to fight an enemy aircraft on the tail of one of his flight's Camels, whereupon the Fokker zoomed and dove on him. He shook the German off his tail by a "vertical spiral." He then was attacked by another enemy aircraft, and in the ensuing dogfight, while he was trying to get a burst of fire at the Fokker, Kindley's Camel stalled and went into a spin. Coming out of his spin, he was able to fire on another Fokker, again on a Camel's tail. The enemy aircraft half-rolled, and Kindley followed him down "until my guns jammed," he reported. "When I last saw him he was spinning at 1500 feet." New York City's 1st Lt. Charles I. McLean was in the Camel with the Fokker on his tail as Lieutenant Kindley came to his aid. McLean then confirmed Kindley's sixth victory. The "Fokker was in a spin when I last saw him. I lost sight of him close to the ground," he noted.[21]

The next day, September 7, Field Kindley went on another patrol, in which he reported "5 E. A. attacked" with one German aircraft indicated as "out of control." In characteristic fashion he drew a German cross on that date in his flight log. This tentative victory was not confirmed, however, and was not added to Kindley's total. For several days following, Kindley's patrols remained uncontested, and it was not until September 15 when on a bombing mission over Dartford Wood Kindley said sixteen enemy aircraft were seen and a "scrap" followed. Field described firing "80 rounds head-on into a Fokker." The German pilot then made a gentle turn. "On the turn, I followed him with both guns and continued to fire until he pulled up in a stall and then in a very slow spin." Kindley concluded his report with, "I last saw him spinning at 2000 ft through a cloud."[22] Again, in his flight log, he noted "one out of control" and drew another black cross. This time Kindley was credited with another downed Fokker, his seventh. Only two days later, on September 17, Kindley recorded an engagement over Epinoy, or a "scrap" as he was prone to call it, with twenty enemy aircraft involved. In his combat narrative he told how he had fired 150 rounds at a Fokker biplane when the German "came head-on for me." In this dramatic face-off, Field stated he "fired head-on at him until we nearly collided." The result was that "he, as well as his engine, was evidently crippled, his manoeuvers were poor while Lt. Creech followed him down, he crashed near Epinoy."[23] Kindley once more had succeeded in attacking a Fokker biplane, Germany's best, and had sent it crashing from 7,000 feet.[24]

Lt. Lawrence T. Wyly, a member of Kindley's "A" Flight, shown with his Sopwith Camel

Photo courtesy Lafayette Foundation; Signal Corps Photo 24245

Meanwhile the German forces continued to withdraw in the face of the Allied offensive, falling back to the Canal du Nord on the British front. To the south, American troops began their attack on the St. Mihiel salient on September 12. Despite clouds and mist, American aircraft went airborne and on patrol as low as 50 feet. "No enemy aircraft were encountered but we had an exciting day flying just over the heads of Germans, shooting into trenches, at retreating columns on the roads, troop trains, and whatever targets we could find," reported one American squadron.[25] A few weeks later, in support of the advancing Americans, Col. Billy Mitchell ordered all squadrons to a special targeting of enemy observation balloons. "The safety of thousands of our attacking soldiers depended upon our success in eliminating these eyes of the enemy," declared Mitchell.[26] The likes of Rickenbacker and Luke responded with balloon kills. By September 27, British General Haig's First and Third Armies prepared to follow up their previous twenty-five-mile advance by mounting an assault on the German Hindenburg Line. The Allied commanders at last sensed victory with continuous pressure on the increasingly desperate German forces.

Because of the success of the Allied offensives and the relatively short range of the Camels, it became necessary to again move the American squadrons forward in the British sector, closer to the new German defensive positions. The 148th was ordered to a new airdrome at Baizieux, near Albert, on September 20.[27]

The Baizieux airdrome was a comparatively short distance from Remaisnil Field, so when the squadron went out on patrol, it was ordered to land at the new airdrome. As the 148th's planes landed, there were "few there to greet them, and the place seemed barren and inhospitable." Adding to the pilot's low spirits was the terrible loss that day of 1st Lt. Harry Jenkinson, Jr., who had been shot down in flames. "He had been the life of the whole Squadron, and everyone liked him . . . so his loss was keenly felt."[28]

Each of these forward moves meant more difficult and primitive living and operating conditions. In addition, there would be even more dangerous strafing, bombing, and reconnaissance missions. As a consequence, the pilot's life became significantly more stressful and unpleasant.

To relieve the combat pressures, one of the squadron's flights would occasionally have a "wash out." This was a half-day release from duty, usually in the afternoon. The pilots during this break would commandeer a touring car and travel to a nearby city to have drinks and dinner. Enlisted men generally had to be content with a relaxing game of horseshoes.

Despite the hot action, Kindley seemed genuinely proud of being a flight leader. He had become "acting commander" of Flight "A" on July 10 and was subsequently confirmed as "commander" on July 30. In his September 30 letter to his cousin Uther he commented, "The last time I wrote you I was acting Flight Commander but now I am honest to god Flight Commander with 6 machines & pilots and 25 men under my charge. However have not received the Captain bars that go with it yet."[29] Kindley was keenly aware that the Air Service's Table of Organization had just changed, authorizing the rank of captain for flight commander.

Pilots readily recognized the responsibilities associated with the position of flight commander. Yeates in his realistic novel *Winged Victory* declared, "Looking after a flight was a hundred times more than looking after an aeroplane. Returns, records, reports, N.C.O.s chasing after him about this and that, being father to his pilots and seeing that new fellows did plenty of target practice, for shooting was nine-tenths of the battle."[30] Captain Bogart Rogers, writing to his girlfriend back home, commented, "I've some new pilots to send up this afternoon and have to dash up to the aerodrome and tell them what to do and what not to do. You see, us flight commanders packs [*sic*] an awful lot of responsibility."[31]

In addition, the role of the flight commanders increased in importance as the aerial battles intensified, and squadron and flight leadership, as in all combat, proved crucial to success and to survival. Leading pilots demonstrated wide-ranging approaches to their aerial missions, which often emphasized their individual characteristics. For example, Edward "Mick" Mannock, Lieutenant Springs's hero and patrol leader with seventy-three victories, although moody and high strung, earned a reputation for tactical success because he planned missions a day in advance and then rehearsed them. He assigned his pilots a specific task at a specific time and "raised merry hell if anyone falls down on his job." He also insisted on a pilot sighting his own guns. "The armorer hasn't got to do the fighting," he said, "and you must learn to shoot. To be good fliers is not enough. It's the shooting that kills."[32] At the same time, Mannock conscientiously cared for his pilots and trained them to survive even to the point of being particularly cautious in the attack. Albert Ball, another noted RAF leader with forty-seven kills, in contrast, used daring, head-on tactics, even diving on enemy formations alone. Ball counted on "surprise, daring, and dead aim to strike quickly and extricate himself from tight situations." Other pilots of note, such as Britisher James McCudden and Frenchman René Fonck, attacked when they had an advantage, usually of surprise, and sped away when they did not. The great French ace, Georges Guynemer, used the opposite tactical approach of a cold-blooded, tenacious, unrelenting pursuit.[33]

In the 148th Aero Squadron, as in other squadrons, the flight commanders were usually selected for their experience, flying ability, leadership qualities, and combat instincts. Yet each flight leader brought a certain personality to his unit and tactics. 1st Lt. Elliott Springs, "B" Flight commander, was judged "more impetuous," willing to take chances, first to take on a fight and last to leave one. He, like Mannock and Kindley, "would never desert a pilot in distress, several times nearly losing his life in vainly trying to save a pilot who was hopelessly fighting against odds." According to one observer, 1st Lt. Henry R. Clay, Jr., commander of "C" Flight, had strengths in aerial strategy and with his "even temperament" was often chosen to lead the squadron's three flights because he seemed to know when to attack and when not to. His "C" Flight, as a consequence, took the lower flight to engineer an attack with the other two to follow.[34]

Field Kindley in his developing leadership embodied elements of some of these celebrated aces and his squadron mates. He totally agreed with, and practiced, Mannock's emphasis on planning, the importance of the guns and shooting techniques, and the constant concern for the survival and welfare of his fellow pilots. At the same time, particularly in the aerial combat, he showed great courage and daring by aggressively closing on his enemy targets to point-blank range, like an Albert Ball. Despite his resemblance to other pilots and leaders, his own personality, and his flying, remained unique if examined closely. He was more quiet, judicious, methodical, and level-headed, and more of a team player in his combat flying and leadership. Burke Davis in his biography of Elliott Springs assessed Kindley as "deliberate, mature and coolly competent."[35] His handling of his flight's pilots showed keen intelligence and a quick discernment of their abilities. Some of his perceived calmness in combat camouflaged an underlying nervousness, as events were to prove, but this often was the case with many of the pilots. Elliott Springs, Field's fellow flight commander, also described being nervous while on the ground awaiting an assigned patrol. Kindley too experienced this uneasy waiting, but when he was in the air and in combat, he focused solely on the battle or the bombing, strafing mission. Perhaps more than anything else, Kindley's success in downing enemy aircraft resulted from quick reactions, skilled machine gun firing, and an aggressive, tenacious, close-quarter attack when the battle began.

An interesting aspect of the aerial warfare was the attachment pilots and units felt for their animal mascots. No doubt this was to some extent a means of fostering unit cohesion and *esprit de corps*. Many individuals, however, had their pets. "Everybody in the squadron has some sort of a dog," said American pilot John Grider. "Cunningham-Reed had a forced landing and came back with a Belgian fox terrier that can do every thing but talk. I have a chow that was born in the hangar at Hounslow—a real dog of war."[36] Lieutenant Kindley was often pictured with his English bullterrier pup, called "Fokker," indicating that the dog occupied an important place in his life at the front. Undoubtedly these dogs provided their owners with a relief from a level of stress that seemed to be growing daily.

Adding to the tension for the pursuit pilots were their premonitions and superstitions. A number of World War I pilots had interesting ones. Elliott Springs stated he had discarded dogs. His new and best lucky piece, undoubtedly the most outlandish, was "a garter taken from the left leg of a virgin in the dark of the moon."[37] Lieutenant Kindley revealed two of his. He felt most uneasy, he said, "about flying after having received orders to go on leave or return to the States or any place that you really want to go."[38] He held this belief "because he saw several men lose their lives when they attempted a flight after being ordered on furlough or to the rear." Another thing he avoided, Kindley confessed, "is to light a cigarette from a match that two others have already used."[39] While these individually held beliefs often seem strange, they nevertheless had impact on the daily life of the aerial warrior.

The last week in September proved to be one of Field Kindley's busiest, most productive, and most frightening. On September 24, at 7:28 A.M., Lieutenant Kindley and his "A" Flight began another of the frequent "offensive patrols," which usually numbered two a day, just west of Cambrai and north of Bourlon Wood. The five-plane

Lt. Field E. Kindley, photographed in France. (Note the wings insignia he wore.) This photo was later used for an oil painting put on display in the Officers' Club at Kindley Air Force Base, Bermuda.
Kindley family photo

"A" Flight and five-plane "B" Flight were providing top cover for Lieutenant Clay's "C" Flight several thousand feet below. Lieutenant Kindley spotted seven German pursuit aircraft diving out of a cloud on top of "C" Flight. Checking his formation and signaling the dive to attack, Lieutenant Kindley hastily moved to break up the German onslaught on the outnumbered Clay unit. Leveling off behind the German planes, he quickly became aware that the enemy machines were Fokker D.VIIs with the "blue tails" of Germany's leading squadrons, equaled perhaps only by Richthofen's Flying Circus. Furthermore, the Germans saw Kindley's attack coming and banked steeply to the right. Elliott Springs's flight joined the dogfight, as did other Fokkers. There were now some twenty Fokkers and the 148th's fifteen Camels in the battle. Field Kindley, in characteristic close-in pursuit, stayed on the tail of a Fokker, and when it stalled

Lieutenant Kindley in his aircraft with pup "Fokker"
Kindley family photo

in a tight turn, he fired tracer bullets from his twin Vickers machine guns, sending smoke pouring from the enemy aircraft's fuselage and engine. Field sent another burst into the Fokker as it went into a slow spin. The Fokker then crashed and burned, and Lieutenant Kindley claimed his ninth victory.[40] Subsequently, he was awarded the U.S. Distinguished Service Cross for his actions and heroism in this engagement (see appendix D).[41]

Although the aerial battle was fierce on September 24, with many Camels badly damaged, the 148th Aero Squadron came out of it with a major victory. It had met some of Germany's finest pilots and best aircraft, and sent seven enemy aircraft down or out of control without loss of a single American. Besides Kindley's kill, Springs, Clay, Knox, and Wyly had each claimed one and Lt. Erroll Zistel of Cleveland, Ohio, had gotten two. Lieutenant Springs now had eleven victories, and Lieutenant Clay, seven. The squadron celebrated.[42]

A mere two days later, two of the 148th's flights again were on offensive patrol, with Lieutenant Kindley leading the top flight. The lower flight, attempting to destroy two enemy aircraft, came under attack by six Fokker biplanes as well as the two they had been chasing. With the lower flight now in serious trouble, Lieutenant Kindley led his flight to the attack. In the ensuing dogfight, two enemy planes were downed, with Lieutenant Kindley accounting for one.[43] Field reported "I saw Lt. Creech go through the clouds close on to a Fokker, a few seconds later I drove an E. A. down into a spin, firing until he went through the clouds, but did not follow him down." Lieutenant Creech confirmed his kill as well as Kindley's. "After I dove through the clouds and crashed the E. A. I was after, I observed another E. A. spin through the clouds and crash east of Bourlon Wood. I believe this to be the E. A. Lt. Kindley shot down," said Creech.[44] Amazingly, the squadron again escaped losses.

September 27 became a special day but started with the usual morning routine in preparation for an offensive patrol and bombing-strafing mission. Kindley's mechanics and flight crew carefully armed and readied his plane for action. At 8:20 A.M. Field Kindley appeared at the flight line ready to go through the Camel checkout before taking off. With a glance and a signal to the other pilots, "A" Flight got airborne for the battle lines at 8:40 A.M.[45] Within minutes, Kindley and his flight were nearing the ground battle area. He described the scene below him: "You see the clouds from the heavy barrage below were just clearing away and the British Tommys were going over the top with the southern outskirts of Cambrai as their objective. The Hun batteries were getting into their stride when my flight and I just reached the frontlines with a load of bombs or better known among the pilots as pills. You could see that the Hun was retreating for miles back of the lines and one would wonder just where his bombs would kill more Boch."[46]

The "wonder" about the appropriate bombing target was soon answered. "At last we located a railway station of Marcoing that seemed to be doing a rushing business and we relieved ourselves of our loads."[47] While dodging anti-aircraft fire, Kindley went down to 800 feet before he released his four 25-pound bombs placed under the fuselage. The rest of the "A" Flight Camels followed, and more than a dozen transports were soon engulfed in flames.[48]

After accomplishing their bombing mission, Lieutenant Kindley and the other "A" Flight pilots turned their attention to the strafing of German troops. "Here we broke our formation for a purpose," commented Kindley, "it was to attack the Hun infantry that had by now commenced to gather at points along the road and were on their way to the rear."[49]

The strafing was interrupted by a balloon sighting. "Directly ahead of me I noticed a captive balloon on the outskirts of Cambrai so it was a race between myself and a few of the others as to who would get it first." This comment merited further explanation, he said. "Don't misunderstand me by thinking that pilots are so crazy about attacking balloons that they race one another to attack them but this morning special orders had been issued to destroy all balloons at all cost as they are such a deadly weapon against advancing troops and this race was only a means to hurry along the fulfillment of orders. We rained explosive lead upon it until that type of ammunition was gone and then continued till other observers were compelled to jump and the balloon was on the ground and out of action so far as being of use against the on-rushing British."[50]

Balloon busting was a dangerous business, as often the balloons were protected by concentrated anti-aircraft weapons and sometimes they were traps to lure planes into anti-aircraft fire or even ambushes by enemy aircraft. Lt. Frank Luke, Jr., of the 27th American Aero Squadron was known as the premier American "balloon buster" because he destroyed fourteen in addition to four aircraft, emerging as the second-ranking American ace of the war.[51] Lt. Kindley was frustrated with only forcing down the balloon near Cambrai. "One must not get the impression that during the attacking of a balloon that the sky is yours even though there are no enemy aircraft about for every balloon has its defence and this one had an exceptionally good one." Kindley successfully avoided the anti-aircraft shells and took a little comfort in observing, "Although the sky was so full of archie that it appeared as a black cloud each of us felt that the Boch was shooting at the other fellow." Nevertheless, he noted, "in the mind of most pilots the most disgusting thing in the world is to shoot all of your explosive ammunition at a balloon and then not getting it. Honestly I believe that it would make a preacher curse to sit in the middle of a barrage for a few seconds and fire a few hundred rounds at a captive and then not get it."[52]

After forcing down the enemy balloon, it was back to the strafing assignment—always hazardous action. Kindley wrote, "I was only a few hundred feet off the ground and the Hun machine gunners were getting at close quarters for now and then you could hear something pierce the fabric of the machine." Kindley then spied another target of opportunity along the road. "Some Hun commander had just gotten his battalion into close formation for me in such a position that I could sweep it with ease." This was too good to be true, thought Lieutenant Kindley. "Indeed it seemed unfair to take advantage of them but my chicken heart did not get the best of me for till this day I can see the little pills along the road from which a few were trying to crawl to safety while those that were lucky were running here and there. One thing that I have wondered about often is whether that Hun commander ever got his men together for a formation again."

"A few miles on down the road towards the front lines I noticed the British tanks working their way towards Cambrai and at the same time a few British machine guns popping away at something but what I could not tell so I ventured over and found it to be in the general direction of some Hun machine guns that were holding up the advance," reported Kindley. "With a few shots from my two Vickers the Huns closed up and the British rolled on."

As Kindley turned to attack another German machine gun nest, he "heard that familiar popping behind." A two-seater Halberstadt had slipped behind him coming out of the west and was right on his tail, firing its front guns, before he was aware of its presence. Kindley took immediate evasive action. "A quick right and an equally quick left placed me underneath his tail," said Kindley, and he was able to bring withering fire on the heavier Halberstadt. "Of course his general direction of flight was for Hunland and at top speed. But this speed did not last long for I had hardly opened fire until I saw a perfectly good Halberstadt carrying two little Fritzies turn into a most wonderful comet." While Kindley might have had some pangs of conscience at the "unfairness" of catching and strafing troops in the open, he seemed to relish the fight in the air. Claiming his eleventh aerial victory, Kindley mused, "That is the most wonderful sight in the world to my mind and regardless of the Hun archie and machine gun fire I had to sit there and watch the slashing of flames as he hit the ground not more than six hundred feet below me."

The morning's work was not over, however. While testing his guns, Kindley discovered he had spent all of his ammunition. At that point, he headed back across the lines and for home base. Kindley then observed two Fokkers “picking upon a lone comrade.” Despite being without ammunition, he audaciously dove straight for them with hopes of frightening them off. The bluff surprisingly worked, and the enemy aircraft fled eastward.[53]

Despite this busy, heroic morning of aerial activity, Kindley had another bombing mission at 2:15 in the afternoon, during which four bombs were dropped on the road between Cantaing and Flesquires.[54]

This momentous day of combat action on September 27, 1918, earned Lieutenant Kindley a Bronze Oak Leaf to the U.S. Distinguished Service Cross.[55] It also led to the British awarding him the Distinguished Flying Cross, which was presented on November 1, 1918.[56] The citation accompanying the British decoration noted that Lieutenant Kindley had “proven himself an excellent patrol leader and has at all times shown gallantry and disregard of danger of a very high order” (see appendix D).[57] In writing about all of the day’s action, Kindley modestly observed, “A strange thing about an Oak Leaf or any other kind of a job is that it takes a few moments and at the time you do not realize that you have done anything out of the ordinary.”[58] He expressed a bit of pride in his accomplishments in his September 30 letter, however. “I don’t know how many Huns I had when I last wrote you but up to date I have 10 ½ officially to my credit. It could be worse.” Then he added, “I understand that soon I am to be wearing a blue & white stripped ribbon on my left breast. That is I have been recommended for the (D.F.C.) the distinguished flying cross which is a British medal.”[59]

Kindley’s late September successes did not in any way ease the strain of the daily patrols and strafing and bombing operations. Indicative of his state of mind was a comment he made to cousin Uther in his September 30 letter. “Shortly I will have been on the front six months after which I should be given home service or at least not war flying because the British do not. The reason being, not many men can stand the nerve strain longer. I must admit my nerves are getting very poor.”[60]

A fascinating account of the effects of this mental combat stress can be found in the “War Birds” diary of American pilot Lt. John Grider, who was flying with a British squadron on the same front as Kindley. There seems to be a progression of despair or fatalism which ultimately undermines the pilot’s abilities. “Here I am, twenty-four years old, I look forty and I feel ninety,” wrote Grider on August 27. Particularly preying on the pilot’s mind was the loss of comrades and the feeling of the inevitability of his own death if combat continued. "It's only a question of time until we all get it. I'm all shot to pieces. I only hope I can stick it. I don't want to quit. My nerves are all gone and I can't stop. I've lived beyond my time already."[61]

An element of this fatalistic thinking was simple fear, which no doubt even the bravest aviators experienced. Grider in his diary expressed it well: "Few men live to know what real fear is. It's something that grows on you, day by day, that eats into your constitution and undermines your sanity." The American pilot claimed he had "even lost my taste for licker." But sadly, he commented, "I haven't a chance, I know, and its this eternal waiting around that's killing me."[62] Tragically, Lieutenant Grider was shot down shortly after these statements. The noted British ace Edward "Mick" Mannock reportedly had waves of nausea from fear when he first served at the front. On one occasion when on patrol his guns jammed and his engine quit, and he still managed to return "with my knees shaking and my nerves all torn to bits," he said.[63]

Lt. Jesse Creech signaling two enemy aircraft downed in combat as he leaves his Sopwith Camel
Photo courtesy Lafayette Foundation

German Halberstadt-type aircraft claimed by Kindley in his eleventh aerial victory
Photo courtesy Lafayette Foundation

Lieutenant Springs, another example, admitted being depressed by the loss of many fellow pilots. "It gives me a dizzy feeling every time I hear of the men that are gone," he said. After a patrol he experienced repercussions from the day's action. "Before I got back, I was shivering so I could hardly land. And I haven't been feeling right since. My heart seems to be trying to stunt all the time," he wrote. Sleeping became difficult, with nightmares that would replay an engagement. "I don't know which will get me first, a bullet or the nervous strain," he complained.[64] Kindley did not record similar details as to his feelings of stress, but he undoubtedly went through similar problems. It seems likely that he, like many other combat pilots, masked his fears, grieving, and worried thoughts with a matter-of-fact, stoic, even detached demeanor. "In the mess, it is an unwritten law for pilots to forget sorrow and assume cheerfulness which give the impression of 'living for today.'"[65] This served a purpose in that it helped reassure the new, replacement pilots and even steadied the emotions of the combat veterans.

Nevertheless, there was ample reason for concern about survival, for by this time some of the best known names in aerial warfare had been lost. Germany's Red Baron, Manfred von Richthofen, age twenty-five, with an astonishing eighty victories, had been shot down and killed in late April. Britain's Mick Mannock, age thirty-one, with seventy-three kills, died in a flaming crash in July. Grider took note of the loss of Mannock in a diary entry on July 20: "Mannock is dead, the greatest pilot of the war."[66] Britisher James McCudden, another leading ace, had been killed. In late September, America's Lt. Frank Luke, Jr., the celebrated Arizona balloon-buster, had crash-landed and been shot dead when he refused to surrender. Little wonder that news of these casualties, and others less noted, had a sobering effect on every pilot's outlook.

Field Kindley's thoughts about relief from war flying proved to be no more than wishful thinking, as patrols and combat continued. More ground strafing and bombing missions were assigned. During the next several days, both morning and afternoon flights were ordered. Lieutenant Kindley, for example, flew morning and afternoon sorties on September 28 in which he fired 500 and 600 rounds respectively on the road south of Masnières and Bois Latéan, and dropped the usual four bombs. The next day there was more of the same, with four bombs on Grevecoeur and 150 rounds fired. On the morning of October 1, Kindley reported seeing three direct hits on a trench running west to east south of Seranvillers.[67] Kindley's flight log noted ground strafing "good targets" on October 3, 1918. On several occasions he also recorded spotting enemy aircraft, as on October 7, when he "saw 7 Fokkers," but no aerial battles developed.

On October 8, Lieutenant Kindley and his flight "were detailed to verify a report that the enemy was concentrating for an immediate attack north of Cattenieres." Responding quickly, Flight "A" located the point and found many troops. Kindley directed an attack, diving to 1,000 feet for bomb drops and then strafing with machine gun fire from 500 feet. Kindley's report stated, "Observed 5 direct hits on troops with bombs."[68] After expending all of their ordnance, the flight returned to base with their report. The squadron's two other flights and several other squadrons took off to attack the troop concentrations. The following morning the Germans did launch a counter-attack, but it had been weakened and the British were alerted.[69]

A factor in the early October air operations was the weather. On October 12, for example, Kindley reported, "O. P. [offensive patrol] with bombs very bad weather."[70] The European fall brought rain, fog, and heavy clouds, making aerial battles less frequent and posing great problems for ground support missions. In addition to the weather difficulties, on October 14 the 148th was ordered to move forward again, this time to an airdrome at Bapaume.[71]

The new airfield had been "covered with shell holes," but they had been filled through the work of Chinese laborers, employed by the thousands by the French. The hangars were not as large nor as permanent as those at Baizieux, but they were useable and British bell tents had to suffice for the quarters of the enlisted men and the officers. The air base was now in the midst of the war-devastated countryside, and with increasingly frequent rain and drizzle there was mud everywhere. "It was not possible to walk about the camp without making walks of corrugated iron and boards from the ruined huts that the Germans had occupied not long before." Squadron personnel believed they had left civilization behind, and it was pointed out that "both officers and men will remember the Bapaume camp as a most disagreeable place."

Bapaume marked approximately the midway point on a nearly straight road between Albert and Cambrai, and for some thirty miles there was a no-man's-land of shell holes, broken trenches, damaged equipment, and ruins on all sides. According to the pilots, this was what the "territory looked like to those who flew over it every day." "Upon the ground its influence was even more depressing. As far as the eye could see out across that rolling plain, nothing but the havoc of war is apparent. All habitations have vanished or lie in ruins, almost level with the ground. The trees like gaunt spectres blackened and shorn of their foliage and branches, stick up uncannily along the skyline. These things one hardly connect in the mind with the human army which fought the battle over these fields so short a time before. It seems more the work of a greater power, an evil supernatural being, than the work of man." The area seemed devoid of life except for the rats, which provided some shooting sport for the pilots and their "forty-fives." Despite the dreary and depressing environment the squadron now found itself in, the move to the new airdrome had gone smoothly, and aerial patrols began almost immediately.

The move to Bapaume had been made possible finally by the Germans' retreat from Cambrai and their effort to straighten their lines to the east. The ground strafing and bombing on the retreating Germans had been meant to harass the enemy withdrawal and, if possible, prevent their forming a new, stabilizing front line. This continuous attacking pressure was in line with RAF Maj. Gen. Hugh Trenchard's concepts of using aircraft as important offensive weapons and applying them accordingly.

Kindley's first days at Bapaume consisted of testing aircraft, but that activity was seriously hampered by the bad weather. Soon enough, however, he was back on offensive patrols. On October 23 he recorded dropping four bombs on "road S. E. of Bois L'Evesque" and on October 26 he performed a ground strafing and bombing mission where he noted, "Dropped bombs on woods" and "fired into transport moving east." The following day he saw twenty enemy aircraft but noted they were "too high."[72] As the war seemed to be winding down, the Germans appeared more reluctant to engage in battle.

In fact, the Germans, feeling the late war pinch in matériel and manpower, were husbanding their resources. This greatly affected their air strategy and tactics. During the last months of the war they had turned increasingly on the defensive, seeking command of the air over their own lines and at times of their own choosing.[73]

On October 28 a plan was developed to lure enemy aircraft into combat. Lieutenant Kindley's "A" Flight would act as a decoy over the lines at 3,000 feet, pretending to be looking for German observation planes or two-seaters. The Squadron's "B" Flight and "C" Flight, now commanded by Lt. Thomas L. Moore and Lt. Lawrence K. Callahan, respectively, were to fly top cover with some 7,000 feet separating them above "A" Flight.[74] This was a dangerous altitude gap, as the "B" and "C" Flights would have to speedily dive in response to a German attack to prevent the destruction of the decoy "A" Flight.

Seven Fokkers were detected some distance to the east, and Lieutenant Kindley, now leading because he was the remaining most experienced flight commander, used a very pistol to signal setting the trap. The precarious altitude separation was maintained for over an hour, with the flights patrolling back and forth over the lines. Lieutenant Kindley gradually directed his lower flight closer to the German planes, which were still a distance to the east and above. The two upper flight commanders continued to keep a watchful eye still above the Fokker's altitude. Kindley hoped that the German aircraft would concentrate on observing his decoy flight and not see the higher flying 148th planes.

The enemy aircraft took the bait over Villers Pol, apparently not aware of the upper flight's position in the fleecy clouds. As the Fokkers dove to the attack, Lieutenants Moore and Callahan hurtled down on the startled Germans almost before they had begun shooting at Kindley's "A" Flight. The surprise was complete. Lieutenant Kindley "held the formation together till the Huns were close on our tail," he reported. However, Kindley then had two Fokkers on his tail. He once again called on all his pilot skill to escape this predicament. "Lt. Creech shot one off and I succeeded in getting into a general dog-fight with the other. After putting a few bursts into him he flew straight east at stalling speed. While stalling, I continued to fire at him at close range, when he suddenly nosed down as though going into a spin. I lost sight of him in the mist. I am confident he crashed." The kill was confirmed for Kindley's twelfth victory.[75] The trap, with the surprise attack from the upper flights, as the scheme had intended, worked with amazing success, and seven Fokkers were shot down and crashed within a radius of 1,000 yards. Besides Lieutenant Kindley's victim, Lts. Tom Moore, Jesse Creech, Larry Callahan, and George Dorsey were credited with one victory each, while Lt. Clayton Bissell was credited with two.

Although a number of the squadron planes sustained considerable damage, only Lieutenant Wyly was forced down behind Allied lines with a bullet in his engine. He managed to return safely to the airdrome that night. This single aerial battle was one of the most spectacular and productive for the Americans in the war. Rather

Lt. Clayton Bissell posing in his Sopwith Camel
Photo courtesy Lafayette Foundation

modestly, Lieutenant Kindley recorded a simple remark in his flight log, "Biggest scrap yet."[76]

Quite unexpectedly, the big October 28 aerial victory resulting from a carefully planned and executed trap turned out to be the culmination of the 148th Aero Squadron's combat action and its time under British command. Orders were issued to stop "war-flying" on October 29, and the 148th and the 17th were transferred to the 4th Pursuit Group in the American-French sector to support General Pershing's Meuse-Argonne offensive. Col. Billy Mitchell, Pershing's aerial combat commander, had formulated plans to mass as many American aerial units as possible to command the air over the battle front and to provide harassing and destructive strafing and bombing runs as the Americans advanced.[77]

On November 1, 1918, the 148th "entrained at Bapaume for their long and tedious journey to Toul." The train trip proved memorable. Officers were crowded into the "usual cattle-cars" without even "room for a cot to be set up." "The first night was very cold, and sleeping was almost impossible. With overcoats and any available covering, even the old green baize of the card table, the officers passed a most uncomfortable night."[78]

Toul airdrome, south of Bapaume and some 150 miles east of Paris, was intended to be the location for outfitting the squadron with the French-built Spad XIII aircraft before returning to combat.[79] Lieutenant Kindley's flight log entry remark on October 31 read, "To Acceptance Park, turning in machine."[80] Most likely he had mixed emotions at this point. Surely this was the needed break in combat flying, but it also meant leaving the known British command structure and war methods, and above all giving up his trustworthy Camel, which up to now had kept him alive and accounted for his twelve victories.

While there is no record of Kindley's feelings about leaving his combat Sopwith Camel, he must have had emotions similar to many pilots when confronted with this situation. Capt. Bogart Rogers, in writing to his girlfriend after the Armistice, stated it well: "The old S E 5s are pretty fine airships and the day mine has to be handed over I know I'd weep copious tears. It's like getting rid of a horse you've had for years. Aeroplanes have personalities. When you've had one for months and months, when it's always brought you home safely and never let you down in a pinch you acquire a small bit of affection for it. I'd like to be able to bring mine home and store it in the barn."[81] Surely Kindley must have been saddened and desirous of holding on to his combat steed.

Once at Toul, one of the last entries in Kindley's flight log indicated he had a twenty-minute flight in the heavier but more powerful Spad. It had a 220-hp Hispano-Suiza engine and could fly 130 mph, plus could perform at a higher altitude. Although by war's end it was considered the premier French pursuit aircraft, Kindley's comments read, "First Solo Spad" followed by "Don't like it." These Spad flights were followed by one of thirty minutes' duration in which he did a "few stunts" at the airdrome.[82]

Other squadron pilots, like Kindley, had misgivings about the changeover to the Spad aircraft. "There is a great difference between the light, manoeuverable Camel and the heavy but powerful Spad. It was like learning to fly over again to take these powerful, little machines up and fly them for the first time. The pilots, one after another, 'soloed' or made their first flight, and came down vowing that the Spad was the worst machine, the most dangerous, and so on, ad infinitum, that they had ever flown. After several flights, they began to be very good Spad 'merchants' in time."[83] Probably unknown to Kindley, RAF Gen. J. N. Salmond had recommended that the American squadrons be "fitted" with British-built S.E. 5 machines, adding, "Their formation flying is good and I consider this type of machine would suit them."[84]

French-built Spad XIII to which Kindley transitioned toward the end of the war

Photo courtesy Lafayette Foundation

General Salmond sent the 148th and 17th Squadrons to American command with praise. "I wish to say how magnificently they have carried out their duties during the time they have been lent to the British Aviation." In a letter to General Patrick, commander of the American Air Service, he added, "Every call has been answered by them to the highest degree, and when they have arrived with you, you will have two highly efficient squadrons filled with the offensive spirit."[85] Indeed, the two American squadrons had established a commendable record in the relatively few months they were on the front. The 148th amassed sixty-six victories, and the 17th, sixty-four.[86]

As the 148th Squadron adjusted to new aircraft and a new command at Toul airdrome in the first days of November, the order came to discontinue aerial offensive patrols, as an armistice was developing, and on November 11, 1918, fighting stopped. Thereupon, Lieutenant Kindley summarized his flying role from November 24, 1917, to November 24, 1918, as follows:

Aircraft	*Dual Time*	*Solo Time*	*"War Work" (hrs)*
M.F.S.H.	3:50	4:05	
AVRO	12:20	13:15	
Pup		27:10	
S.E. 5		1:35	
Spad		:50	
Camel		73:15	210:25

Total Time In Air: 346:45
Total Huns Officially Credited: 9 Crashed, 3 Out of Control
Total Pounds Bombs Dropped: 1440 lbs.
Total Fired At Troops: 3550 Rounds

Kindley had this data dutifully authenticated by the signature of Capt. M. L. Marshall, then commanding officer of the 148th Aero Squadron.[87]

With the November 11, 1918, Armistice, World War I came to an end, and the book closed on tallying aerial victories. Lt. Field Kindley's 12 downed aircraft paled in comparison to those of some others: on the German side, Richthofen with 80; France's René Fonck, 75; Great Britain's Mick Mannock, 73; and America's Eddie Rickenbacker, 26. Nevertheless, Kindley's aerial success in becoming the fourth-ranking

American ace of World War I,[88] in the relatively few months on the battle front and in combat, compared favorably with that of many of the other leading aces of the war. Furthermore, the exploits of the American pilots flying under British command, such as the 148th Squadron's Kindley, Springs, and Clay, and the 17th's Lt. George Vaughn, firmly established their names in the Allied lists of aces and decidedly earned the attention of the RAF.

Although battle-tested late in the war, the American pilots, like the U.S. ground forces, provided the extra push needed to reach an Allied victory and the end of the conflict. A big part of that effort was not only clearing the German Jastas out of the sky and dominating the air, but also providing crucial ground support to the advancing Allied troops.

The stated mission for the pursuit squadrons was quite clear: "Pursuit aviation has for its object the destruction of the enemy air service and the protection of our own observation aviation. When opportunity offers it will take part in the battle on the ground, inflicting maximum casualties upon and weakening the morale of the enemy's ground troops."[89] The 148th and 17th Aero Squadrons accomplished this task and helped bring the war to a close.

Lieutenant Kindley's combat experience with the 148th Aero Squadron, from July 1 to October 31, 1918, continued to be a time of self-discovery. He found, for example, courage to battle against great odds, through life-threatening moments, and with dangerous decoy tactics. He experienced being shot-up, having Fokkers on his tail, and dealing with heart-stopping stalls and gun jams. He learned life-saving skills in mastering his flying machine, the Sopwith Camel; firing his twin-synchronized Vickers machine guns; maneuvering for the close-in attack; and when needed, engaging in the escape tactics necessary to survive. He found success in downing enemy aircraft by combining the aggressive press-the-attack with judicious selection of the right moment for battle. In his strafing and bombing missions, he proved adaptable and opportunistic, with an eagle eye for targets.

The greatest learning and personal achievement involved Kindley's leadership. As a flight commander he became a take-charge person, giving signals and directions to his pilots and at the same time effectively leading by example. With usually five and sometimes six aircraft in the flight's offensive patrols, Lieutenant Kindley had to develop a strong sense of teamwork. Insight into his role in this regard is contained in his evaluative comments about Lt. Lawrence T. Wyly, who served as his deputy flight leader, flying wing on his right in formation. He lauded Wyly's teamwork, initiative, and "consistent punch." Kindley wrote, "He put teamwork and co-operation as first and individual honors second." At another point he said, "This is clearly a case of putting the welfare of the Flight first."[90] These same characteristics could be ascribed to Field Kindley himself. On several occasions Kindley stated, "I am proud to have led my flight in a manner as to destroy 27 of the enemy and yet only lose one of my flight."[91] Like other flight commanders, he earned high respect for diving into the fray to assist a beleaguered comrade. Kindley's squadron commander commented in summary fashion, "Lt. Kindley has shown splendid ability as a Scout Pilot and as a Flight Commander has led his flight with excellent judgment combined with rare skill and courage."[92]

Lieutenant Kindley conscientiously showed concern not only for his fellow pilots but also for his enlisted flight crews and the mechanics who kept the planes flying. His flying skills and his down-to-earth attitude, along with his modest, self-effacing manner, gained him admiration in the enlisted ranks. He, in turn, appreciated their role. According to one postwar newspaper account, "Captain Kindley eulogized his mechanics, declaring it was their continuous vigilance and careful work that counted most in achieving victory."[93] At that time and age such comments were not uttered to be politically correct but were spoken from the heart.

Lt. Field E. Kindley, along with the other American pilots, had participated in and witnessed a new age of warfare in the use of aircraft as weapons. The military lessons in the employment of warplanes would be studied and analyzed in the postwar period, but they would not be totally absorbed. The postwar period would see rapid dismantling of U.S. military forces, including the Air Service. The American Expeditionary Force in Europe would soon melt away, with a clamor for airmen and troops to get home to the United States. Lieutenant Kindley, in the midst of this demobilization, would face some new challenges and a new struggle.

Chapter Seven

The Postwar Experience

To defeat the enemy we must meet his improvement by improving ourselves.

Lt. Field E. Kindley,
lessons-learned report, in Mauer,
U.S. Air Service in World War I

THE REASSIGNMENT of the 148th Aero Squadron to Toul, France, on November 1, 1918, and the subsequent November 11 Armistice ending World War I may have saved Lt. Field Kindley's life. As has been noted, he had expressed concern about his fraying nerves and wished for a break in his combat flying. It seems highly possible that if Kindley's move to Toul and the process of transition to a new aircraft had not occurred, he might have been on that psychological downward spiral wherein that dreaded one last offensive patrol could have been his last.[1] This thought is reinforced by a medical evaluation that Kindley received by the Office of the Surgeon, Air Service Examination Board, on November 24, 1918. Capt. D. S. Edwards, the examiner, stated in his report: "Examination of the Lieut. (1st Lt. Field E. Kindley) finished this date shows he is suffering from a typical case of flying fatigue." The examination detailed "low blood pressure," "high pulse rate," "nervous tremor marked," "reflexes markedly exaggerated," "very restless," and "History of nervous head aches." The doctor's recommendation was that "Lieut. Kindley be given two or three months leave, at the end of this time to be returned to duty."[2]

Four days later, on November 28, Kindley wrote to his father in the Philippines that "because of my health or nerves I was given by an Army medical board three months leave. Through this I was given orders for home." He added that he "had dreams of being home in two or three weeks." But the thrust of his letter continued with a complete about-face. He had elected not to return to the United States "because I thought it best for you."[3]

In truth, Field Kindley had made a momentous career decision rather than thinking what was best for his father. His late November letter told the story. "Two hours before I was to board a train enroute home the Chief of the Air Service called me into his office. Understand I have been trying to get a commission in the regular army and this Chief of Air Service has been very kind to help me etc. He said that if I wanted a regular commission he thought he had a proposition that it would make it better for me. He offered me the command of a very popular Aero Squadron over here. I could take it or leave it. I took it."

According to Kindley's letter, the chief of the Air Service promised him a captaincy leading eventually to the rank of major. "So I guess it was best I took it," he concluded. "However it was mighty hard to refuse going home. He has given me seven days leave in England to get my D. F. C. (Distinguished Flying Cross). Shall enjoy myself." Thus, Kindley got a much shortened leave, which probably didn't matter so much since combat flying had ceased, and he decided to remain in the Air Service. On the same date, November 28, he also wrote his cousin Uther and said, "You see I have had a funny idea of wanting to stay in the army so if I do stay over here, till the thing is over, I shall stand a better show."[4]

Lt. Field Kindley got his coveted squadron command on December 21, 1918, when Special Orders 39 from Headquarters 4th Pursuit Group assigned him as commanding officer of the 141st Aero Squadron.[5] His promotion to captain, equally sought, would not come until February 24, 1919.[6] The third element in Kindley's career decision-making, a permanent or regular officer's commission in the U.S. Army, was initiated November 20 when he wrote a letter formally requesting that status. The request went upward through military channels with endorsed recommendations for approval. In addition, Kindley secured personal letters of support. In a "To Whom It May Concern" letter from Captain Newhall, the 148th commander, he had the ringing supportive comment: "I cannot recommend him too highly for a Captaincy in the Regular Army. . . . He has shown the qualities of an officer in the air and on the ground." Newhall went on to say, "He has a record as Flight Commander in leading his Flight into combat for three (3) months with the loss of only one (1) man and yet his Flight crashed twenty-one and one-half (21 1/2) Huns and seven (7) driven down out of control. He, himself, accounting for nine (9) crashed and three (3) out of control."[7]

When the correspondence reached General Headquarters for the American Expeditionary Forces, it was sent back to Kindley at the 148th Aero Squadron on November 30, 1918, with the remark, "It is not known at these headquarters that any examination for appointment in the Regular Army is scheduled."[8] Thus, Kindley was frustrated in this endeavor. He was farsighted and correct in seeing the need for a regular commission in postwar times as it provided far better career path security than continuing with a reserve officer's commission. The reserves would always be the first to be demobilized and relieved from service. If he wanted to have a career as a military pilot, he would eventually have to attain a regular army commission. Lieutenant Kindley, along with other members of the 148th Aero Squadron, turned in their equipment and cleaned up their area at the end of October in preparation for their move to Toul and the American front. By November 4, the squadron was quartered in barracks at Toul and had begun the familiarization process with six Spad XIII aircraft. Members anxiously waited to hear if the Germans were going to accept Allied peace terms. On November 9 they heard rumors the Kaiser had abdicated, and then on Monday, November 11, they celebrated the Armistice. "Much rejoicing. Happy moment of our lives," wrote one squadron member in his diary.[9] The flying continued, however. "Routine carried on as though war was still in progress," reported a 148th member. But it was also noted that "a spirit of let-down is evident."[10]

On Saturday, December 7, 1918, at Toul Airdrome, Kindley was honored with a big decoration ceremony that included a pass-in-review of squadron personnel. Lt. Gen. Robert L. Bullard, Second Army Commander of the American Expeditionary Force, presented Lieutenant Kindley with his previously earned Distinguished Service Cross with Oak Leaf Cluster.[11] Col. Frank P. Lahm, described the presentation:

> Sat, Dec. 7. This morning Gen. Bullard, with Col. De Boisanger and one of his aides, Curry, Poivillers and myself went to the 4th Pursuit Group where Gen. B. was to present a Distinguished Service Cross, with a bronze oak leaf added, to Lt. Kindley of 17th for some great work he had done on the British front, and a Croix de Guerre to Lt. David W. Lewis, U.S. 25th Pursuit

> Squadron, presented by the French Govt. for some good work Aug. 1 when he was in a French squadron. Davis had borrowed a band and had the 4 squadrons in line with the colors in the middle. The command was presented by Davis, the band played the Star Spangled Banner. Then I read the citation, we went forward and the General pinned on the decorations,—we withdrew & the command marched in review in a very creditable manner.[12]

No doubt this award ceremony must have been a highlight in Kindley's life and his military service. When combined with the British award of the Distinguished Flying Cross on November 1, these presentations, his leave, and the end of combat flying must have eased some of Kindley's diagnosed nervousness and flying fatigue. Little wonder that he must have thought he was momentarily on top of the world. He had achieved recognition that was way beyond any he could have imagined when he volunteered for the Air Service in 1917 in Kansas.

Lt. Field E. Kindley (*right*) with Lt. Gen. Robert L. Bullard at the presentation of Field's Distinguished Service Cross with Bronze Oak Leaf at Toul, France, December 7, 1918
Signal Corps Photo 37913

Lieutenant Kindley's assignment as commander of the 141st Aero Squadron on December 21 constituted a major challenge. He was quickly named that squadron's leader after the tragic death of legendary Hobart Amory "Hobey" Baker. Captain Baker, who had been in command of the 141st since September 10, 1918, was a celebrated football player, hockey star, and all-around athlete at Princeton University. He was well known on the East Coast not only for his sports accomplishments but also for his appearances in Manhattan society news.[13] His pre–Air Service reputation, friendly and considerate personality, and adventuresome flying, with two German planes to his credit, had established him as a highly regarded commander. On December 21, Capt. Hobey Baker died in a crash of Spad No. 7 near Toul airfield at 11:55 A.M. It was a "one last flight" accident just when he was to leave for the United States. Col. Frank P. Lahm, the pioneer Air Service pilot, recorded in his World War I diary the scene at Toul airdrome on that fateful day:

> Sat, Dec. 21. This has been a sad day, but in war time it is a case of ending up with 'Here's to the next one that dies.' I was flying the dual control 'Avro' at the Toul field this morning with Krout. We were just coming in for a landing when a Spad started out, giving us a little bump from the wash of its propeller as it left the ground. I landed, stopped and was about to take off again when Krout said 'the Spad crashed.' I looked around and there it was, lying on the field, not far from us. We taxied over, I helped get the pilot out—had to use an axe to get his foot loose. He probably died as he was laid on the stretcher. His face was badly cut up, and it was not until some one said 'It is Capt. Baker,' that I realized it was Hobey Baker, C. O. of the 141st Pursuit Squadron. Baker, the former captain of the Princeton foot-ball team, one of the best if not the best hockey player in the U.S., came to the front with the 94th last February, was transferred to the Lafayette (103rd) where he made a great reputation—then came here as C. O. of the 141st, the first pursuit squadron to join the 2nd Army Air Service. He was anxious to get home—finally, yesterday, his order came, he was going out for a farewell spin in his Spad, shot up, motor evidently died and he was too low to recover so crashed on the field.

> Sun, Dec. 22. Baker's funeral was at 11 o'clock this morning from Evacuation No. 1. A band led the cortege, then the firing squad, then a Q. M. truck with the casket, then officers of the 4th Pursuit Group followed by the 141st, Baker's squadron. We marched to the cemetery just beyond where Lufbery, John Mitchell and so many of our aviators are buried. It was a mournful procession in the rain. The chaplain read a prayer, then spoke very eloquently for a very few moments, the firing squad fired their volleys over the grave, the trumpeter sounded taps and it was all over. Another aviator buried at Evacuation No. 1. Another one of us gone. But somehow this seemed a particularly sad case. Hobey Baker stood out from others—and just as he was ready to start home. Newhall, Eckert, Landis, and Kindley, all of them and many others are left, the lucky ones—they are more fortunate, that is all. Baker makes the seventh to pass out since the Armistice—it seems like a good many, now that there is no more war.[14]

Kindley's orders to assume command of the 141st Aero Squadron on that same tragic day of the Hobey Baker death meant he must cope with the squadron's deeply emotional situation. He would be replacing a popular squadron commander, a noted national athlete, and another one of the Ivy League graduates. All the 141st Squadron would be watching to see if he measured up to his revered predecessor and how he would direct unit affairs in a period of genuine grief. Leading in combat was one thing, but moving an organization forward after stepping into someone else's big shoes was totally different. The challenge became all the more difficult because of the natural letdown after the war. Combat no longer held the squadron together in unity of purpose. A postwar leader had to find ways to motivate his men and keep a careful balance between discipline and relaxation. The one thing Kindley had in his favor was that the 141st anticipated and had prepared for a new commander (Baker was headed home).

Kindley's new unit, the 141st Aero Squadron, had been organized at Rockwell Field, southern California, on October 8, 1917, by Special Orders 132. It was first named as a Provisional Aero Squadron and then given a numerical unit designation later. Training progressed with the Curtiss JN- 4 aircraft, and on January 2, 1918, the squadron was ordered to France, traveling across the United States via train. Thirteen days

Lieutenant Kindley shortly before he received his promotion to captain. Note ribbons under wings for his U.S. and British medals.
Kindley family photo

later, on January 15, the 141st and four other squadrons boarded the famous *Titanic* rescue vessel *Carpathia* for the voyage to Glasgow, Scotland. Squadron flights were dispersed to various British aerodromes to continue their training, and it was not until August 18, 1918, that the 141st arrived in France to be a part of the 5th Pursuit Group based at Romorantin. On October 19 the squadron moved by truck convoy and by air to Toul and settled in concrete barracks at Gengault Airfield, three miles east of the city. Four days later, on October 23, the first patrols, flying Spads, began over the front lines with pursuit and protection missions the main duty. Capt. Hobey Baker won the first victory for the 141st on October 28, and the squadron recorded a second kill on November 5. Bad weather and the Armistice on November 11 brought an early end to the unit's combat.[15]

In the days following the Armistice, the 141st Aero Squadron pilots continued to fly their planes once a day, weather permitting. Formation flying and target shooting were emphasized. A small lake had been designated for the target area and a man stationed nearby cared for the target and reported on firing accuracy. Drills and parades became a part of the postwar routine, although it was later recorded they "seemed to lack appeal." Sports, along with visits by groups and individuals to nearby battle sites and to Toul, Nancy, and Metz, relieved some of the boredom. The Thanksgiving dinner of 1918 became a very memorable occasion for the men, who were increasingly thinking about returning to the United States.

No account of a 141st Aero Squadron celebration on Christmas 1918 has been noted, perhaps because the spirit of the unit had been dampened by the recent death of Hobey Baker. Meanwhile, however, Kindley's old organization, the 148th, had a Christmas disaster. Their "long expected Xmas turkey dinner went a-glimmering" when two of the kitchen staff went AWOL with the dinner funds. "The day was saved, however, by the 17th Aero who provided an evening of beer and entertainment."[16] Quite likely, Kindley joined his former combat comrades in hoisting a few holiday toasts.

Despite holiday celebrations and thoughts of home, the 141st Aero Squadron faced a more depressing situation. That the squadron had gone into combat late meant that it was a prime candidate for further duty with the occupation forces.[17]

The 141st, now commanded by Lieutenant (soon to be Captain) Field Kindley, kept flying out of Toul Airdrome in the early part of 1919. On April 11, 1919, General Pershing conducted a unit inspection, and the squadron marched in review in the afternoon. The 2nd Army and the 4th Pursuit Group were dissolved on April 15, and the 141st, along with several other squadrons, became elements of the 5th Pursuit Group. The Toul-based 25th Aero Squadron headed for the United States, and its S.E. 5 aircraft went to the 141st. The next day, part of the 141st left by truck convoy for Coblenz, Germany, and the balance went by train. The truck convoy arrived in Coblenz on April 20, and the squadron was reconstituted and billeted in old Fort Alexander.[18]

Kindley's squadron now became part of the Army of Occupation and the 3rd Army, tasked with dismantling and disarming German air units. Besides its two flights of S.E. 5 planes, it now had one flight of eight Fokker D.VIIs, which had been turned over to the Army of Occupation in accordance with the aviation stipulations of the Armistice. The Allies had great interest in the Fokker D.VIIs because their advanced design had made them a formidable enemy weapon. The U.S. Air Service eagerly received a total of 142 Fokker aircraft as partial reparations.[19]

The total American force in the Army of Occupation, some 200,000 strong, was also holding a Rhine River bridgehead until the Germans signed the peace treaty in June 1919. In addition, the Allies based on German soil would represent a visible reminder of victory.[20] Writing to his cousin Uther, Kindley said, "It seems good for our boys to be moving upon Hun soil."[21]

Coblenz, a city of more than fifty thousand people, was strategically situated at the point where the Moselle flowed into the Rhine River, and had railroads and factories. There were barracks and facilities available to accommodate the occupying forces, including the air elements.[22]

Lt. Kindley's late December assignment as 141st Aero Squadron commander meant he would be spending another Christmas in Europe. He sent a colorful Christmas card to cousin Uther with an airplane dropping letters. On the reverse side he scribbled the following note:

> Hello Sport: Was on my way home but now I guess I am stuck for going up into Germany. Am to command a squadron up there. May not be home for Xmas 1919. Why don't you write. Do you think because the war is over you don't need to write over here any more or what?[23]

While Field was again away from home for Christmas 1918, he received authorization in late January for a two-week leave, effective February 1, with travel to London. This allowed Kindley to return to some of his favorite English haunts.[24] After his relaxing leave and after his squadron's move to Coblenz, he got in some German sightseeing. On March 24 he was given leave to visit Cologne and return via auto.[25] Then in April Kindley, along with four other officers, was ordered to proceed to Paris, via airplane, landing at Orly Field, to attend a "gala performance at the Opera House" on April 12, 1919, where there was to be a ceremony of presenting flags to the American Air Service.[26]

Colonel Frank Lahm played a part in the Opera House ceremonies, and his colorful description provides a glimpse of what Kindley must have experienced:

> Sat, Apr. 12. Reported at the Opera Comique at 10 A. M. and rehearsed until nearly noon for the ceremony, then hurried out to Parc des Primes, brought K. in with me—she dropped me at the Place du Carrousel, where the 225 officers of the three Army Air Services were formed—I had the pleasure (?) of marching them up the Ave. de 1'Opera and the Boulevard to the Opera Comique where the "Gala" performance started at 2 P. M. First they gave "La Coupe Enchante," a pretty one act opera. Then 48 of our officers, representing that many squadrons and balloon companies, took seats on the stage, about 25 French aviators, including my friend Petit, now a major, Fonck and a number of other celebrities, Gen. Patrick, General Duval, Chief of the French Air Service & Lt. Co. Gros. Gen. Patrick made a very eloquent address in which he told of the help France gave us thru Lafayette, then down to the present day—after which Col. Gros read it in French. Then M. Lausanne, editor of Le Matin, (distinguished Paris newspaper) made the presentation address in English, the number of each squadron was called, the name of the aviator representing it, then one of the French aviators handed him a banner, saluted and they shook hands. There was great applause from the French each time that one of their "aces" rose, great applause from our Air Service in the audience each time a banner was handed to one of our "aces." Between acts we visited. Katherine and I called on Gen. Patrick who had Mrs. Wilson (wife of President Wilson) in his box. Father, K. & I talked to Besancon, Mr. Deutsch de la Meurthe (Pres. of the Aero Club de France) and his daughter—de la Voulx was there. The ceremony was typically French, arranged with the greatest nicety as to details, and went off very well. These banners had been distributed to all Air Service men in the audience, and at the appointed time we all waved them vigorously. Mlle. Alavoine sang the 'Star Spangled Banner' with tremendous feeling, that is the only way to describe it, and the last thing a Frenchman sang 'La Marseillaise,' the chorus of the Opera joining in on the chorus. Each little banner had been embroidered by some particular one or

> ones, whose name was announced as it was handed out. The one I carried had a note pinned to it, signed by four little girls all 11 or 12 years old, saying they had gone back to school every day during Christmas holidays to work on the banner! They deserve a letter from the squadron or company that receives their banner.[27]

Another of Field Kindley's postwar tasks was to contribute to an effort by the chief of the Air Service to compile "lessons learned" from the war, particularly deploying and operating aerial units. There had been early recognition that the build-up of the Air Service, along with its employment in combat, had been marked with many problems and a steep and time-consuming learning curve. The contributions of the British and the French in their more advanced machines and air operations had been clear, but the American experience needed to be captured in a more formal sense and hopefully rendered into some form of air doctrine. The order to submit "lessons learned" was comprehensive in nature but spotty and uneven in response. Field Kindley complied by forwarding a relatively short written essay. Because of the demobilizing of the aero squadrons, his submission was among the few at that level of organization.

In his "lessons learned" report, prepared while he was commanding officer of the 141st Aero Squadron in Coblenz, Field touched on the following subjects: manufacture, training, discipline, aerial tactics, and care and treatment of pilots at the front. He focused his harshest criticism on manufacturing: "The greatest failure of our entire air program is that of manufacturing." He believed the production failure stemmed from U.S. manufacturers who were "selfish and tried at first to perfect their own type of machine while later no one seemed to know just what type they wanted." Perhaps Kindley's pursuit-flying bias showed when he wrote, "It seemed they were partial to the two seaters and neglected the scout. This was probably due to the fact that they could appreciate the work of a two seater observation machine, but could not appreciate the work of a scout. They could not understand that a scout was very necessary in order for a two seater to work."[28] What Kindley was noting, of course, was the slow acceptance of aircraft from serving as aerial cavalry, eyes for the Army, to being aircraft fighting each other to control the skies and to deny the same observation to the enemy.

Kindley criticized training primarily because of the lack of schools to train a war pilot. "We had thousands of pilots but very few of which were fit for the front," he declared. "One of the greatest faults of our advance training is that our instructors were not experienced war pilots and did not know the 'game.'" He believed the answer to that problem was to send a war pilot to lead and instruct the advanced training. "A good war pilot is of greater value at the advance training school than he would be at the front," offered Kindley. No doubt he made a comparison with what he had experienced with his combat-trained British instructors.

Kindley had some rather strong opinions about the handling of pilot trainees who had crashes. He took exception to a fear he felt was created by holding over a pilot's head the specter of being punished and being removed from the Air Service. He also thought that in the case of a crash it was a "bad mistake" to punish a pilot by taking him off flying a week or two. "I honestly believe that the sooner a pilot gets back into the air after a crash the better it is for him. I have actual experience along this line," reported Kindley. Discipline in the Air Service became controversial in the postwar assessments, as it was during the war. Kindley took the typical pilot's view. "The Air Service is entirely different from any branch of the army and the same should be considered in the required discipline," he wrote. "In many training camps an officer under instruction is made to feel like a third class private and not like an officer in the United States Army. Many think that this has no effect upon results, but I am sure that a satisfied and comfortable pilot will make a better air man." The solution to this, according to Kindley, was to instill loyalty and respect emanating from a "good commanding officer." "Loyalty will also demand team work among the pilots in combat," Kindley emphasized. "Understand me I do not mean to say a pilot should be allowed to call his commanding officer by his first name or such as that but I do mean to say the iron infantry hand should not be used."

Not all associated with the Air Service or in the American Expeditionary Force shared Captain Kindley's opinions on discipline. Typical of an opposing view was one expressed by Maj. Howard S. Curry, commanding officer of Headquarters Detachment Third Aviation Instruction Center at Issoudun. "The most important lesson I learned is the power of discipline or lack of it for good or poor results," he said. "Training has been hampered by extreme lack of discipline among flying officers, particularly those undergoing instruction. Few of them have ever handled any men either in civil life or in the Army, and have [no] conception of the responsibilities of an officer." 1st Lt. Richard H. Merkel, also at Issoudun, made the following remark in his "lessons learned" report: "In my opinion student flyers should receive more military training to make them better soldiers." Probably no other issue created as much controversy as flier discipline. It often appeared to create a tension, especially between army regular officers and new officers created in the mobilizing of the Air Service. In addition, some pilot experiences with the British and French were considered destructive to good order and discipline.

Although the differing views about aviator discipline in the U.S. Army and the Air Service were never completely resolved, at least in the minds of various individuals, the more lenient approach seemed to be signaled in the "Final Report of the Chief of Air Service, AEF." That report stated: "The discipline enforced must be of a character which will not only keep the pilot out of trouble at the school, but will fit him to assume heavy individual responsibility. It must be remembered that in action the pilot is necessarily his own master and that treatment of him as a school boy and not as a man during the course of his instruction, though it may save trouble at the time, will tend to produce an irresponsible worthless officer."[29] Kindley could totally agree with this conclusion.

As for the matter of "aerial tactics," Kindley clearly incorporated his flight leader experiences, but with a broader perspective, in his report: "It seems that we had no system at the front, that is to say we did not keep a consistent patrol on the lines, to work at different heights, nor did the pursuit squadron know just how to cooperate with the observation and bombing machines to the best advantage." Perhaps recalling his last aerial battle, on October 28, Kindley wrote, "They did not use the system of trapping the enemy and out-maneuvering him." In his view, "they seemed to go to the lines blind folded and butted into the enemy and fought the best they could." He also noted that by September–October 1918 a "squadron patrol of three flights became necessary" because of the introduction by the enemy of the Fokker biplane.[30]

Kindley offered two thoughts, consistently important to him, in "Care and Treatment of Pilots at the Front." The first involved rest from combat flying. "Of course because we were so short of good men at the front they were kept there for very long periods, but every effort should be made to give a pilot the necessary rest in the form of leave or other duties such as instructing or lecturing at the training schools." With his own diagnosis of flying fatigue in mind, Kindley added, "Many pilots broke down in health and others were shot down because their efficiency had gone down." His second observation, certainly touching on morale, concerned promotions. "There is no better tonic for a soldier than that of promotion on the grounds he had done good work. This tonic was very scarce."[31]

Captain Kindley's views may not have received favorable acceptance in all cases, but at least he was being heard. A diary entry by Col. Frank Lahm for May 18, 1919, indicated he was being consulted. "After working many hours, I to-day finished up going over the material for the Air Service manual, flew to Chaumont from Colombey with Schirra in D. H. I went over the manuals with Reinburg, McNarney & Kindley, flew back & reached Toul in time for dinner."[32]

Among Kindley's other postwar duties, besides filing "lessons learned" reports, was handling inquiries about various personnel, particularly those lost during the war. For example, he had to respond to a request for information about Lt. Linn H. Foster from Buffalo, New York, who had disappeared during the 148th Aero Squadron's aerial battle on September 2. Field recalled that "Lieut. Foster was a personal friend of mine" and that a "diligent search for information regarding him" had not been successful. Although Lieutenant Foster was a member of Lieutenant Springs's "B" Flight, Kindley related what he believed happened:

> "B" Flight in command of Lieut. Springs, and "A" Flight at my command left the ground at 11:00 A. M., September 2, 1918. "B" Flight was to lead and "A" Flight was to form protection. The clouds were so low it was necessary to fly just underneath them at 3,000 feet. A short time after crossing the lines we were engaged by some of the enemy and immediately more of the enemy came up. The enemy numbering twenty-five, attacked the lower flight, that is "B" Flight which Lieut. Foster was in and it seemed certain death for them and us as well if we went to their rescue. However we did go in to do our bit and to help our comrades below. I noticed one of our machines which I believe to be Lieut. Foster's with three enemy machines attacking him so I went to his assistance and luckily shot down one of the enemy.

> By this time I was attacked by three of the enemy and of course had my hands full trying to defend myself. Just then I noticed a machine in flames pass me on it way to the ground. I could not identify it as it was in flames. . . . I was sure a few of my comrades were not going to return but how many I did not know and of course would not learn for days, for often many land just back of the lines and do not return for days. There was only one out of "B" Flight that returned (Lieut. Foster's flight), and that was Lieut. Springs the Flight Commander. He did not know what had become of the rest of his flight, other than they had started to fight with him. Out of "B" Flight Lieuts. Foster, Mandel, and Kenyon were missing, and out of my Flight, Lieut. Frobisher was missing.

Kindley concluded his letter by giving the time of the fight as 11:50 A.M. located west of the Canal du Nord along the "straight road from Cambrai to Arras."[33] Such communication to pass along to relatives, in this case Lieutenant Foster's mother, might have been some comfort, but as sometimes happens, it did not bring the full closure she or others desperately sought.

Meanwhile, Kindley's father in the Philippines was both proud of his son's wartime accomplishments and curious about his future plans. In his January 11, 1919, letter to Field he acknowledged his October 1 correspondence and declared, "You must be a very good fighter to get ten of the bloody beasts and not get wounded." He was puzzled how his son could be credited with 10 $^{1}/_{2}$ planes and anxious to know, "When are you going home? Tell me all about it." "Will you remain in the flying service or will you go back to your old Cine?" he asked.[34] In a February 23, 1919, letter to Field, his father reported receipt of letters dated November 14 and 28. The latter had conveyed Field's intention to stay in the Air Service, and his father responded with concern. "While I am glad to note that you are now in the regular army I have some fears for your safety as so many flyers have been killed in training camps. You must be exceedingly careful and don't get hurt. Let me hear from you as often as possible and everything." George Kindley then told of a change in his status. He was leaving Malaybalay and going to Baguio to "talk over propositions with the Director and if nothing looks good I shall take my retirement" and return to the United States. Then he added, "I shall be very lonely in U.S. if you are not there but you must do what you think best for your future good."[35]

In a similar vein, George Kindley wrote on March 2 indicating he had seen an article in a New York newspaper about his son's receiving the Distinguished Service Cross. "I am very proud of you Field and you have done nobly. Hope that you may not have any accidents now that the war is over but you must be careful and don't take too much risk in cutting shines." He added, "Write me often. I will leave here first of May never to return. Write me addressing me at Manila."[36] Later, in mid-April, the father again noted, "You certainly have been well advertised thru the Philippines for your good work against the Hun."[37] Still later in July George Kindley reported he was now "Superintendent of the Camarines Agri School" at Ambros, Camarines, P.I.[38]

In stark contrast to the exciting and tense days of combat flying over the front lines, the postwar period posed boredom problems. Commanders, like Kindley, faced serious challenges in keeping squadron men occupied. One of the answers to this difficult peacetime situation was an occasional air show. These performances or competitions included mock dogfights, aerial acrobatic maneuvers, and firing at ground targets. Kindley participated in some of these during his time at Coblenz.

From April 25 through April 27 a "Third Army Carnival" was held at Coblenz. It included a horse show and extensive aerial exhibits. Col. Frank Lahm, who was there, said, "It is excellent." He reported there were "two inflated balloons, one is an exhibit; the other to take up passengers." Also, "a line of planes stands on the ground, one of every type, one Salmson entirely stripped to show the construction. Two hangars were filled with aero exhibits—a Liberty motor assembled, another disassembled, aerial armament exhibit, aerial photography, balloon parachute suspended over a basket, all instruments and accessories used in the balloon and heavier-than-air service. The hangars were crowded with men, all of whom were intensely interested in the exhibits." Of course, the highlight was the flying.

> The aerial exhibit was great—at least twenty planes were in the air at once, S. E. 5's flying formation, Sops, Spads and Fokkers engaged in aerial combats, others doing acrobatics, message-dropping contests for Salmsons and DH-4's. Even a hail storm did not stop their flying. . . . But the grand finale to the whole show was when they let up an old captive balloon, dropped the basket with its parachute which floated off toward the Rhine and

> then the four pursuit squadron commanders attacked the balloon in turn with incendiary bullets. [Clayton] Bissell with his Spad failed to get it, [Forester] Marshall in his Sop-Camel failed, Kindley in an S. E. missed it, Fauntleroy in a Spad VII failed—just as Schirra and I were about to take off in the 'Bug,' a Spad dove in close and the balloon burst into flames, coming down and continuing to blaze long after it reached the ground. It was a fitting finale to a great 4-days show.[39]

Despite the remark about Kindley's failure to down the balloon, one account claimed Kindley triumphed over some other top air aces in the April 1919 Coblenz air competition. Coffeyville's Bruce Bentley, who had joined the Kansas National Guard with Kindley, met his friend once again at Coblenz with the Army of Occupation. He witnessed the Coblenz air show and reported that the competition between ace pilots of the British RAF and the AEF Air Service finally narrowed down to a few finalists, including Captain Kindley. Bentley declared the "Coffeyville man won hands down."[40] Kindley did receive a silver cup inscribed "Third Army Carnival, Chasse Airplane Exhibit, Coblenz, Germany 1919 First Prize."

Captain Kindley received some good evaluations on his leadership of the 141st Aero Squadron. On April 20, 1919, Maj. M. F. Davies, commanding officer of the 4th Pursuit Group at Toul, France, wrote that "as commanding officer of the 141st Squadron Captain Kindley has worked conscientiously and has at all times kept his Squadron at a high state of efficiency and proven his ability as a Squadron Commander."[41] Later, on May 12, 1919, he was recommended by Headquarters, 5th Pursuit Group, Coblenz Airdrome, for promotion to major. It was pointed out that a vacancy existed per Air Service Tables of Organization. Supporting comments included this accolade: "Capt. Kindley has done excellent work as Squadron Commander and has had long service over the front, and is credited with 12 official planes by the British, brought down while serving with the 148th Aero Squadron."[42] Much to the disappointment of Kindley, this promotion recommendation went nowhere. The American Expeditionary Forces were in a state of flux, as indeed the whole army and Air Service were, as a result of the rapid demobilization measures and the uncertainties of future U.S. military strength.

With progress in completing the terms of the Armistice and the peace treaty, the decision was made to return the 141st Aero Squadron to the United States for demobilization. Thus, Captain Kindley now became exceedingly busy with preparations for the long journey of the unit from Coblenz, Germany, to New York. Operations Orders 172 on May 12 by Headquarters Third Army, Germany, directed the route across Germany, Luxembourg, and France to the port of embarkation of St. Nazaire.[43] Later, Troop Movement Order 157 by the Headquarters American Embarkation Center, dated June 6, 1919, further directed one officer, Captain Kindley, and 124 enlisted men of the 141st Aero Squadron to board the U.S.S. *Tiger* for transport to the United States.[44] On June 9, 1919, Field signed a detailed memorandum regarding the move for men in his squadron. The instructions touched on baggage handling, policing of the billets, and responsibilities of the mess sergeant and kitchen. The last item said, "There will be no drill tomorrow."[45]

The long move to the French port of St. Nazaire had been an ordeal with men billeted in pup tents and haylofts—punctuated with several rounds of lice ("cootie") and physical inspections, craps and poker games, and marches. On June 14, the 141st troops were the first to board the U.S.S. *Tiger*. Some of the squadron officers, who had now been detached from the unit, came down to bid the men goodbye and good luck. The next day, June 15, the U.S.S. *Tiger* with Captain Kindley and 2,548 other officers and men aboard departed France. After twelve days at sea, on June 27 the U.S.S. *Tiger* docked at Brooklyn, New York.[46] Captain Kindley had brought his first squadron command home, and it fittingly marked the end of another phase of his life and the beginning of a new one.

It would be a grave mistake to believe these postwar months were mundane and unimportant. First, Kindley's life in this postwar phase in Europe provided an especially concise and telling account of the turmoil that U.S. armed forces went through following World War I. The traditional demobilization, complicated in this case by such large forces overseas, created a multitude of problems. First, the necessity for an occupation army on German soil pulled reluctant troops in one direction and then, with the peace treaty, pushed them in the opposite in the rush to get them back quickly to the United States. Managing this shift in personnel and material frustrated those in charge. Second, in the immediate postwar period, armies typically move toward a retrospective analysis. There were surely lessons to be learned. Kindley became a player in this attempt to determine what worked and what didn't, and what changes might worthily be considered. Kindley's status as an air ace gave importance to his voice in lessons-learned reports. Third, these postwar months revealed significant information about the role of leadership and specifically Kindley's role. Maintaining discipline and *esprit de corps* in postwar times taxes the very best. With the absence of purpose for the army draftees and volunteers, now that the war is over, the men think only of going home and bemoan the nonsense often associated with "make work" and "keeping busy" activities. Motivation of postwar troops becomes a true art. Kindley directly dealt with these leadership problems and through his responses revealed yet another facet of his character and command.

Chapter Eight

Return to the United States

We had more fun in the old days when pilots flew those old crates covered with fabric and held together with wire, without parachutes or pushbuttons. And as they say, those men were a race apart; those jacketed, goggled knights, those airborne warriors lived and fought and died according to all the rules of chivalry. War in those days was a test of valor.

Charles Batty, 141st Aero Squadron, quoted in Brown and Dodds, *History of the 141st Aero Squadron in World War I,* 4

The *New York Times* headline, June 28, 1919, read: "Famous Ace Returns. Capt. Kindley Brings Home Two Hard-Earned Decorations." The New York newspaper went on to say, "Captain F. E. Kindley, next to 'Eddie' Rickenbacker, America's greatest ace, returned yesterday on the transport *Tiger,* which brought 2,546 troops into port. Captain Kindley, who is officially credited with downing twelve German planes, was in command of the 141st Aero Squadron, which was also on board."[1] In another newspaper and in an article filed by the Associated Press, Kindley and his exploits were featured.

> He fought twenty-seven battles near Cambrai and Amiens as a squadron flight leader. One of the most thrilling of these, he said, occurred last September 28 near the Canal du Nord. After he had been transferred from the British squadron to the

> One Hundred and Forty Eighth American Pursuit Squadron, he started out with three other fliers in single-seater planes and at an altitude of 5,000 feet, near the German lines, the four aviators discovered that another American pursuit squadron was being attacked by twenty-five German machines. The quartet flew to their comrades' aid. The fight lasted seven minutes, during which one of the Americans was shot down. Capt. Kindley's machine was struck forty-seven times, his pilot's cap pierced, his goggles knocked off, and his leather jacket perforated, but he escaped injury.

More Kindley heroics were noted: "A machine gun bullet struck his gasoline tank, but the hole was above the fluid. Four of the Germans were sent down and the others flew back to their own lines, allowing the Americans to return to their hangars." The newspaper account, apparently based on an interview with Kindley, concluded with the remark, "Capt. Kindley eulogized his mechanics, declaring 'it was their continuous vigilance and careful work that counted most in achieving victory.'"[2]

Another newspaper quoted Field more extensively regarding his flight crew. "I could not make any statements about flying without paying a tribute to the mechanics of the air force who worked night and day behind the lines to enable the flying men to take the air," he said. "The life of the pilot is in the hands of his mechanics, and every moment of safety depends upon the carefulness and skill with which they have done their work. The best friends I had in France were the two men who kept my machine in order. If the mechanics understood their business and are faithful, the pilot with a little luck has a chance to come through with a whole skin."[3] Kindley's remarks reflected a true modesty on his part and a sincere appreciation for his ground support.

Such attention by the press must have been pleasing to Captain Kindley upon his arrival in New York. He had become more newsworthy because he was the highest ranking U.S. air ace still remaining in the Air Service. Also, the arrival home of such a large military contingent, signaling the near-end of the European pull-out and the approaching conclusion of the World War I demobilization, made the debarkation of the troop ships more significant. It also marked a new period in Captain Kindley's life. His high adventure in Europe had come to an end. His

141st Aero Squadron was to be demobilized at Hazelhurst Field, New York, so he would no longer have a command.[4] He had an uncertain career ahead, and he had no assurance that the flying he loved would necessarily continue. Even though he was back in the United States, he was a considerably different individual than when he had left it in 1917, and his more mature perspective toward life, jobs, and family relations meant he must be ever more on his own. The Air Service represented the continuity in his life, at this point, and his fame as a ranking World War I air ace could be his ticket for success in this new phase. Shortly after arriving in New York, Captain Kindley wrote Uther Kindley, "I am back and in one sense of the word I am glad but would be more satisfied if I only knew what I was going to do for a living in the months to come." He had previously telegraphed to Uther when he landed in New York, reporting that he was back in the country and mentioning that he might get a peacetime assignment to the Philippines. In his follow-up letter, he explained further: "I said something in my wire about going to the Philippines and the reason that I said it was that I hoped to get placed in command of the 4th Aero Squadron which is leaving for the Philippines on the 28th of this month. If I'm with it I will be able to work my way into the regular army and at the same time I will be able to see father and get him into the notion of coming home at the end of two years when my time is up."[5]

On July 8 Field Kindley wrote to his father, informing him of his arrival back in the United States, but his letter was not acknowledged by George Kindley until September 18, 1919.[6] However, the father wrote his son on September 1, saying he had received word from Margaret, his older sister and Field's aunt, that Field had arrived in New York on June 27 and would be in Gravette, Arkansas, by July 15.[7] In the same letter he referred to the possibility of Field being assigned to the Philippines for postwar duty, a prospect that delighted George Kindley: "I want you to take me out for a fly," he wrote.

The War Department decided not to deploy a squadron to the Philippines; therefore, Captain Kindley's speculative planning for going to the islands came to naught. This no doubt proved a major disappointment for both father and son. A reunion after so many years would not happen.

Captain Kindley's first task upon his return was to manage the demobilization of the 141st Aero Squadron. In his letter to Uther Kindley he said, "I am working hard trying to get my squadron discharged so that I will be free for a little leave in which I hope to get down to Gravette for a day or so before I go to the Islands if I go." He closed his letter with the remark, "I believe since I wrote you last that I have been promoted to Captain and also been awarded the Aero Club of America Medal but they don't mean anything in civilian life."[8] After taking care of the move of the 141st from the port to Hazelhurst Field No. 2, Long Island, New York, and its subsequent deactivation on July 9, Field was assigned to Hazelhurst Field on July 12, 1919.[9]

Consideration of life in the civilian world in contrast to that of a career military aviator may have entered into Field Kindley's thinking, though how seriously is difficult to judge. One temptation for the handsome aviator was to do a movie. "I have been offered a little money to go into pictures and make one picture for a firm here in New York but it is not a lasting proposition and the results are that I do not feel like taking it," Kindley informed his Arkansas cousin. "Then from what I can tell they want to picture me in an aero drama picturizing the act that won for me the Distinguished Service Cross and I am sure that they will not be able to picture it as it should be pictured and then that would hurt me more than it would do me good." Also, there were the financial aspects. "They have offered me $60 a day for the first picture which would take about two weeks but they will not promise me more work so I am not going to take it."[10]

While making a movie must have been an exciting thought, Kindley's military duties became more mundane headquarters tasks. On August 16, 1919, Captain Kindley was detailed as assistant to the executive officer of the Command Headquarters, Hazelhurst Field, Long Island, New York, an assignment he held until October 3.[11] On that October date he was designated as adjutant of the command.[12] During his headquarters duty he became subject to a variety of responsibilities, such as acting as summary court officer and serving on boards.[13]

In mid-July, he was able to take a fifteen-day leave during which time he traveled to Coffeyville, Kansas, to visit friends and to Gravette, Arkansas, to see his relatives. At both locations he received a hero's welcome. En route to Kansas, he received newspaper attention in Kansas City. "All Credit Goes to Company, Says Arkansas Ace in K. C.: Captain Field E. Kindley, Second Only to Eddie Rickenbacker, Refuses to Commit Himself to Heroism," read the headline. "All credit goes to the 148th, we fought together. I was just a member of the squadron," Kindley was quoted as saying. This newspaper interview had

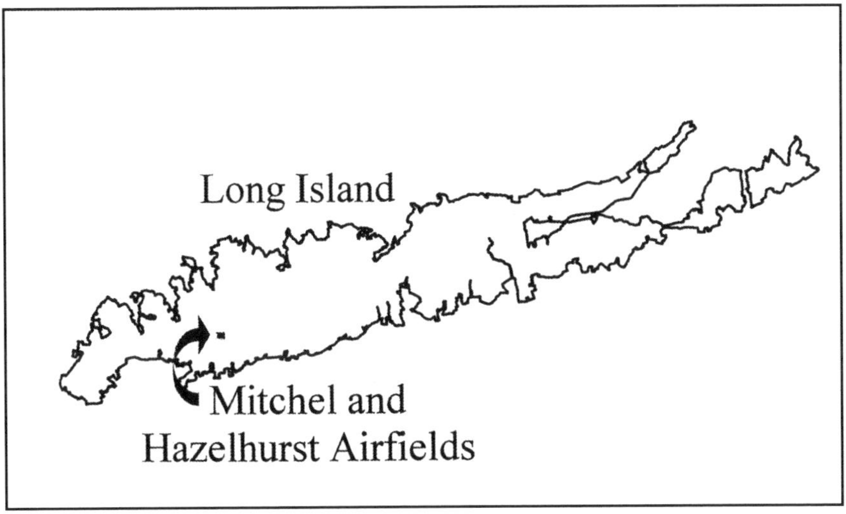

an interesting revelation. It reported that Kindley was "known in his squadron as the pilot of the 'Luck Bus' because of his narrow escapes from death."[14] Kindley recognized the value of maintaining hometown, down-to-earth relationships, for on July 21 he became a member of the Coffeyville, Kansas, post of the American Legion, by paying one dollar in dues.[15] He no doubt became a star member. Various groups, such as the American Legion, eagerly sought contact with such decorated veterans of World War I aerial combat. Kindley's return to his early roots in Arkansas and Kansas developed differently than he anticipated. He had left as one of the many young men going off to war, and he now returned as a celebrity. Upon completion of his leave of absence and return to Long Island, Captain Kindley got back into flying in a new way. He started participating in air races, largely because he enjoyed flying, but also as part of an effort to keep flying before the American public. A highlight of this activity occurred in August with his entry in the New York–Toronto Air Race. This was heralded as the first "big aeronautical event of the year in North America." "Many of the leading aviation personalities, military and civil, and from Canada and the United States, entered and for five days it was the subject of front page stories in the newspapers of Toronto and New York."[16] The *New York Times* of August 24 carried the headline: "Prince of Wales and General Menoher to Speed Aviators on 1,000-Mile Contest—Noted Airmen to Compete." The paper went on to report, "What aeronautical experts expect to be the greatest race in the history of aviation will start at 9 o'clock tomorrow morning, when Gen. Charles T. Menoher, head of the Air Service, will give the signal for the first of more than forty airplanes to leave the ground at Roosevelt Field, Long Island, and speed toward Canada on the first leg of the New York–Toronto and return course of 1,000 miles." The Prince of Wales, visiting Canada, was to be the starter in Toronto for the Canadian entries.[17]

The race was apparently the idea of Chance M. Vought, with sponsorship by the American Flying Club, which had been formed in New York earlier that year. Vought became chairman of the Contest Committee. In a June 25 meeting between the Canadian National Exhibition, the Aero Club of Canada, and the American Flying Club, plans were developed and prizes agreed on for the big race. Cash prizes totaling $5,000 were later increased to $10,000, with trophies awarded for the American and Canadian entries that recorded the best time either way between New York and Toronto, and with a Canadian National Exhibition trophy going for the best round-trip time. The U.S. Air Service ruled that military pilots would be ineligible for cash prizes. As originally envisioned, the flights were to have been nonstop, but later considerations of simulating airline service prompted a route with three stops at Buffalo, Syracuse, and Albany. Each contestant would be required to stay thirty minutes and refuel at each of the stops. Weather and nightfall delays would not be counted against a contestant's time, but an aviator forced down at another point would be charged that full time. Various handicap provisions were also included.[18]

Roosevelt Field, Mineola, Long Island, would be the U.S. start point or terminus, and the round trip would be 1,044 miles with legs of 149 miles from New York to Albany; 141 miles, Albany to Syracuse; 146 miles, Syracuse to Buffalo; and 86 miles, Buffalo to Toronto. The race could be begun at either the New York or Toronto terminus and could take place anytime beginning August 25 and the closing time of midnight, August 29. The airfields at the race stops were satisfactory except for Syracuse where refueling had to be done by pails and at Albany where the field had been a polo ground and was small and poorly situated. There was a woods on one side, a slope on the other, and a shallow ditch at each end.

Captain Kindley, like most of the Americans, prepared to take off from Long Island on the starting date of August 25. Major delays occurred because of weather at New York, and it was nearly 2:00 P.M. before

Captain Kindley in his S. E. 5a awaiting takeoff in the New York–to–Toronto air race

Kindley family photo

the first contestant took off. Some twenty-seven others got airborne at three- to five-minute intervals. Kindley had race number 15 and was flying an S.E. 5. He left Roosevelt Field at 3:10 P.M., the eighteenth contestant to get in the air. His old 148th Aero Squadron colleague, Elliott Springs, now a test pilot for L.W.F. Engineering Company and flying one of their aircraft, took off as number three over an hour ahead of Kindley.[19] All aviators had to circle the Commodore Hotel and Pershing Square in New York City before flying to the first stop. Upon approaching Albany, Kindley discovered problems at that city's Quentin Roosevelt Memorial Field. Col. H. B. Claggett had overturned his D.H. 4 when it rolled into one of the ditches; J. D. Hill, flying a Curtiss "Oriole," had demolished his aircraft; Lt. Ben Adams had upset his D.H. 4 upon landing; and Elliott Springs had run off the end of the field but was unhurt.[20] According to Lieutenant Holland, one of the contestants, "The broken machines at Albany reminded one of an aviation graveyard." Both sides of the narrow field were lined with spectators, including the mayor and head of the Albany Chamber of Commerce.[21]

The *Knickerbocker Press* of Albany reported that the crowd excitement over the preceding crashes "had only subsided when Captain F. E. Kindley arrived with a huge machine." "His thirteen victorious fights with Hun airmen in France had made him a favorite with all flying men, who sent up a cheer as they recognized his machine." According to the newspaper's account, Kindley's troubles then began. "The famous ace flew low just outside of the east boundary of the field, and as he turned hit an air pocket and one wing sagged. The machine headed directly for the crowd in the earthward plunge. With screams, they scattered, women clutching children, trampling one another in a wild dash for safety. Realizing the danger to the crowd, Kindley turned his plane toward the hill east of the field. The machine, passed within three feet of several hundred persons, and crashed into junk when it struck the ground. Several women fainted."[22]

Another version of what happened at the Albany field came some forty years later from Elliott Springs. He wrote, "In mid-summer of 1919 I was a test pilot for L.W.F. Company and flew one of their planes in the New York to Toronto Air Race. When I landed at Albany I had no brakes or flaps and ran off the runway and down a cliff. The crowd rushed to see what happened to me. Kindley was coming in for a landing behind me. In order to avoid hitting the crowd, he kicked the rudder and deliberately crashed his S.E. 5. I thought that was a pretty stout effort and we both had tears in our eyes when I congratulated him. He was unhurt but his plane was a wash-out."[23]

The *New York Times* report of the Albany situation as Captain Kindley attempted to land provided even more graphic detail and drama:

> With a strong south wind blowing at the shorter side of the rectangular municipal landing field here (Albany's Quentin Roosevelt Memorial Field), the "reliability test" feature of the American Flying Club's international handicap airplane race seemed to apply to pilots more than to the machines. The crowd which lined the longer sides of the field had four times the thrill which comes with the spectacle of an airplane crash, and they had the additional and unasked for tingle of a narrow escape from slaughter, despite the fact that one of the four airplanes here is recorded against Captain Kindley, his judgement and nerve alone were responsible for a lack of fatalities among the hundreds who pushed against the police line at the edge of the airdrome. As Captain Kindley's plane lost speed in landing, a suddenly increasing wind caused a drift that carried him almost to the crowd of spectators, which stood just on the edge of a sharp embankment. As the plane drew closer the crowd rushed in an effort to get out of the way. Children and women were shoved aside, some of them falling in the drifting path of the plane. Captain Kindley seeing the crowd, opened his throttle in the hope of gaining momentum to carry him into the air again. Enough power was generated to pull his plane slightly out of its wind-driven course, until the edge of the wings did no more damage than brush a few of the frightened spectators, but insufficient strength was given to the machine to lift it from the ground, and the hundreds of people on the far side of the landing station saw the Dehaviland [*sic*] suddenly swerve over the embankment and crash. Captain Kindley escaped with a slight flesh wound over his eye, but his machine was a total wreck. In the opinion of aviators at the field this pilot would have escaped personal injury had he allowed his machine to continue its drifting course, but he would probably have injured many of the crowd in saving himself. It is one of the miracles which so astound non-fliers, but which aviators take as a matter of course,

> which saved Captain Kindley from being killed. The appearance of his wrecked airplane was such as to make escape seem impossible. The Captain had unstrapped his safety belt, and landed with both feet on the ground almost before the dust had cleared. He received immediate medical attention.[24]

Lt. Col. Harold E. Hartney, a World War I pilot and later commander of the 1st Pursuit Group in France, had entered the air race, also flying an S.E. 5, and had landed at Albany before Kindley. He observed Kindley's sacrificial crash landing and dispatched a telegram to Maj. Gen. Menoher at Hazelhurst Field commending Kindley's actions:

> Am Albany all night. Race going nicely but Albany Field too small. Several crashes. Wish [to] commend spirit self sacrifice of Captain Kindley, Hazelhurst, officially second American ace who deliberately and in face of almost certain death zoomed and stalled over crowd saving from propeller the lives, crashing badly but luckily only slightly hurt. No commendation from you to high, view of his previous keen appreciation personal risk taken by so doing. Am leaving for Toronto early in morning.[25]

Maj. Archie Miller, commander of the Long Island flying field, provided copies of the telegram for the press so it was reported in the newspapers.

While the *New York Times* account had praise for Captain Kindley in his handling of the landing and crash, it found fault with Albany's airport:

> The disasters at this station are attributed to two things—the irregular shape of the landing station and the uncertain, varying speed of the wind. The gusty outbreaks made it impossible for the fliers attempting the difficult crosswind landing to estimate correctly the amount of drift for which they had to allow. . . . But the greatest lesson taught by the contest here was the necessity for suitable landing stations. Albany claims one of the few municipal fields in the country. The city's enterprise may be commendable, but it has gone only far enough to endanger the lives of the pilots who may have occasion to use the airdrome. A restricted field such as this is almost as dangerous as none at

> all under the conditions which prevailed today. The pilots who crashed are not to be blamed; rather does more glory go to those who landed safely.[26]

At least momentarily, the New York–Toronto Air Race captured public attention, one of its goals, and in the view of a number of commentators it served to strengthen aviation's role in the future. Out of some fifty-two entries twenty-eight finished the round trip, with Lt. Belvin W. Maynard of the Army Air Service declared the speed winner with a time of 7 hours, 45 minutes, and 15 seconds. Lieutenant Maynard, a "bespectacled divinity student turned soldier who is going back to his classes in the seminary," flew a DeHaviland 4 (D.H. 4), which was duly noted as American built, powered by an American Liberty engine (400-hp), helping to prove the relative "reliability and efficiency" of competing aircraft and engines, another stated goal of the race.[27] In addition, Robert J. Kennedy of the American Flying Club predicted the race would lead to a "permanent air mail service between New York and Toronto."

"Businessmen believe that the international race had proved the feasibility of commercial air travel," he stated, "and the necessity for an aerial mail route is apparent."[28] On September 2 the *New York Times*

British S. E. 5a–type aircraft, which Kindley flew while ferrying planes and later in postwar air races
Photo courtesy Lafayette Foundation

editorialized that the air race "will give a much-needed stimulus to aviation in this country." "In fact, it was one of the most successful tests of an airplane ever made," declared the paper. "The question of primacy in speed having been settled, there remains to be determined the really more important factors of reliability and efficiency," and "security is of no less importance," said the editorial.[29]

In early October Captain Kindley received orders to participate in another air race, an imposing transcontinental race from Long Island to San Francisco or vice versa. The purpose of this contest was a test of "reliability and endurance." By Air Service orders dated October 2, 1919, Field Kindley was to "proceed by airplane from Hazelhurst Field, Mineola, Long Island, New York, to Buffalo, New York; thence to Chicago, Illinois; thence to Omaha, Nebraska; thence to Cheyenne, Wyoming; thence to Salt Lake City, Utah; thence to Reno, Nevada; thence to San Francisco, California." Upon completion of this cross-country flight, he was to return to Hazelhurst Field by rail. He was to receive "actual and necessary expenses not to exceed eight dollars ($8.00) per day."[30]

The coast-to-coast "aerial derby" was to begin simultaneously from Mineola, Long Island, and San Francisco on October 8. According to the newspaper accounts, thirty-six pilots of the Army Air Service and one British pilot, an attaché at Washington, prepared to compete. The aircraft being flown were all foreign machines except for two Glenn L. Martin Company bombers. Capt. Roy N. Frances, one of the Martin bomber pilots, reported to have "flown in the air more hours than any other living American," was considered a favorite to win the handicapped race. Capt. Field E. Kindley, to fly an S.E. 5, was also believed to be a likely winner. One newspaper said Kindley had been one of the favorites in the New York–Toronto Air Race, but "he lost his chances for first honors when he pancaked his 'bus' over the crowds on the field." The paper added, "He was cited by General Menoher of the Air Service for his heroism and bravery in endangering his own life to avert hitting persons in the crowd."[31] Still another favorite was Lt. Belvin W. Maynard, "the Flying Pastor," speed winner of the New York–Toronto race.

Shortly before the contest was to have begun, newspapers reported that six U.S. Army aircraft had arrived from Europe to enter the transcontinental reliability airplane derby. "Two of the machines are of the S.E. 5 type, two of them are Spads and two Nieuports. The SE-5's are new and have 180-horsepower Hispano motors. The Spads which have

220-horsepower Hispano motors, have seen a little service, the Nieuports are equipped with rotary motors." One newspaper went on to state that "Captain Fred [*sic*] Kindley, who participated in the recent aerial derby between New York and Toronto, will pilot one of the SE-5's and Captain O. D. Donaldson the other." It was confirmed that Roosevelt Field on Long Island would be used for the eastern starting point.[32]

Besides keeping aviation in the news, the Air Service had multiple reasons for staging this ambitious transcontinental air race, officially titled the "First Transcontinental Reliability and Endurance Test." According to the concluding report, "it was to be an examination of the personnel efficiency, a close scrutiny of the existing mode of organization, and administration, a precursory but penetrating survey of the supply system as it stood, its distribution and control, a test of American methods and communications, a sweeping experiment of machines, motors, and instruments, far-reaching exploration into new fields of air travel, with its attendant search for landing fields, and research into things meteorological, in so far as concerns navigators of the air." "Three styles of competition each way" and various rules were specified in an encompassing telegram sent throughout the Air Service by General Menoher. The contest winners would be determined as "first, shortest time across, irrespective flying time; second, fastest actual time calculated between control compulsory stops each type machine; third, fastest flying time based handicap given each class machines." The race attracted 73 entries, 48 at New York and 15 at San Francisco, but after a number of incidents and accidents, a total of 59 airplanes actually competed.[33]

Captain Kindley, flying one of the S.E. 5s, was listed as entry No. 49 at the eastern starting point at Mineola, Long Island. Just as in the case of the New York–Toronto Air Race, he experienced early difficulties and was scratched from the race. The major winner turned out to be 1st Lt. Belvin W. Maynard, the divinity student who had won the New York–Toronto contest. Lieutenant Maynard registered the best time on the east-to-west leg and the best round-trip elapsed time (9 days, 4 hours, 25 minutes, and 12 seconds).[34] In an interview on October 18, 1919, Brig. Gen. William Mitchell enthusiastically commended Lieutenant Maynard. "As an individual performance, Maynard's record stands second to none. His judgement, ability, grit and determination exhibit the quality shown by our pilots in the European War, and are typically American," he said.[35]

Although Captain Kindley disappointingly was not a participant, the Air Service believed the "Reliability and Endurance Test" had been a success in more ways than one. "It is recognized by everyone that this country is considerably behind other nations in its aerial forces. If this contest contributes one small portion toward helping us to 'catch up' it will have more than accomplished its purpose and justified the expenditure made upon it," stated the 1920 final report. It concluded that "this test was designed not only to show the potentialities, but to reveal the problems." With the resulting news coverage across the breadth of the nation, the Air Service recognized that "probably one of the greatest results of the test was the stimulus given to aviation in the country."[36]

Despite entering and participating in the fall 1919 air races, Captain Kindley had other duties to perform. In November 1919 he served as adjutant at Headquarters Mitchel Field on Long Island. Such administrative positions would occupy much of his time. However, flying remained his great joy. He was detailed to the 1st Aero Squadron at Mitchel Field to maintain his flying proficiency—a necessity in his view.[37]

On November 12, 1919, Kindley's father wrote from the Philippines that he had been given a clipping of a New York paper "giving an account of your 'smash up' at Albany." He expressed sorrow about the accident but relief that his son had not been hurt. He went on to admonish him, "Don't you think you had best quit that hazardous business? You were lucky in France but if you keep it up you may get killed in the states."[38]

In December 1919 Field Kindley, along with other aviation notables, took part in a congressional hearing in Washington, D.C., on reorganization of the army and more specifically the formation of a united air service. Captain Kindley testified before a House Military Affairs Subcommittee on Aviation on December 12. The subcommittee was chaired by Rep. Fiorello H. LaGuardia of New York, a fellow aviator of World War I. LaGuardia warmly greeted Captain Kindley and seemed to lead him in his questioning along opinion lines they both shared. After a few preliminary questions from the committee, establishing that Kindley was a World War I ace with twelve victories and that he was still on active duty with the Army Air Service, Captain Kindley made an opening statement. Somewhat bluntly he said, "I think it is a decided fact that aviation should be combined; that the Army and Navy are, instead of cooperating with each other, in one sense of the word bucking each other, and twice as much money being spent where one-half the amount would serve the same purpose if the Army and Navy and other government branches of aviation were under one head."[39]

Kindley went on to point out what the British had done in their consolidation. Although the Air Service was currently in its infancy, he believed, "in the future we will have so much aviation that it is going to be necessary for us to patrol the air just as we patrol the border" and that will be "too big a job for either the Army or the Navy alone to undertake." Kindley was very clear: "So far as a separate air service is concerned, my opinion is that everything that goes into the air should be under one head, known as a combined air service."

Representative LaGuardia touched on another, related subject on which Kindley had a strong opinion, the training of aviators. LaGuardia asked, "Captain, it would also be very useful, would it not, if we were to keep a large number of men flying at all times?" Kindley replied, "It is absolutely necessary." "And the best way to make a flier is to let him fly?" asked LaGuardia. Kindley answered, "It is the only way to make one and keep one." In a prescient thought, Kindley concluded his congressional testimony: "It is possible in the next war, as has been suggested, that the first battle will be in the air. We do not know where it will be. It may be 25 or 50 miles or 200 miles inside the enemy's lines, or it may be just the other way—it may be inside our lines. If war was declared now it would probably be that way. If a battle in the air is carried on 200 miles away from the Navy or the Army, it is decidedly up to the Air Service to carry that out." While LaGuardia was obviously supportive of such a view, Rep. Harry E. Hull of Iowa retorted, "Of course, these gentlemen are giving us good testimony, but some of the statements they make we might take exception to."

The *New York Times* on the next day, December 13, took note of the Committee on Military Affairs hearing. "Five American aces, credited with having brought down more than fifty German airplanes, advocated today before a House subcommittee the creation of an aeronautical department of the Government to co-ordinate all aerial activities," the paper reported. "The group included Captain 'Eddie' Rickenbacker, officially credited with twenty-seven air victories in France; Major Charles J. Biddle, Philadelphia; Captain F. E. Kindley, Gravette, Ark.; and Captain J. A. Healey, Washington. All asserted that the air forces in France would have been much more efficient if administered by a Department of Aeronautics." The paper indicated that Glenn L. Martin, a spokesperson for the ailing aircraft manufacturers, believed the American aircraft industry would "soon become extinct without early and substantial aid from the Government." In summary, the *Times* said, "Recommendations made during the hearing included establishment of a national flying academy, Government subsidies to manufacturers, and preliminary training of army and navy fliers under the same system."[40]

Captain Kindley had another cause that he carried to the halls of Congress. He strongly believed that there was some injustice in the awarding of Distinguished Service Crosses and Oak Leaves to that medal. In a letter to Rep. James A. Frear on December 24, 1919, he offered a comparison of the number of Distinguished Service Crosses awarded to American pilots on the British front versus those flying elsewhere. The great preponderance of decorations going to Americans flying on the French and American fronts indicated a discrimination against Americans flying on the British sector. "In my opinion," Kindley wrote, "this was not the result of someone's intent to commit an injustice, but it was the fault of someone, and the matter should be rectified."[41] Captain Kindley, as one who had been awarded the Distinguished Service Cross with Oak Leaf, could speak out on this subject with some moral authority. But as with his advocacy for one air service, his quest for more medals to be awarded to those Americans that had flown under British control would not achieve success.

Captain Kindley maintained a close relationship with the American Flying Club in New York City. That organization had been a sponsor of the New York–Toronto Air Race and had a goal of promoting aviation information and activities. On December 20, 1919, Field wrote to Maj. Maurice Connelly of the club inquiring about rumors that there would be a change in club officials. Kindley went on to say, "If there is to be, I have a mighty fine suggestion to make to you, with regard to a secretary who would be a wonderful agent to you in your work. I do not think that I need to go into detail, but I would be very glad to talk to you on this subject the next time I see you." There was no further hint as to the person Field had in mind.[42]

In the same letter, Kindley made an interesting revelation. "You will probably be surprised to learn that I have been ordered to Ft. Sam Houston, Tex. However, you can not be any more surprised than I was to receive the order. They have been trying to transfer me for a long while, and the Colonel and I have been endeavoring to prevent it. The orders are here now, and, as the old saying goes 'orders are orders.' I shall be leaving about the first of the year."

Thus, an element of mystery entered into the last days of Captain Kindley's time on Long Island. There are no indications of why the Air Service wanted to reassign him and why he objected to it. Furthermore, it is unclear who might have been pushing the move. Billy Mitchell had created a storm with his pushing for an independent air service, and perhaps Captain Kindley was being sent to Texas to mute another voice arguing for the same. Regardless, in typical fashion, Kindley reacted positively even if he did not want the new assignment.

En route to Fort Sam Houston in San Antonio, Captain Kindley stopped at Coffeyville to see old friends again. His modesty when asked about his feats in the war impressed the citizens. According to one account, he responded to questions about the medals he had earned by self-consciously pulling them from a pocket and dumping them on a table for display.[43]

Although Captain Kindley's orders directed his move to Fort Sam Houston, his real destination was to be to the 1st Pursuit Group at Kelly Field.[44] Upon arriving at Kelly Field, he had further orders to the 94th Aero Squadron.[45] The 94th Aero Squadron was Eddie Rickenbacker's old "Hat in the Ring" Squadron and considered one of the best squadrons on active service after the war. It seems likely that Captain Kindley knew he was to command this prestigious organization when he left New York. Certainly, it would have eased some of his expressed qualms about leaving Mitchel Field. In addition, he would be returning to an operational flying unit and would once again be in command. Field Kindley was ambitious, and this new assignment could lead to a promotion to major. It might not have been his first career choice, but it could not have been all bad in Kindley's eyes. Like the new assignments of most military men, the move to San Antonio marked the closure of still another phase of his life and the beginning of a new one.

Kindley's return to the United States and his subsequent activities in the postwar Air Service illustrate the continuing transition troubles of the demobilizing army. In particular, all aviation experienced a severe letdown. Kindley, along with other leaders, sought to rekindle public interest and support by staging air races. Although Kindley failed in such competitions, he nevertheless lent his name to those endeavors, thereby increasing public interest and media attention. He continued to speak out via congressional hearings on matters of national air policy and specifically zeroed in on the perceived medal discrimination between Americans flying with the British versus those flying with the French. These events in the latter part of 1919 reveal how Kindley and the nation struggled to define the future direction of aviation in general and air power in particular. They also clearly show Kindley's personal and professional growth as his vision expanded to one with a more national perspective.

Chapter Nine

Fallen Aerial Warrior

> *His nature was generous, loving and appreciative. He was brave, daring and courageous and adored by his men and fellow officers.*
>
> Gravette News Herald, February 13, 1920

EN ROUTE to his new assignment in Texas, Capt. Field E. Kindley stopped in Gravette, Arkansas, to visit relatives and friends. Once again, his hometown celebrated his arrival. At one point he was honored by the citizens with the presentation of a "handsome gold watch." One young townsman remembered his very shiny brown boots.[1] Others were impressed with his modesty and his military bearing. During his short stay there he expressed the wish to bring his father back from the Philippines to join him and perhaps to live in Gravette.

Captain Kindley's destination, Kelly Field in San Antonio, Texas, and his assignment as commander of the 94th Aero Squadron seemed a promising beginning of the year 1920. Only a few years earlier, the young pioneer military aviator Benjamin Foulois had been ordered to survey a landing field in the San Antonio area. He chose a 700-acre site to the south of the city, which would become Kelly Field, named after the first American military aviator killed while flying a military aircraft. On April 5, 1917, the former cotton field received the inaugural four JN-4 Jenny trainers. During World War I it became a training center for mechanics and specialists of various kinds, as well as pilots.[2] After the war, Rickenbacker's famed 94th Aero Squadron was stationed there, and Captain Kindley now would be in charge of this well-known and important Air Service organization. Kelly Field had become a lively and major Air Service aerodrome.

Kindley scarcely had time to settle himself in his new community and new aero unit when he was confronted with the major task of preparing for a visit by Gen. John J. Pershing, the noted World War I commander of the American Expeditionary Force in France. In addition, Kindley had been ill with the flu since his arrival and had been ordered to stay in his quarters. The doctor had trouble keeping him there, so Kindley soon began the urgent preparatory work in the squadron.

There was much excitement over Pershing's forthcoming inspection. Kelly Field was in a celebratory state of mind, and the 1st Pursuit Group and its squadrons rejoiced in the opportunity to "show itself at its best." Practically all the aces who had survived World War I and had remained in the Air Service were at Kelly Field. Some had been decorated by the general, and they would again be able to see the famed commander. They were to fly at the head of their squadrons as they had done in Europe. There would be an aerial pass-in-review, and then they would execute maneuvers as they had against the Germans.[3]

Each of the Kelly Field squadrons planned some stunt or operational tactic to impress and honor the general. The 94th Aero Squadron had S.E. 5s, and Kindley decided to demonstrate a flight of five aircraft flying in formation and firing at a ground target. Kindley, leading the flight, practiced the unit's maneuver on the Saturday preceding the Tuesday arrival of Pershing, but on that day he was not satisfied with the tightness of the formation.[4]

Although it was the custom at Kelly Field to "cease work from Saturday noon until Monday morning," the Pursuit Group elected to continue their practice maneuvers and take time off after Pershing's visit. On Sunday, February 1, 1920, Kindley's flight took off in good formation. Experiencing mechanical problems, one of Field's aircraft came back to the field and landed, and Kindley circled the airdrome and then approached the firing demonstration area. As the formation began its dive toward the designated area, Kindley saw some enlisted men in the vicinity of the target. Sensing that other formation pilots might not see the men and might open fire, Field went full throttle and skimmed over the target at low altitude to warn the men on the ground. Three passes were made over the designated point.

On the last pass Captain Kindley's aircraft appeared to be working perfectly as he eased his throttle off, turned slightly, and glided at high speed over some mesquite woods. According to Kindley's friend and fellow pilot, Capt. Clayton Bissell, who was watching on the ground, Field appeared not to realize how fast he was losing his speed as he looked back to pick up his formation and see if the men had left the target area. "The machine quivered for a fraction of a second and one wing dropped . . . and the machine began to settle in a slideslip stall." Kindley had an estimated 40–75 feet of altitude. Although Field put his "motor on full and it took in good shape," he didn't have enough altitude, and the aircraft hit the ground with full motor just as it began to get forward speed.

Kindley's aircraft "broke at the cockpit and the streamline behind his head fractured the base of his skull and caused death instantly." He therefore probably lost consciousness immediately when the plane struck the ground. A fire followed, and exploding bullets prevented the recovery of Kindley's burned body for some minutes.

Another ground observer, Harry A. Johnson, who would become an Air Force major general later, reported he "was on the flight line watching a flight of S.E. 5s diving on and firing at a ground target at the south end of the Kelly Field. On one pass the lead plane, diving at about a 45 degree angle went into the ground and burst into flames. Never did know what happened, if he was hit by a wing man, or passed out, or just misjudged the ground," stated Johnson.[5]

Thus, at 1:35 P.M., Sunday, February 1, 1920, Capt. Field E. Kindley was killed in a peacetime accident. He had defied death in so many other crashes and life-threatening incidents in training, battle, and postwar races, but, just as his father feared, he could not escape them all. Field Kindley's luck had finally run out. Characteristically, however, he died in heroic fashion, ignoring his own safety in concern about possible harm to others. In an echo of his near-fatal crash at Albany, New York, in avoiding the crowd of spectators, he flew too low at Kelly Field warning away enlisted men from a target. The resulting crash was horrific.

The tragic death of Captain Kindley, like that of Hobey Baker, hit the remaining Air Service veterans hard. The "In Memoriam" document, written by a war colleague and presented to a solemn gathering of fellow fliers, read, "Britain can mourn, France may weep, all the Allies may indeed express their sorrow, but America must bow its head in deeper mourning than all; for with this simple crash, America, The Army, The Air Service loses one of its best." Then the statement turned more poetic and eloquent:

Picture the glorious combat of the air! Sometimes single-handed against many; at other times while accompanied by friends, but always ready to do or die. Sometimes the flight over the lines meant escorting some untried pilot—a helping hand. At other times it meant diving to the rescue of some brother, hard pressed by the enemy. Then again, there were times without number when it meant a flight through raking shrapnel, when every moment might be the last. But the greater number of times was when the enemy was met and the result of combat could be only death. This meant skill against skill and courage against courage, but there never was a question. Field E. Kindley was always superior, always better, always more skillful, always possessed of more courage. For all that he was awarded the highest honors possible by both Great Britain and America. It was not so much the deeds that were rewarded but the conception of duty which made these deeds possible. Yet tonight all that was mortal of Field E. Kindley—man amongst men, courageous amongst the courageous—lays crushed and broken at Kelly Field. . . . Another life has gone—once more the finger of Death has beckoned. This time it took one of the best, but the spirit of Field E. Kindley will forever live on.[6]

The New York Times on February 2 carried the headline: "Air Captain Kindley Killed—Leading American Ace Falls to His Death in Texas." The article reported that Kindley "was killed instantly in aerial maneuvers at Kelley [*sic*] Field No. 2" and that "the accident occurred while a group of airplanes were in practice formation, preparing for an exhibition scheduled in honor of General Pershing's visit next Tuesday." It continued, "Captain Kindley's machine fell when he was about fifty feet above the ground. He was crushed and burned." The *Times* also noted that "Captain Kindley was the premier American ace remaining in the service, having twelve German planes to his credit" and that he "was one of the air service officers summoned before the House subcommittee investigating the air service recently."[7]

On the tragic day of February 1 Uther Kindley, the cousin in Gravette, Arkansas, with whom Field Kindley had corresponded so frequently, received the following dreaded telegram:

> Regret to inform you of the death of Captain Field Kindley in aeroplane accident at this field at one thirty five pm today. Request information by wire of your desire as to disposal of remains which will be sent with an attendant at Government expense if so desired.[8]

A similar notification went to Field Kindley's father in the Philippines. Uther Kindley also cabled him shortly thereafter. In a letter to Uther dated February 8, George Kindley indicated he had received word of the "death of my dear boy" from Kelly Field and from Gravette. A pained and deeply saddened father wrote: "It is needless for me to tell you that I am broken hearted and at drift. I have nothing in view and nothing that I want to do. This takes the last of my family. Could I have gone instead and left his young life to continue in the defense of his country I could be satisfied. It is awful. The dear boy was all the world to me and now I can see him no more. I am thankful that, as death had to come to him, it was in his own country and that the bloody Huns did not have the satisfaction of taking his life."[9] Capt. Clayton Bissell, the 148th Aero Squadron comrade who was a ground observer of Kindley's crash, became the Air Service officer to take care of Kindley's personal effects. He took charge of the notification of key people and became the "attendant" to escort Kindley's body back to Gravette, Arkansas, for burial. Once in Kindley's hometown, he handled most of the military funeral details.[10]

On Thursday, February 5, according to Kindley's hometown newspaper, the *Gravette News Herald,* "by far the most ostentatious funeral ceremony in the history of Northwest Arkansas was enacted." Kindley's casket had been taken to the place he called home—the residence of his late uncle and his aunt, Mrs. A. E. "Mollie" Kindley. "The large room in which the body was laid was not sufficient to accommodate the flowers which poured in from everywhere." Among the many dispatching flowers and condolences were Elliott White Springs, Kindley's friend and comrade who had served as 148th Aero Squadron Flight "B" commander, and Morton L. Newhall, Field's 148th squadron commander. Tributes also came from many other former colleagues. A great crowd of relatives, friends, and citizens, larger than could be housed inside the building, gathered on the lawn at 11:00 A.M. for the beginning of the solemn ceremony.[11] Reverend Gillespie of Fayetteville, who was to have opened the ceremony, was delayed, and services did not commence until 12:30. Following the remarks at the Kindley residence, members of the old 142nd Field Artillery Band of nearby Bentonville formed an honorary band and led a funeral march to the cemetery. An honor guard made up of former enlisted men in the area and commanded by Captain Ingerton, a local veteran, accompanied the hearse. A long line of cars followed the marching party and the funeral procession stretched for a mile from the town to the International Order of Odd Fellows cemetery. At the cemetery, the honor guard deployed for the final salute, appropriate music was played, commitment was made by Reverend Hay of Bentonville acting as chaplain, taps were played, and the firing squad rendered the last respects as Capt. Field Kindley's body was lowered to rest. Three of Captain Kindley's Air Service comrades, Captain Bissell, Lieutenant Applegate, and Lieutenant McFarlin, were present at the funeral, and the two lieutenants joined Lieutenants Steele, Williams, Michael, and Huffman to serve as pallbearers. Representatives of the U.S. Army, the U.S. Navy, and the Air Service were included in the funeral ceremony, with some eighty-five officers and men paying last respects to the fallen hero.[12] Many local people vividly remembered the impressive funeral for years to come.[13]

While Captain Kindley's body was laid to rest in the Gravette cemetery, a formal accident investigation had begun at 9:30 A.M. on February 4, 1920, at Kelly Field.[14] A three-member board of officers, all captains, called nine witnesses, including 1st Lt. Sam L. Ellis, 2nd Lt. Harry W. Brokaw, and 2nd Lt. Bushrod Hoppin, who were flying in formation with Captain Kindley at the time of the crash. Other witnesses were on the ground, with Maj. Reed W. Chambers, commanding officer of the 1st Pursuit Group being the key observer. All witnesses reported that Captain Kindley's plane, after flying low over the firing target to warn the men in the area, had made a sharp right climbing turn and then suddenly nosed down into the fatal crash. Several estimated the plane's altitude at only about 75 feet at that crucial moment. In the board's questioning several opinions emerged as to the cause of the accident. Major Reed said he believed it was "a broken control, probably an aileron control" that was at fault, and this notion received support by an officer's testimony stating, "All of the controls were intact with

Captain Kindley's funeral procession from the Kindley house to the IOOF Cemetery in Gravette, Arkansas, February 5, 1920
Kindley family photo

the exception of the lower end of the RAF wire connecting the two right ailerons. This wire had broken off where the threads enter the socket of the clevis." Another officer reported, "I have heard and understand that the aileron control wire was found broken on this ship of Captain Kindley's. There has been a great deal of trouble experienced at this field with the present type of RAF wire breaking just above the clevis fixture." Other testimony offered the possibility that Kindley's aircraft had been "placed in a stalling position" with subsequent "falling off on its right wing and the controls refused to act at the necessary altitude." Still another mentioned that in the area of the crash site, "The air was very bad around there, which might tend to throw him off." This witness further added, "I have heard other pilots mention the fact that at that particular place it is bumpy and a plane could be thrown into an unnatural position at that point."[15]

The investigative board could not come to any definitive single cause of the Kindley accident. Its "Findings" declared:

Captain Field E. Kindley, A.S.A., met his death in an airplane crash and conflagration, due to any one of the following reasons, in the opinion of the Board:

(a) Breaking of the RAF aileron control wire.
(b) Stall in climbing right turn.
(c) Due to gullies, a gust of wind my have rendered the plane temporarily out of control.

The "Findings" section of the investigative report closed with the key statement: "That, the deceased's death was in line of duty, and was not the result of the deceased's own misconduct."[16]

There was an outpouring of sympathy letters and telegrams as the news of Kindley's death spread. Captain Bissell, now returned to Kelly Field, wrote to Uther Kindley on February 8, stating, "Enclosed are all the wires I received from people relative to Captain Kindley." In addition, he said, "I am enclosing some Weekly News Letters for February 7th which have an account of Captain Kindley's death. The Weekly News Letter is an official organ and is sent all over the country. You may publish the part relative to Captain Kindley if you desire."[17]

Among the correspondence addressed to Uther Kindley was an intriguing letter from Kathryn Seibold, widow of Lt. George Seibold, a colleague of Kindley and Captain Bissell, and a member of the 148th Aero Squadron. Lieutenant Seibold had been killed in France. On February 12, 1920, Mrs. Seibold wrote, "I had expected to write you before this, before coming to Fort Worth, but the shock of Field's death has made things so different." She went on to say, "I don't know whether or not Field ever told you about me or not. I was with him for a short time in New York during the holidays and am now so glad to have seen him there. He was so blue about his transfer to Texas and then his sickness there no doubt unfitted him for flying." Kathryn Seibold asked for George Kindley's address, commenting, "I should like very much to write Field's father, because I believe that I have been in closer touch with him in these last months than anyone else and I know how Field wrote to people." She concluded, "If there is anything that I can tell you that you might want to know, please call on me, for Field was dearer to me than anyone in the world."[18] The words and tone of this letter would seem to indicate that Kathryn Seibold was a serious romantic interest of Field

Kindley. If so, that relationship, too, was cut short by the tragic and untimely death of Kindley.

Captain Bissell, obviously sincerely interested in easing the impact of Kindley's death on the Arkansas relatives, continued correspondence for some months. On February 14 he sent a letter to Uther Kindley touching on the subject of Field Kindley's attempt at getting redress on the inequities of awarding the World War I aerial medals. Bissell wrote, "I am also enclosing a copy of a letter which Kindley had written to Representative Frear. Field was doing all in his power to get this injustice straightened out, and I would like to carry on his work. Frear has evidently done nothing. I desire your permission to have this letter published in the Air Service Journals, and I believe we can bring about a rectification of this matter for which Field worked so hard." Bissell concluded his letter by asking if Kindley's effects had reached Gravette.[19]

Unfortunately, but as might be expected, closure did not come rapidly or easily to Kindley's father in the Philippines. He wrote to Uther on February 16 expressing his heartache: "I cannot recover from this awful loss of Field. . . . I loved him so much and he did me. In the last letter I had from him written soon after his return to the states he pled with me to go to him and it was my intention to do so this year but now I shall never see him again. It is awful. How can I go home any more. My dear brother is gone and now my dearest son. When I return instead of seeing my two best friends I can only see their graves. Write me everything about Field."[20] The request for more information about his son became a recurring theme in George Kindley's future letters.

The Kindleys' father-son relationship remains an intriguing subject. On the surface, it appeared to be a mutually loving one, and the correspondence between the two indicated a respect and caring for each other. In Field Kindley's days of involvement in the war, his father displayed great pride in his son's accomplishments and worried about his safety. The son, in turn, dutifully wanted to keep his father informed as to his actions in Europe. George Kindley, in his grieving for the loss of his son, depicted genuine emotional pain and regret at not seeing him again. At the same time, one wonders about the father dispatching his young, impressionable, only child to live with relatives half the world away. In addition, as the war neared a climax, Field Kindley expressed a rare criticism to Uther about his father remaining in the Philippines, seemingly stubbornly so. The trailing off of the correspondence between the two indicated a likely cooling of the relationship. Field Kindley, maturing and back in the United States with other adventures, increasingly concerned himself with career over family matters. However, the Kindleys' father-son relationship differed markedly from that of Elliott White Springs and his father. That relationship remained consistently quarrelsome and almost a bitter contest of son versus parental authority.[21] A key element in thoroughly understanding the Kindley father-son relationship remains missing given the absence of Field Kindley's side of the correspondence. The many and varied letters after Captain Kindley's death provide valuable insights into the life and character of Field Kindley and his association with some of the key people in his last years. They remind us not to lose sight of the human dimension. Captain Bissell typified the military bond that tightly tied Field Kindley with his aviation colleagues in life and in death. Letters and telegrams from acquaintances and even strangers showed the fame that Captain Kindley had earned at that time and revealed an admiration, affection, and respect that only a relatively few individuals could command. The correspondence from and to relatives, particularly to and from the father, decidedly communicated the impact Field had on their lives and how the tragic end brought an emotional pain, slow to heal. Included also was the surprise surfacing of romance, but it too was destined to fade to fleeting memory.

The mentioning of "character" as an outstanding attribute of Captain Kindley in several letters of condolence and sympathy did not come by chance or as only a nice memorial comment. Field's inner strength, however variously defined, attracted notice. Although carrying a reputation as a relatively quiet and unassuming young man, he became a respected leader for his perseverance and his calm, steady courage in the face of combat and in postwar events. Throughout, he showed an inquisitive willingness to learn, self-initiative, and personal integrity, coupled with a humility that endeared him to many. These core qualities marked his brief life.

Field Kindley faced major challenges in his short mortal time. His childhood was not easy, absent a mother and a father for many of his early years. He became a high school dropout but demonstrated an entrepreneurial spirit. He joined the army in patriotic World War I fervor but hated the drill. He learned to fly and to survive the ever present training accidents, even though he was not particularly mechanically inclined. He developed into a skilled, admired pilot and leading aerial fighter even though he lacked the Ivy League education and elite background of many of his peers. He downed twelve German planes in aerial dogfights, although he was not among the typical flamboyant fighter aces in their daring and aggressiveness. He faced near-certain death on several occasions, but never turned away from what he saw as duty. After the war he remained in the Air Service, commanded squadrons, earned the esteem of his men, but retained the semblance of Ozark charm as a country boy. He spoke out boldly on postwar aviation issues that mattered to him, yet maintained a gentlemanly demeanor. He loved and continued to fly, entering postwar air races, despite being plagued with accidents. He sought justice for inequities for medals awarded to British front pilots despite possible career damage to himself. These various and lifelong challenges molded and built Field Kindley's character. A lesser man would have been defeated without the inner strengths and traits he brought to bear on those same challenges.

Kindley's development into a World War I air ace, although relatively short in time, remains the heart and the most engaging part of his life's story. His flight training with the British and his subsequent task of ferrying aircraft for the Royal Air Force provided thrills and death-threatening incidents. The details of this experience drive home the great risks associated with learning to fly in the early days of aviation. Furthermore, Kindley exemplified the remarkable perseverance of World War I pilots in mastering training despite the accidents and severe losses of comrades. Through it all, Kindley obviously became a product of the British training system, and that would mark him forever as a British admirer and imitator. When he was assigned to the RAF 65th Squadron for combat flying, he readily applied his British indoctrination and found easy accommodation to their tactics, organization, and personnel. The downing of his first German aircraft while flying with the British and in the British-built Sopwith Camel established him as a shining example of one of the labeled "War Birds." This designation would always be a defining one for him and others, in contrast to the Americans flying with the French.

A greater appreciation of Kindley's combat flying skill comes with the review of the aerial characteristics of his pursuit plane, the Sopwith Camel. As has been noted, the Camel had a number of strengths and weaknesses, and was generally considered a difficult plane to fly. Kindley truly liked the aircraft and mastered its deficiencies to the ultimate success of shooting down a dozen Germans. This feat becomes all the more remarkable when considering he battled against the best German aircraft, the Fokker D.VII, and some of Germany's best pilots.

Kindley's flight missions, particularly during his time with the American 148th Aero Squadron, illustrated the changing nature of aerial warfare and ground support in World War I. At the time of his combat duty, the war on the ground evolved into a more fluid state. The 1918 German offensives followed by Allied counter-offensives brought movement in contrast to the stalemated trench warfare. Air operations became critical in support of the ground forces, and air tactics changed accordingly. Kindley experienced the range of the new challenges from the fight for air superiority to the strafing and bombing of advancing or retreating ground forces. As frequently emphasized, the thread of leadership development courses through Kindley's brief life. He learned to follow, and then he gradually advanced to flight commander and to squadron commander. His leadership skills were honed primarily in the heat of combat; in the postwar period he faced different but still demanding, difficult circumstances. He exhibited in the war and postwar months a consistent courage and drive toward his mission and his duty. At the same time, he did not diminish his caring concern for his men and colleagues. Most dramatic were the incidents of willing, deadly sacrifice for the benefit of others. It appeared in the early 1920s that he was destined for still greater accomplishments. It is little wonder that the reaction to his tragic final accident provided further evidence that he succeeded in being the respected and admired figure in the public eye as well as in the esteem of his flying companions.

Although Capt. Field Kindley never commanded national attention, as did Capt. Eddie Rickenbacker, he nevertheless attained a high rank as an American air ace of World War I. His record, and the award of the Distinguished Service Cross and Britain's Distinguished Flying Cross for valor, marked his special place in aviation history. In addition, however, when one carefully examines the details of his twenty-three years of life, Kindley's character and exploits convincingly point to an authentic, although neglected, American hero.

Appendix A

Capt. Field E. Kindley's Victories

Number	Date	Time	Squadron	Enemy Aircraft	Location
1	26 June 1918	8:28 P.M.	65th RAF	Pfalz D.III	Albert
2	13 July 1918	8:57 A.M.	148th	Albatros D.III	Ypres
3	3 August 1918	9:30 A.M.	148th	Fokker D.VII	Ostend
4	13 August 1918	1:50 P.M.	148th	Two-seater*	Roye
5	2 September 1918	11:50 A.M.	148th	Fokker D.VII	Romaucourt
6	5 September 1918	5:20 P.M.	148th	Fokker D.VII	St. Quentin Lake
7	15 September 1918	10:55 A.M.	148th	Fokker D.VII	Dartford Wood
8	17 September 1918	1:00 P.M.	148th	Fokker D.VII	Epinoy
9	24 September 1918	7:28 A.M.	148th	Fokker D.VII	Cambrai
10	26 September 1918	1:25 P.M.	148th	Fokker D.VII	Cambrai Road
11	27 September 1918	9:20 A.M.	148th	Halberstadt C	Marcoing
12	28 October 1918	12:05 P.M.	148th	Fokker D.VII	Villers Pol

* Some publications indicate the German aircraft was a Fokker D.VII. Field's combat report says "two-seater."

Appendix B

Airfields or Bases Named for Capt. Field E. Kindley

Kindley Field—Philippines

In 1921 the first airfield to bear the Kindley name was designated on the little island of Corregidor, commanding the entrance to Manila Bay in the Philippine Islands. It appropriately carried the Kindley name due to Field Kindley's time spent in the Philippines and his father's long career in education positions in those islands. Kindley Field was once "considered one of the most desirable stations to which Air Corps personnel in the Philippines could be assigned," as it was "free of the mosquitoes found on the mainland and, being entirely surrounded by water, was cool at night."[1]

> Pilots assigned to Kindley Field flew airplanes and amphibians, since there wasn't enough room on the little island for a regular landing field. The airplanes were hangared ashore, but were rolled or taxied into the water for take-off. The Air Corps officers flew missions for the Coast Artillery Corps, spotting the fire of the huge guns guarding the entrance to Manila Bay.[2]

Kindley Field in the Philippines was abandoned by the Air Service about 1930. The six or seven officers and their families and the supporting enlisted personnel to maintain three or four aircraft returned to the United States, and the station was then turned over to the Coast Artillery. The last commanding officer of the old Kindley Field was Lt. Col. Vincent J. Meloy.[3]

Kindley Field/Kindley Air Force Base—Bermuda

War Department orders designated Kindley Field on the British Atlantic island of Bermuda on 25 June 1941. Only the runway portion of a base called Fort Bell bore the Kindley name in the beginning. It was held fitting to honor World War I ace Capt. Field E. Kindley on the British possession due to Field's wartime assignment with the RAF's 65th Aero Squadron and his aerial successes with the 148th Aero Squadron under British control and in the British sector of the Western Front in 1918.

Preceding this official Kindley Field designation was an American naval survey mission in October 1940, followed by arrival of U.S. engineers and architect-engineers in early 1941. All of this activity was part of the agreement reached by the United States and Great Britain in September 1940 concerning Western Hemisphere military bases for fifty U.S. Navy destroyers. By March 1941 construction, using thousands of civilian workers, had started on the military airfield. In April the Bermuda Base Command was activated, with the first U.S. troops arriving shortly thereafter on board the U.S. transport *American Legion.* The Americans were quartered in Bermuda's Castle Harbour Hotel while the construction progressed. On 4 July 1941 the American flag was raised as runway pavement was laid. The first aircraft landed at Kindley Field on 15 December 1941, off the aircraft carrier *U.S.S. Long Island,* followed by the first land-based aircraft landing on 20 December, an RAF B-24 from Canada. The first Army Air Forces troops did not arrive until February 1942, and the first land-based operational aircraft to land was a B-17, which came in April. Wartime air operations at Kindley Field were mainly twofold: to serve as an air transport stop, especially when the more northerly route was hampered by weather, and to provide anti-submarine patrols by Kindley-based B-17s and B-24s, which continued to early 1944. During World War II Kindley Field served as a major "intermediate station and refueling stop for aircraft going between the United States and the war zones." In 1943 there were some 200 landings, but by 1944 that number increased to 4,000. By January 1945 weather reconnaissance flights by B-25s also became an important operation.

In January 1946 the Fort Bell name was dropped as U.S. Army ground troops had been returned to the United States and the entire base became known as Kindley Field and later as Kindley Air Force

Base. During the 1950s and 1960s the base, at various times, had an air transport squadron, air rescue squadron, Strategic Air Command (SAC) and Tactical Air Command (TAC) air refueling squadrons, and NASA space operations support. As the only airfield in Bermuda, the Kindley runways were also used by commercial airlines.[4] Kindley Air Force Base was deactivated in July 1970.

Appendix C

Civic Memorials to Field E. Kindley

Captain Field E. Kindley Memorial Park, Gravette, Arkansas

On 20 April 1920 a group of Gravette women, including Mrs. A. E. Kindley (Field's Aunt Mollie), met at the Kindley home to discuss organizing a Civic Improvement Club. Nora A. Buffington, wife of a prominent Gravette businessman, was elected president. Mrs. Buffington appointed a committee "to find out if the lots known as the Park and owned by Mr. Covey of South West City, Mo. could be bought."[1] This was the beginning of the project to establish a memorial park to carry the Field Kindley name.

At the Civic Improvement Club meeting on 25 May the park committee reported that Mr. Covey was willing to sell the Covey Park for fifteen hundred dollars and would give the club until 7 June to arrange the purchase. The club thereupon proposed to contact the city council and "present the matter of buying the Covey Park, and take-up the matter of selling the city park and apply the funds on the purchase of the Covey Park."[2] The proposal was granted, and during the 1 June meeting the park committee reported that the city council had authorized sale of the city park and had approved application of the funds therefrom for the purchase of Covey Park. The Civic Improvement Club then decided to proceed with the proposed purchase, paying an amount between seven and eight hundred dollars, and borrowing the remainder. A new committee was charged to secure a bank loan. A week later, on 8 June, the group gave a favorable report on getting the loan.

With the project nearing successs, President Nora Buffington suggested that the "park be made a memorial park for Field Kindley and be named and dedicated to his memory." After discussion, a motion carried that "the lots that C.I.C have purchased be made into a Field Kindley Memorial Park" and that members confer with the city council regarding it.[3] The proposal met with council approval, and the Covey Park purchase occurred officially on 16 June 1920, with the town of Gravette taking possession.[4]

In subsequent meetings the Civic Improvement Club appointed a "landscape committee" to look into beautifying the park and embarked on a campaign to solicit funds to support the purchase and landscaping efforts. A brochure outlining the Kindley memorialization was prepared and distributed, and some copies were sent to aviation fields. A notable contribution of a one-hundred-dollar Liberty Bond came from Long Beach, California, on 21 October 1920, in memory of Mrs. Isadore Spraker, Field's maternal grandmother. The accompanying note said, "I am sorry your communication did not come before her death (September 16th, 1920) for she loved Field so & would have delighted in doing something her self in his memory."[5] Thus, a Gravette city block became a Captain Field E. Kindley Memorial Park not only initiated by local civic-minded ladies and city councilmen but supported by people elsewhere who fondly remembered Field Kindley.

Many years later, on 12 August 1966, a U.S. Air Force T-33A jet trainer was placed in the Kindley Memorial Park and dedicated to remembrance of Kindley's heroics. A fly-over by four F-84s and a program led by Arkansas Rep. Jim Trimble rekindled recognition of the World War I air ace and provided a modern salute during the annual and traditional Gravette "Ole Settlers Picnic."

Field Kindley Memorial High School, Coffeyville, Kansas

On 29 January 1931 the Coffeyville, Kansas, Post No. 20 of the American Legion wrote to Uther Kindley at Gravette, Arkansas, announcing that the city's new high school nearing completion was to bear the name of Field Kindley Memorial High School. A picture of Field Kindley, three by four feet in size, was to be placed inside the main entrance accompanied by a bronze tablet giving his military record. The letter asked for the air ace's medals and citations so that they could also be displayed in a "suitable case in the building."[6]

In a subsequent letter, dated 6 February 1931, Coffeyville attorney and school board president, Charles D. Ise, wrote to "Mrs. Mollie Kindley" inviting her to attend the 26 February dedication of the new $500,000 building as the Field Kindley Memorial High School. Mr. Ise's letter also requested on behalf of the Coffeyville American Legion and the Board of Education Kindley's medals, service badges, and any personal effects for display in "an air tight school glass case" to be placed near Kindley's picture.[7]

Only eight days later, Charles Ise again wrote to Mollie Kindley saying he was pleased to have received Kindley's personal effects. He reported that the Kansas governor could not be present on 26 February, so the dedication would be delayed until 6 March. The American Legion would be in charge of the ceremony, to be followed by an open house for the high school. He added that he had heard from E. E. Kindley advising that he expected to attend. He also revealed that he himself had gone to school together with Field Kindley's cousins, children of Sam Kindley, at Downs, Kansas.[8]

On 16 February 1931 still another communication from Mr. Ise to Mollie Kindley expressed his hope that she could come to the high school dedication. Significantly, he also wrote:

> We have this day received the medals of honor which Field won in the service. These were sent to us by his father, with the information that they were to remain in the care and custody of the high school so long as it bears his son's name. These, together with the souvenirs which you sent me, are being placed on exhibit in one of our main stores in this city. There is a great deal of interest being created in our high school, and more especially in Field Kindley, and I am sending you a copy of our city paper which will keep you informed in a way of what is being done along this line.[9]

This was remarkably high recognition and honor for a young man who had spent such a short time in the Coffeyville community. Also, it reflected the strong sentiment, even as late as 1931, of appreciation, respect, and commendation believed due those men who had served in World War I.

Appendix D

Citations to Field E. Kindley's Medals

U.S. Distinguished Service Cross and Bronze Oak Leaf

The commander in chief, in the name of the President, has awarded the Distinguished Service Cross to the following named officers and soldiers for acts of extraordinary heroism herein described after their names:

> First Lieut. Field E. Kindley, Air Service. For extraordinary heroism in action near Bourlon Wood, France, September 24, 1918. Lieut. Kindley attacked formation of seven hostile planes (type Fokker) and sent one crashing to the ground. A Bronze Oak Leaf is awarded to Lieut. Kindley for the following act of extraordinary heroism in action near Marcoing, France, September 27, 1918. Flying at a low altitude, this officer bombed the railway at Marcoing and drove down an enemy balloon. He then attacked German troops at low altitude and silenced a hostile machine gun, after which he shot down in flames an enemy plane (type Halberstadt) which had attacked him. Lieut. Kindley has so far destroyed seven enemy aircraft and driven down three out of control.

Distinguished Flying Cross for Service with 65th Squadron, Royal Air Force

On September 24th, Lt. Kindley led his flight down on seven Fokkers north of Bourlon Wood, one of which he followed down and saw crash and burst into flames. On September 26th, while working in conjunction with another of our flights, Lt. Kindley's flight accounted for two EA crashed, one of which he got. On September 27th this officer on low flying duty dropped bombs on railways near Marcoing, then attacked a balloon near Noyelles-sur-L'Escaut, driving same down and compelling the two observers to jump. He then, at an altitude of 600 feet, attacked and silenced an enemy machine-gun and shot up troops. Being then attacked by a Halberstadt he engaged it and brought it down in flames. Lt. Kindley's ammunition then being used up, he started for the lines but on the way back he saw two EA which he dived on. They turned and went east. This officer has been on active service in France since 23 May 1918. His work in this squadron has been consistently good and since 30 July, he has been leading "A" Flight with marked success. He has accounted for a total of seven and one half EA destroyed and has driven down out of control, three.[1]

Notes

Preface

1. John H. Morrow Jr., *German Air Power in World War I* (Lincoln: University of Nebraska Press, 1982), 2.

2. John R. Cuneo, *Winged Mars* (Harrisburg, Pa.: Military Service Publishing, 1947), preface.

Chapter 1: The Early Years

1. A British interception of a German message proposing that Mexico enter the war.

2. *Congressional Record,* Vol. 55, Part 1, 65th Cong., 1st sess., 2–24 April 1917: 120.

3. "Over There" became a popular song during the time.

4. Interview reported in *The Denver Post,* 30 May 2005, 2A.

5. Kindley listed theater "proprietor" on several military forms when asked his business or occupation. Kindley lived at 109 West Ninth Street in Coffeyville.

6. *Coffeyville* [Kansas] *Journal,* 22 February 1953, 10. Kindley "was associated with Jay Perry in the old Drexel theater on the south side of 9th Street in the 100 block."

7. "Application for Examination," 1 May 1917, Kindley Personnel File.

8. A "To Whom It May Concern" letter of recommendation from the advertising manager of the *Daily Earth,* Coffeyville, Kans., 1 May 1917, clipping, Kindley Personnel File.

9. National Guard Form No. 525–1, A.G.O. "Enlistment Record," 10 May 1917.

10. Interview, Bruce Bentley by James J. Hudson, Coffeyville, Kans., 2 January 1958. Reported in "Captain Field E. Kindley: Arkansas' Air Ace of the First World War," *Arkansas Historical Quarterly* 18, No. 2 (Summer 1959): 6. Also, *Coffeyville Kansas Journal,* 22 February 1953, 10. "Bruce Bentley recalled that Capt. Kindley was on the same train which took him, Frank Sutton and Clement Reed to Ft. Riley for infantry training. All of them, with the exception of Mr. Reed were billeted in the same barracks."

11. National Guard State of Kansas form by which Private Field E. Kindley is "Honorably Discharged from the National Guard of the United States and the State of Kansas," signed and dated 16 August 1917. Also, letter, 1st Lt. Field E. Kindley to Chief of Air Service, American E. F., Subject: Permanent Commission, 20 November 1918, Kindley Personnel File.

12. Clipping from a Coffeyville newspaper, unidentified and undated, in Kindley Personnel File.

13. Questions for Examination of Applicants Aviation Section, Signal Officers' Reserve Corps, Fort Riley, Kans., 17 July 1917. Interestingly, Field was asked, "Have you ridden horseback to any extent?" His reply, "Not lately."

14. Benton County Heritage Committee, *History of Benton County, Arkansas* (Dallas: Curtis Media, 1991), 583–85.

15. Ibid., 586.

16. Letter, George C. Kindley, Malaybalay, Bukidnon, Philippine Islands, to A. E. Kindley, Gravette, Ark., 13 August 1915.

17. Letter, George C. Kindley, Malaybalay, Bukidnon, Philippine Islands, to Field E. Kindley, 7 July 1918. Also, *Mindanao Herald,* Zamboanga, Mindanao, 1 March 1919, 1. Both in Kindley Personnel File.

18. Questions for Examination of Applicants Aviation Section, Signal Officers' Reserve Corps, Fort Riley, Kans., 17 July 1917, Kindley Personnel File.

19. The Bank of Gravett was incorporated before the Post Office Department added the final *e* to the town's name and thus the bank retained the original spelling in its commercial name.

20. The *Gravette News Herald,* 12 February 1898, reported the election of A. E. Kindley as bank cashier. Also see *Gravette News Herald,* 5 September 1919, 1.

21. Benton County Heritage Committee, *History of Benton County, Arkansas*, 585–86. The *Gravette News Herald,* 13 February 1920, 1, reported that "Mrs. A. E. Kindley was always a mother to him."

22. Interview, Lena Chatfield by Jack Ballard, Gravette, Ark., 12 August 1966.

23. "Pupil's Certificate" (report card), 1911–12, Special Collections Division, University of Arkansas Libraries, Fayetteville.

24. James J. Hudson, "Captain Field E. Kindley: Arkansas' Air Ace of the First World War," *Arkansas Historical Quarterly* 18, No. 2 (Summer 1959): 5.

25. Questions for Examination of Applicants Aviation Section, Signal Officers' Reserve Corps, Fort Riley, Kans, 17 July 1917. Field also mentioned swimming, running, and jumping as "forms of athletic exercise." Also, "Field E. Kindley Memorial Supplement," *Gravette News Herald,* 10 August 1966, 1.

26. Interview, Olga Oswalt by Jack Ballard, Gravette, Ark., 11 August 1966. Olga was about sixteen, and Field Kindley was about the same age.

27. Interview, Mrs. Marion (Genevieve Kindley) Wasson by Jack Ballard, Fayetteville, Ark., 8 August 1966. Genevieve was a daughter of Uncle "Bob" Kindley in Gravette.

28. Interview, Dick Oswalt by Jack Ballard, Gravette, Ark., 12 August 1966.

29. U.S. War Department Certificate of Identity, No. 53, 20 May 1918, Kindley Personnel File.

30. Benton County Heritage Committee, *History of Benton County, Arkansas*, 586.

31. Interview, Dick Oswalt by Jack Ballard, Gravette, Ark., 12 August 1966; interview, Lena Chatfield by Jack Ballard, Gravette, Ark., 10 August 1966; interview, Charles F. Kenney by Jack Ballard, Gravette, Ark., 10 August 1966.

32. Interview, Dick Oswalt by Jack Ballard, Gravette, Ark., 12 August 1966.

33. Questions for Examination of Applicants Aviation Section, Signal Officers' Reserve Corps, Fort Riley, Kans., 17 July 1917, Kindley Personnel File.

34. *Gravette News Herald,* 7 August 1996, 1.

35. Interview, Dick Oswalt by Jack Ballard, Gravette, Ark., 12 August 1966.

36. Questions for Examination of Applicants Aviation Section, Signal Officers' Reserve Corps, Fort Riley, Kans., 17 July 1917, Kindley Personnel File.

37. Interview, Charles F. Kenney by Jack Ballard, Gravette, Ark., 10 August 1966.

38. *Southwest Times Record,* Fort Smith, Ark., 10 May 1925, 9.

39. Interview, Gary Phipps by Jack Ballard, Gravette, Ark., 28 October 2001.

Chapter 2: Training for the Big Show

1. *Jane's Fighting Aircraft of World War I* (London: Random House, Studio Edition, 1990), 226.

2. Ibid.

3. Ibid. Also, James J. Hudson, *Hostile Skies: A Combat History of the American Air Service in World War I* (Syracuse: Syracuse University Press, 1968), 28.

4. Howard L. Scamehorn, *Balloons to Jets: A Century of Aeronautics in Illinois, 1855–1955* (Chicago: Henry Regnery, 1957), 117.

5. Russell F. Weigley, *History of the United States Army* (New York: Macmillan, 1967), 363.

6. U.S. Schools of Military Aeronautics, Certificate of Graduation, 1 September 1917, Kindley Personnel File.

7. Letter, 1st Lt. Field E. Kindley, A.S., USA, to Chief of Air Service, American E.F. (Thru Military Channels), Subject: Permanent Commission, 20 November 1918. In this letter Field listed important chronological events in his career to this date.

8. Grider, *War Birds,* 9–15.

9. Hudson, *Hostile Skies,* 30–33.

10. Letter, Field E. Kindley to George C. Kindley (father), Philippine Islands, 28 November 1918. In this letter Field gives a chronology of his experiences for his father's information.

11. Grider, *War Birds,* 25.

12. Hudson, *Hostile Skies,* 33.

13. Grider, *War Birds,* 26.

14. Ibid., 28.

15. Field Kindley's Machine Gun Training Centre and School of Military Aeronautics Training Record, Kindley Personnel File.

16. Grider, *War Birds,* 48–49.

17. James J. Hudson, "Captain Field E. Kindley: Arkansas' Air Ace of the First World War," *Arkansas Historical Quarterly* 18, No. 2 (Summer 1959): 7.

18. Grider, *War Birds,* 55–56.

19. Field E. Kindley Flight Log Book, Kindley Personnel File.

20. Ibid. "Undercarriage" was the landing gear.

21. Ibid.

22. Grider, *War Birds,* 59.

23. *Jane's Fighting Aircraft of World War I,* 50.

24. Field E. Kindley Flight Log Book, Kindley Personnel File.

25. Field E. Kindley Letters 1913–19, Special Collections Division, University of Arkansas Libraries, Fayetteville.

26. Field E. Kindley Flight Log Book, Kindley Personnel File.

27. Grider, *War Birds,* 75–76.

28. Hudson, *Hostile Skies,* 33. In contrast to the French flying training system (called Penquin), the British believed in faster training even if it meant greater casualties.

29. Interview, Lena Chatfield by Jack Ballard, Gravette, Ark., 12 August 1966. Also, these comments were contained in an unidentified newspaper clipping in materials owned by Lena Chatfield. Kindley's comment about an "Immelmann drop" probably referred to an aerial maneuver named after its developer, German Lt. Max Immelmann. The Immelmann turn or maneuver was a half-roll on top of a half-loop. Some British sources argue it originally came from an Allied pilot.

30. Ibid.

31. Field E. Kindley Flight Log Book, Kindley Personnel File.

32. Field E. Kindley, Royal Flying Corps Training Record, Kindley Personnel File.

33. Grider, *War Birds,* 64.

34. Field E. Kindley Flight Log Book, Kindley Personnel File.

35. Grider, *War Birds,* 56–57.

36. *Jane's Fighting Aircraft of World War I,* 85.

37. Field E. Kindley Flight Log Book, Kindley Personnel File.

38. Grider, *War Birds,* 60.

39. Marvin L. Skelton, "Flight 'C,' 148th Aero Squadron, USAS," *Cross & Cockade Journal* 17, No. 3 (Autumn 1976): 268.

40. Grider, *War Birds,* 60.

41. Ibid.

42. Ibid., 109.

43. Ibid., 84.

44. Ibid., 86.

45. Letter, Capt. Field E. Kindley to Commanding Officer Mitchel Field, Subject: Military Record, 7 July 1919. Field states, "Commissioned First Lieut per cable No. 1008 dated March 29, Ordered into active duty April 13th, 1918."

46. Royal Flying Corps Graduation Certificate No. 10172, 29 January 1918, Kindley Personnel File.

47. Field E. Kindley Flight Log Book, Kindley Personnel File.

48. Ibid. Also, Letter, Field E. Kindley to George C. Kindley, Malaybalay, Bukidnon, Philippine Islands, 28 November 1918.

49. *Jane's Fighting Aircraft of World War I,* 85.

50. Norman Franks, *Sopwith Camel Aces of World War I* (Oxford: Osprey Publishing Limited, 2003), 7.

51. V. M. Yeates, *Winged Victory* (London: Jonathan Cape, 1934; reprint, 1961), 25.

52. Burke Davis, *War Bird: The Life and Times of Elliott White Springs* (Chapel Hill: University of North Carolina Press, 1987), 74.

53. Ibid. A comment attributed to Larry Callahan, a friend of Springs and fellow 148th pilot.

54. Yeates, *Winged Victory,* 31.

55. Davis, *War Bird: The Life and Times of Elliott White Springs,* 74.

56. *Jane's Fighting Aircraft of World War I,* 85.

57. Yeates, *Winged Victory,* 292.

58. See comments in John H. Morrow, Jr., and Earl Rogers, eds., *A Yankee Ace in the RAF: The World War I Letters of Captain Bogart Rogers* (Lawrence: University Press of Kansas, 1996), 9.

59. Yeates, *Winged Victory,* 29.

60. Ibid.

61. Skelton, "Flight 'C,' 148th Aero Squadron, USAS," 268; interview, Lt. Thomas L. Moore by Skelton.

62. Field E. Kindley Flight Log Book, Kindley Personnel File.

63. Grider, *War Birds,* 80, 85.

64. Don T. Roger, "1st Lieut. Raymond Watts: Another of the War Birds," *Cross & Cockade Journal* 5, No. 3 (Autumn 1964): 271.

65. Ibid.

66. Grider, *War Birds,* 60.

67. Ibid., 48.

68. Ibid., 86.

Chapter 3: Ferrying Aircraft

1. Letter, George C. Kindley, Malaybalay, Bukidnon, Philippine Islands, to Mollie Kindley, Gravette, Ark., 28 December 1917.

2. Don T. Roger, ed., "1st Lieut. Raymond Watts: Another of the War Birds," *Cross & Cockade Journal* 5, No. 1 (Autumn 1964): 270.

3. Ibid., 271.

4. Ibid.

5. John MacGavock Grider, *War Birds: Diary of An Unknown Aviator* (College Station: Texas A&M University Press, 1988), 138.

6. Roger, "1st Lieut. Raymond Watts: Another of the War Birds," 271.

7. Field E. Kindley Flight Log Book, Kindley Personnel File.

8. Roger, "1st Lieut. Raymond Watts: Another of the War Birds," 271.

9. Letter, Lt. Field E. Kindley to "Cousin Uther & All," Gravette, Ark., 12 May 1918, copy in the University of Arkansas Special Collections.

10. Ibid.

11. Roger, "1st Lieut. Raymond Watts: Another of the War Birds," 272–73.

12. Ibid., 273.

13. Letter, Lt. Field E. Kindley to "Cousin Uther & All," Gravette, Ark., 12 May 1918.

14. Roger, "1st Lieut. Raymond Watts: Another of the War Birds," 273.

15. Ibid.

16. Letter, Lt. Field E. Kindley to "Cousin Uther & All," Gravette, Ark., 12 May 1918.

17. Ibid.

18. Letter, George C. Kindley, Malaybalay, Bukidnon, Philippine Islands, to "Dear Mollie," Gravette, Ark., 28 December 1917.

19. Letter, George C. Kindley, Malaybalay, Bukidnon, Philippine Islands, to Field E. Kindley, 7 July 1918.

20. Honorable Discharge from the U.S. Army, Cadet Field E. Kindley, 15 April 1918, Kindley Personnel File. Field in a later Air Service letter indicated 13 April as the date when he was ordered into active duty.

21. Field E. Kindley Flight Log Book, Kindley Personnel File.

22. The Royal Flying Corps had become the Royal Air Force.

23. Field E. Kindley Flight Log Book, Kindley Personnel File.

Chapter 4: First Combat

1. James J. Hudson, *Hostile Skies: A Combat History of the American Air Service in World War I* (Syracuse: Syracuse University Press, 1968), 35. Also, see Edward M. Coffman, *The War to End All Wars* (Madison: University of Wisconsin Press, 1986), 199–200.

2. John H. Morrow, Jr., *German Air Power in World War I* (Lincoln: University of Nebraska Press, 1982), 95.

3. Martin Middlebrook, *The Kaiser's Battle* (London: Penguin Books, 1978), 124.

4. John Toland, *No Man's Land: 1918—The Last Year of the Great War* (Garden City, N.Y.: Doubleday, 1980), 7.

5. See David T. Zabeski, *Steel Wind: Colonel Georg Bruchmüller and the Birth of Modern Artilley* (Westport, Conn.: Praeger, 1994).

6. Toland, *No Man's Land,* 15.

7. Zabeski, *Steel Wind,* 72.

8. Ibid.

9. Toland, *No Man's Land,* 19.

10. Zabeski, *Steel Wind,* 74.

11. Middlebrook, *Kaiser's Battle,* 182. Also, John Keegan, *The First World War* (New York: Alfred A. Knopf, 1999), 376.

12. Toland, *No Man's Land,* 23.

13. Middlebrook, *Kaiser's Battle,* 279–80.

14. Toland, *No Man's Land,* 63–64.

15. Maj. Georg Paul Neumann, comp., *The German Air Force in the Great War* (Portway, Bath, U.K.: Cedric Chivers, Ltd., 1969), 229, 232; Toland, *No Man's Land,* 26–27. John H. Morrow, Jr., in *The Great War in the Air from 1909 to 1921* (Washington, D.C.: Smithsonian Press, 1992), uses the figures of 750 German aircraft versus 580 British planes (311).

16. Neumann, *German Air Force in the Great War,* 232.

17. Toland, *No Man's Land,* 26–27. A "bitter aerial battle" on 21 February 1918, by von Richthofen's squadron near Le Cateau "lasted over thirty minutes, and involved as many as sixty or seventy machines, thirteen of the enemy's machines and only one of our own being destroyed," as reported by Georg Neumann. This action, a month ahead of Ludendorff's spring offensive, occurred as the Germans were conscious of wanting to conserve their strength to support the ground attack. Neumann, *German Air Force in the Great War,* 200–201.

18. Toland, *No Man's Land,* 87.

19. Middlebrook, *Kaiser's Battle,* 281, 284.

20. Toland, *No Man's Land,* 147, 158.

21. Ibid., 247.

22. Hew Strachan, *The First World War* (New York: Viking Penguin, 2004), 298.

23. John H. Morrow, Jr., *The Great War in the Air: Military Aviation from 1909 to 1921* (Washington, D.C.: Smithsonian Press, 1993), 311.

24. Ibid., 301.

25. Letter, Capt. Field E. Kindley to Commanding Officer, Mitchel Field, 7 July 1919, Kindley Personnel File.

26. Jack S. Ballard, "Ace from the Ozarks," *Aerospace Historian* 16, No. 4 (Winter 1969): 25–27. The description in the following paragraphs is drawn from this source.

27. Field E. Kindley Flight Log Book, Kindley Personnel File.

28. Ibid.

29. Ibid.

30. These comments come from a diary-like document contained in the Field E. Kindley papers held by Field Kindley Memorial High School, Coffeyville, Kans. It will henceforth be referred to as the Kindley diary document.

31. Kindley diary document.

32. V. M. Yeates, *Winged Victory* (London: Jonathan Cape, 1934; reprint, 1961), 18–19.

33. Kindley diary document.

34. Morrow, *Great War in the Air,* 165.

35. Romantic notions of chivalry originated from such accounts as that of Georges Guynemer, the great French ace. Noticing that his German adversary's gun had jammed during a dogfight, he supposedly waved farewell and broke off the fight. See Morrow, *Great War in the Air,* 202, 241–42. Unfortunately, writers of the time created erroneous impressions that this was the way of aerial combat.

36. Letter, Lt. Field E. Kindley to Uther Kindley, Gravette, Ark., 4 June 1918.

37. Letter, Lt. Field E. Kindley to Uther Kindley, Gravette, Ark., 28 June 1918.

38. William R. Puglisi, "Jagdstaffel 5," *Cross & Cockade Journal* 1, No. 3 (Autumn 1960): 63.

39. Letter, Lt. Field E. Kindley to Uther Kindley, Gravette, Ark., 28 June 1918.

40. Ibid. Field sometimes closed his letters to Uther Kindley with the phrase "Honorable Cousin."

41. Ibid.

42. Ibid.

43. Kindley diary document.

Chapter 5: Four Victories

1. Kindley diary document.

2. Maurer Maurer, ed., *The U.S. Air Service in World War I,* vol. 1 (Washington, D .C.: Office of Air Force History U.S. Government Printing Office, 1979), 45.

3. William Taylor and Francis L. Irvin, *History of the 148th Aero Squadron* (Lancaster, S.C.: Tri-County Publishing, 1957), 3. There are a number of published documents of this squadron's history.

4. Ibid., 5–13.

5. *148th Aero Squadron Bulletin,* No. 20, July 1959, 1, Lafayette Foundation Archives.

6. Taylor and Irvin, *History of the 148th Aero Squadron,* 8–20.

7. Ibid., 20. Also, Marvin L. Skelton, "Flight 'C,' 148th Aero Squadron, USAS," *Cross & Cockade Journal* 17, No. 3 (Autumn 1976): 251.

8. H. Hallock Brown and Arthur D. Dodds, *History of the 141st Aero Squadron,* pamphlet, 1968, 16, Lafayette Foundation Archives.

9. James J. Hudson, introduction to *Francis L. "Spike" Irvin's War Diary* (Manhattan, Kans.: Aerospace Historian, 1974), 6.

10. Taylor and Irvin, *History of the 148th Aero Squadron,* 21.

11. Hudson, introduction to *Francis L. "Spike" Irvin's War Diary,* 6–7.

12. Taylor and Irvin, *History of the 148th Aero Squadron,* 21.

13. Kindley diary document.

14. Taylor and Irvin, *History of the 148th Aero Squadron,* 21–22.

15. Captain Newhall, with "quiet reserve," "likeable and considerate," earned the respect of the men of the 148th. He had a reputation for being at the flight line when the men took off and greeting them when they returned, showing great concern about pilot safety. Taylor and Irvin, *History of the 148th Aero Squadron,* 56–57.

16. John MacGavock Grider, *War Birds: Diary of An Unknown Aviator* (College Station: Texas A&M University Press, 1988), 76, 170.

17. James J. Hudson, *Hostile Skies: A Combat History of the American Air Service in World War I* (Syracuse: Syracuse University Press, 1968), 205.

18. Lt. Col. Raymond H. Fredette, "Luke: Watch for Burning Balloons," *Air Force Magazine,* September 1973, 79. Also, Ezra Bowen, *Knights of the Air* (Alexandria, Va.: Time-Life Books, 1980), 153–56.

19. Skelton, "Flight 'C,' 148th Aero Squadron, USAS," 269. Skelton interviewed Lt. Thomas L. Moore.

20. Kindley diary document.

21. Ibid.

22. Norman Franks, *Sopwith Camel Aces of World War I* (Oxford: Osprey Publishing, 2003), 38.

23. Taylor and Irvin, *History of the 148th Aero Squadron,* 22.

24. Kindley diary document.

25. Bowen, *Knights of the Air,* 137.

26. John Toland, *No Man's Land: 1918—The Last Year of the Great War* (Garden City, N.Y.: Doubleday, 1980), 330.

27. James L. Stokesbury, *A Short History of World War I* (New York: William Morrow, 1981), 283.

28. John Keegan, *The First World War* (New York: Alfred A. Knopf, 1999), 410–12.

29. Hudson, *Hostile Skies,* 205.

30. Kindley Flight Log Book, Kindley Personnel File.

31. John H. Morrow, Jr., and Earl Rogers, eds., *A Yankee Ace in the RAF: The World War I Letters of Captain Bogart Rogers* (Lawrence: University Press of Kansas, 1996), 131, 137. Bogart Rogers flew an S.E. 5 with the 32nd Aero Squadron.

32. Taylor and Irvin, *History of the 148th Aero Squadron,* 24.

33. Morrow and Rogers, *Yankee Ace in the RAF,* 173.

34. Burke Davis, *War Bird: The Life and Times of Elliott White Springs* (Chapel Hill: University of North Carolina Press, 1987), 4.

35. Maj. Georg Paul Neumann, comp., *The German Air Force in the Great War* (Portway, Bath, U.K.: Cedric Chivers, Ltd., 1969), 141.

36. Kindley diary document.

37. Franks, *Sopwith Camel Aces of World War I,* 52.

38. Yeates, *Winged Victory,* 27.

39. Bowen, *Knights of the Air,* 136.

40. Special Order No. 36, Headquarters American Air Service, France, 1 October 1918: "1. The appointment of 1st Lieutenant Field E. Kindley, A.S.U.S.A. flight commander of 'A' flight, 148th Aero Squadron, as of July 30, 1918 is hereby confirmed." Kindley Personnel File.

41. Kindley diary document.

42. Yeates, *Winged Victory,* 19.

43. Kindley diary document.

44. Ibid.

45. Bowen, *Knights of the Air,* 139. Recent research supports downing by ground fire.

46. Kindley diary document.

47. Franks, *Sopwith Camel Aces of World War I,* 52.

48. Maurer, *U.S. Air Service in World War I,* 1:45.

49. Combat report, dated 13 July 1918, Field E. Kindley Personnel File.

50. Kindley Flight Log Book, Kindley Personnel File.

51. Telegram, Brig. Gen. E. R. Ludlow-Hewitt, 10th Brigade, RAF 65th Wing, to 148th American Aero Squadron, 13 July 1918. Also, Kindley diary document; Taylor and Irvin, *History of the 148th Aero Squadron,* 23.

52. Kindley diary document.

53. Hudson, *Hostile Skies,* 206–7.

54. 148th Aero Squadron, "Combats in the Air" Report, 3 August 1918. Also, Kindley Flight Log Book, Kindley Personnel File.

55. Hudson, *Hostile Skies,* 209.

56. Kindley Flight Log Book, Kindley Personnel File.

57. Ibid.

58. Taylor and Irvin, *History of the 148th Aero Squadron,* 27–28.

59. Hudson, *Hostile Skies,* 211.

60. Bowen, *Knights of the Air,* 164.

61. Taylor and Irvin, *History of the 148th Aero Squadron,* 27.

62. 148th Aero Squadron, "Combats in the Air" Report, 13 August 1918. Also, Taylor and Irvin, *History of the 148th Squadron,* 26–27.

63. Hudson, *Hostile Skies,* 212.

64. Ibid.

65. Taylor and Irvin, *History of the 148th Aero Squadron,* 27.

66. Kindley Flight Log Book, Kindley Personnel File.

67. Taylor and Irvin, *History of the 148th Aero Squadron,* 32.

68. Letter, Lt. Field E. Kindley to Uther Kindley, Gravette, Ark., 30 September 1918.

1. Letter, George C. Kindley to Lt. Field E. Kindley, France, 19 August 1918.

2. Letter, George C. Kindley to Lt. Field E. Kindley, France, 14 July 1918.

3. Letter, George C. Kindley to Lt. Field E. Kindley, France, 4 August 1918.

4. Letter, Lt. Field E. Kindley to Uther Kindley, Gravette, Ark., 4 June 1918.

5. William Taylor and Francis L. Irvin, *History of the 148th Aero Squadron* (Lancaster, S.C.: Tri-County Publishing, 1957), 30–34; John H. Morrow, Jr., and Earl Rogers, eds., *A Yankee Ace in the RAF: The World War I Letters of Captain Bogart Rogers* (Lawrence: University Press of Kansas, 1996), 9.

6. 148th Aero Squadron, "Attack on Enemy Ground Targets" reports, Nos. 24 and 27, 1 September 1918. Copies of these reports can be found in Taylor and Irvin, *History of the 148th Aero Squadron.*

7. Letter, Lt. Field E. Kindley to Uther Kindley, Gravette, Ark., 30 September 1918.

8. Ibid. Some 1919 newspaper accounts reported Kindley's plane was hit forty-seven times.

9. 148th Aero Squadron, "Combats in the Air" report, 2 September 1918.

10. Taylor and Irvin, *History of the 148th Aero Squadron,* 34.

11. Ibid., 33–34. Also, James J. Hudson, *Hostile Skies: A Combat History of the American Air Service in World War I* (Syracuse: Syracuse University Press, 1968), 218.

12. 148th Aero Squadron, "Combats in the Air" report, 2 September 1918.

13. The term *ace* was defined by the Air Force as a "fighter pilot who destroys five or more enemy aircraft in aerial combat." The word *ace* apparently originated in the French *escadrilles* (squadrons) of World War I and was applied to some of the American pilots who fought for the French before the U.S. Air Service entered combat. "When the American Expeditionary Force (AEF) were sent overseas, the term was bestowed informally on members of its aero squadrons" (Air Force Fact Sheet 73–7, "AF Aces/1918–1972," May 1973).

14. Hudson, *Hostile Skies,* 215–19.

15. John MacGavock Grider, *War Birds: Diary of An Unknown Aviator* (College Station: Texas A&M University Press, 1988), 227.

16. Richard Duiven, "Royal Prussian Jagdgeschwader II," *Over the Front* 9, No. 3 (Fall 1994): 216.

17. Richard Duiven, "Royal Prussian Jagdgeschwader II," *Over the Front* 10, No. 1 (Spring 1995): 12–13.

18. Taylor and Irvin, *History of the 148th Aero Squadron,* 28.

19. Richard Duiven, "Royal Prussian Jagdgeschwader II," *Over the Front* 9, No. 4 (Winter 1994): 351.

20. John R. Cuneo, *The Air Weapon 1914–1916* (Harrisburg, Pa.: Military Publishing, 1947), 260.

21. Kindley's flight log records this engagement on 6 September 1918; however, the 148th Aero Squadron "Combats in the Air" report indicates a date of 5 September 1918.

22. 148th Aero Squadron, "Combats in the Air" report, 15 September 1918.

23. 148th Aero Squadron, "Combats in the Air" report, 17 September 1918.

24. Kindley Flight Log Book, Kindley Personnel File; 148th Aero Squadron, "Combats in the Air" reports, 15 September and 17 September 1918.

25. John Toland, *No Man's Land: 1918—The Last Year of the Great War* (Garden City, N.Y.: Doubleday, 1980), 420.

26. Ibid., 431.

27. Taylor and Irvin, *History of the 148th Aero Squadron,* 35–36.

28. Ibid., 35.

29. Letter, Lt. Field E. Kindley to Uther Kindley, Gravette, Ark., 30 September 1918. Portions of this letter were published in the *Gravette News Herald,* 15 November 1918, 1.

30. Yeates, *Winged Victory,* 353.

31. Morrow and Rogers, *Yankee Ace in the RAF,* 150.

32. Burke Davis, *War Bird: The Life and Times of Elliott White Springs* (Chapel Hill: University of North Carolina Press, 1987), 66.

33. John H. Morrow, Jr., *The Great War in the Air* (Washington, D.C.: Smithsonian Press, 1992), 202–3, 239–41.

34. Taylor and Irvin, *History of the 148th Aero Squadron,* 22.

35. Davis, *War Bird: The Life and Times of Elliott White Springs,* 82.

36. Grider, *War Birds,* 166.

37. Davis, *War Bird: The Life and Times of Elliott White Springs,* 64.

38. Lt. Field E. Kindley Comment Sheet, "Definitions What and Why," Kindley Personnel File. Copy in Special Collections Division, University of Arkansas Libraries, Fayetteville.

39. Unidentified newspaper clipping in Kindley Personnel File. Kindley was probably aware of soldiers' concern that a match used by three men could give an enemy time to sight and fire on the light.

40. Kindley Flight Log Book, Kindley Personnel File. Also see Hudson, *Hostile Skies,* 223; and 148th Aero Squadron, "Combats in the Air" report, 24 September 1918. A letter of recommendation for Distinguished Service Cross, 23 November 1918, indicates a different version of events: "while leading the lower flight of four machines, he was attacked by seven Fokkers."

41. Statement on Presentation of the Distinguished Service Cross, 25 November 1918.

42. Hudson, *Hostile Skies,* 224.

43. Letter, Commanding Officer, 148th Aero Squadron, to Commander-in-Chief, American E. F., Recommendation for Distinguished Service Cross, 23 November 1918.

44. 148th Aero Squadron, "Combats in the Air" report, 26 September 1918.

45. Hudson, *Hostile Skies,* 224–25.

46. Statement, "An Oak Leaf Job," Kindley Personnel File. Also see 148th Aero Squadron, "Combats in the Air" report, 27 September 1918; 148th Aero Squadron, "Attack on Enemy Ground Targets" reports, No. 32, 27 September 1918.

47. Statement, "An Oak Leaf Job," Kindley Personnel File. Also, 148th Aero Squadron, "Attack on Enemy Ground Targets" reports, No. 32.

48. Hudson, *Hostile Skies,* 225.

49. Statement, "An Oak Leaf Job," Kindley Personnel File.

50. Ibid. Also, 148th Aero Squadron, "Combats in the Air" report, 27 September 1918.

51. Dr. Daniel L. Haulman and Col. William C. Stancik, eds., *Aerial Victory Credits: World War I, World War II, Korea, and Vietnam* (Montgomery, Ala.: U.S. Air Force Historical Research Center, 1988), 18.

52. Statement, "An Oak Leaf Job," Kindley Personnel File. The description in the following paragraphs is drawn from this source.

53. The *Kansas City Star*, 14 February 1928, 13, carried this report.

54. 148th Aero Squadron, "Attack on Enemy Ground Targets" reports, No. 33, 27 September 1918.

55. Letter, Hqs. 148th Aero Squadron to Commander-in-Chief A. E. F., Recommendation for Bronze Oak Leaf to be worn with Distinguished Service Cross for 1st Lt. Field E. Kindley, 13 November 1918.

56. Message, 13th RAF Wing to 148th American Aero Squadron, 1 November 1918. "Under authority granted by His Majesty the King C.C. awards D. F. C. to Lieut. Field E. Kindley AS. USA. please convey C.O.C. Third Army and O. C. 13th Wing congratulations."

57. General Headquarters American Expeditionary Force, Citation to Accompany the Award of the Distinguished Flying Cross by the British Government to 1st Lt. Field E. Kindley, undated.

58. Statement, "An Oak Leaf Job," Kindley Personnel File.

59. Letter, Lt. Field E. Kindley to Uther Kindley, Gravette, Ark., 30 September 1918.

60. Ibid.

61. Grider, *War Birds,* 267.

62. Ibid.

63. Ezra Bowen, *Knights of the Air* (Alexandria, Va.: Time-Life Books, 1980), 165.

64. Davis, *War Bird: The Life and Times of Elliott White Springs,* 5–6.

65. Morrow, *Great War in the Air,* 239.

66. Grider, *War Birds,* 233.

67. 148th Aero Squadron, "Attack on Enemy Ground Targets" reports, Nos. 34 and 35, 28 September 1918; No. 36, 29 September 1918; and No. 37, 1 October 1918.

68. 148th Aero Squadron, "Attack on Enemy Ground Targets" reports, No. 48, 8 October 1918.

69. Letter, Hqs. 148th Aero Squadron to Commander-in-Chief, American E. F., Recommendation for Bronze Oak Leaf to be worn with Distinguished Service Cross, 13 November 1918, Kindley Personnel File.

70. Kindley Flight Log Book, Kindley Personnel File.

71. Taylor and Irvin, *History of the 148th Aero Squadron,* 42–52. Information on Bapaume airdrome in the following paragraphs is drawn from this source.

72. 148th Aero Squadron, "Attack on Enemy Ground Targets" reports, No. 56, 23 October 1918, and No. 59, 26 October 1918. Also, Kindley Flight Log Book, Kindley Personnel File.

73. John H. Morrow, Jr., "The War in the Air," in *World War I: A History,* ed. Hew Strachan (Oxford: Oxford University Press, 1998), 271.

74. Lt. Elliott Springs and Lt. Henry R. Clay, Jr., the previous flight commanders, had been reassigned to take command of other U.S. squadrons in the American-French sectors.

75. 148th Aero Squadron, "Combats in the Air" report, 28 October 1918.

76. Kindley Flight Log Book, Kindley Personnel File.

77. Edward M. Coffman, *The War to End All Wars* (Madison: University of Wisconsin Press, 1986), 204–11.

78. Taylor and Irvin, *History of the 148th Aero Squadron,* 53.

79. Ibid., 50–57.

80. Kindley Flight Log Book, Kindley Personnel File.

81. Morrow and Rogers, *Yankee Ace in the RAF,* 240.

82. Kindley Flight Log Book, Kindley Personnel File.

83. Taylor and Irvin, *History of the 148th Aero Squadron,* 54.

84. Ibid., 51–54.

85. Ibid.

86. Maurer Maurer, ed., *The U.S. Air Service in World War I,* vol. 1 (Washington, D.C.: Office of Air Force History U.S. Government Printing Office, 1979), 45.

87. Kindley Flight Log Book, Kindley Personnel File.

88. Kindley's total of twelve victories was equaled by Elliott White Springs, thus he tied for the fourth position. See Haulman and Stancik, eds., *Aerial Victory Credits.*

89. Maurer, *U.S. Air Service in World War I,* 2:352.

90. Letter, 1st Lt. Lawrence T. Wyly to Commanding Officer, 148th Aero Squadron, A.E.F., Subject: Decoration, with endorsements, 30 November 1918.

91. Letter, Capt. Field E. Kindley, Headquarters 141st Aero Squadron, to Commanding Officer Mitchel Field, 7 July 1919.

92. Handwritten remark by Capt. M. L. Newhall, Officer Commanding, 148th Aero Squadron, on 1st Lt. Field E. Kindley's identity card, Kindley Personnel File.

93. Unidentified newspaper clipping, Kindley Personnel File.

Chapter 7: The Postwar Experience

1. A tragic example of the "one last flight" fear of pilots was Capt. Hobey Baker's death in a December 1918 crash. Captain Baker was commander of the 141st Aero Squadron, and Kindley replaced him. See John Davies, *The Legend of Hobey Baker* (Boston: Little, Brown, 1966).

2. Letter, Capt. D. S. Edwards, MC. USA, to Commanding Officer, 1stAir Depot, Subject: 1st Lt. Field E. Kindley, 24 November 1918, Kindley Personnel File.

3. Letter, Lt. Field E. Kindley, Toul, France, to George C. Kindley, Philippines, 28 November 1918.

4. Letter, Lt. Field E. Kindley to "Cousin Uther and All," Gravette, Ark., 28 November 1918.

5. Special Orders 39, Headquarters, 4th Pursuit Group, 2nd Army, American Expeditionary Force, 21 December 1918.

6. Special Orders 55, General Headquarters, American Expeditionary Force, 24 February 1919.

7. Letter, To Whom It May Concern from Capt. M. L. Newhall, 148th Aero Squadron, Commanding, 29 November 1918.

8. Letter, 1st Lt. Field E. Kindley to Chief of Air Service, American Expeditionary Force (Thru Military Channels), Subject: Permanent Commission, 20 November 1918, fifth endorsement, GHQ, AEF, France, to 1st Lt. Field E. Kindley, Hq. 148th Aero Squadron (Pursuit), AEF, 30 November 1918.

9. Diary comments of Lt. Francis (Spike) L. Irvin, 148th Aero Squadron, Lafayette Foundation Archives, Denver.

10. Ibid.

11. Ibid. This portion of Irvin's diary was quoted in 148th Aero Squadron Bulletin No. 52, Christmas 1964, 1, in Lafayette Foundation Archives.

12. *The World War I Diary of Col. Frank Lahm, Air Service, A.E.F.* (Maxwell AFB, Ala.: Historical Research Division of Air University, 1970), 153. Col. Frank Lahm was the first American military man to go aloft in an airplane and held Airplane Pilot License No. 2.

13. Davies, *Legend of Hobey Baker.*

14. *World War I Diary of Col. Frank Lahm, Air Service, A.E.F.,* 156–57.

15. Ibid., 16–27.

16. 148th Aero Squadron Bulletin No. 19, May 1959, 3, Lafayette Foundation Archives.

17. H. Hallock Brown and Arthur D. Dodds, *History of the 141st Aero Squadron,* pamphlet, 1968, 33, Lafayette Foundation Archives.

18. Ibid., 42.

19. Corky Meyer, "Flying the D.VII: A Fabulous Fokker Fighter," *Flight Journal,* October 2003, 62. Anthony Fokker, the aircraft designer, surreptitiously sent six train-loads of Fokker D.VIIs to the Netherlands.

20. Edward M. Coffman, *The War to End All Wars* (Madison: University of Wiscon-sin Press, 1986), 359.

21. Letter, Lt. Field E. Kindley to Uther Kindley, Gravette, Ark., 28 November 1918.

22. Maurer, *U.S. Air Service in World War I,* 4:360.

23. Christmas card, Lt. Field E. Kindley to Uther Kindley, Gravette, Ark., n.d. (Christmas 1918).

24. Special Orders 26, Headquarters Second Army, American Expeditionary Force, 26 January 1919.

25. Pass, Headquarters Third Army to Capt. Field E. Kindley, 24 March 1919.

26. Special Orders 100, Headquarters Second Army, American Expeditionary Force, 10 April 1919, Special Collections Division, University of Arkansas Libraries, Fayette-ville.

27. *World War I Diary of Col. Frank Lahm, Air Service, A.E.F.,* 180.

28. Maurer, *U.S. Air Service in World War I,* 4:57–58, 337, 345. The discussion in the following paragraphs also draws on this source.

29. Ibid., 1:113.

30. Ibid., 4:58–59.

31. Ibid., 4:59.

32. *World War I Diary of Col. Frank Lahm, Air Service, A.E.F.,* 188.

33. Letter, 1st Lt. Field E. Kindley, Commanding Officer 141st Squadron (Pursuit), to Home Communications Section, American Red Cross, Paris, Subject: Lt. Linn H. Foster, 148th Aero Squadron, 17 February 1919.

34. Letter, George C. Kindley, Malaybalay, Bukidnon, Philippine Islands, to Lt. Field E. Kindley, 11 January 1919.

35. Letter, George C. Kindley, Malaybalay, Bukidnon, Philippine Islands, to Lt. Field E. Kindley, 23 February 1919.

36. Letter, George C. Kindley, Malaybalay, Bukidnon, Philippine Islands, to Capt. Field E. Kindley, 2 March 1919.

37. Letter, George C. Kindley, Malaybalay, Bukidnon, Philippine Islands, to Capt. Field E. Kindley, 19 April 1919.

38. Letter, George C. Kindley, Naga, Camarines, Philippine Islands, to Capt. Field E. Kindley, 10 July 1919.

39. *World War I Diary of Col. Frank Lahm, Air Service, A.E.F.,* 184–85.

40. Interview, Bruce Bentley by James J. Hudson, Coffeyville, Kans., 3 January 1958. Also see James J. Hudson, "The Air Knight of the Ozarks, Capt. Field E. Kindley," *American Aviation Historical Society Journal* 4, No. 4 (Winter 1959): 250; and *Coffeyville Kansas Journal.* A silver cup trophy is displayed, along with other Kindley artifacts, at the Arkansas Air Museum, Drake Field, Fayetteville.

41. Handwritten note, Kindley Personnel File.

42. Letter, Commanding Officer, Headquarters, Fifth Pursuit Group, Coblenz Airdrome, Third Army, American E.F., to Adjutant General, A.E.F. (Thru Chief of Air Service), Subject: Recommendation for Promotion of Capt. Field E. Kindley, AS., 141st Aero Squadron, to Major, 12 May 1919, Kindley Personnel File.

43. Operations Orders No. 172, Headquarters Third Army, American Expeditionary Force, Germany, 12 May 1919, Kindley Personnel File.

44. Troop Movement Order No. 157, Headquarters American Embarkation Center, 6 June 1919; Special Orders 165, 14 June 1919; both in Kindley Personnel File.

45. Memorandum, Headquarters, 141st Aero Squadron (Pursuit), 9 June 1919, Kindley Personnel File.

46. Brown and Dodds, *History of the 141st Aero Squadron in World War I,* 44.

Chapter 8: Return to the United States

1. *New York Times,* 28 June 1919, 16.

2. Unidentified newspaper clipping, Kindley Personnel File. The *Gravette News Herald,* 4 July 1919, 1, gave much the same story. Some of these details appear to exaggerate accounts recorded at the time.

3. Unidentified newspaper clipping, Kindley Personnel File.

4. Special Orders 85, Headquarters, Camp Mills, Long Island, N.Y., 28 June 1919, Kindley Personnel File.

5. Letter, Capt. Field E. Kindley, Hazelhurst Field, Mineola, Long Island, N.Y., to Uther Kindley, Gravette, Ark., n.d. (ca. early July 1919), Special Collections Division, University of Arkansas Libraries, Fayetteville.

6. Letter, George C. Kindley, Naga, Camarines, Philippine Islands, to Capt. Field E. Kindley, 18 September 1919.

7. Letter, George C. Kindley, Naga, Camarines, Philippine Islands, to Capt. Field E. Kindley, 1 September 1919.

8. Letter, Capt. Field E. Kindley, Hazelhurst Field, Mineola, Long Island, N.Y., to Uther Kindley, Gravette, Ark., n.d. Capt. Kindley received two large, elaborate certificates from the Aero Club of America, one for "Valor and Distinguished Service" on 10 February 1919, and another one dated 9 May 1919.

9. H. Hallock Brown and Arthur D. Dodds, *History of the 141st Aero Squadron in World War I,* 44–45, n.p., 1968, pamphlet, Lafayette Foundation Archives; Special Orders 115, Headquarters, Mitchel Field, Long Island, N.Y., 12 July 1919.

10. Letter, Capt. Field E. Kindley, Hazelhurst Field, Mineola, Long Island, N.Y., to Uther Kindley, Gravette, Ark., n.d. (ca. early July 1919).

11. Special Orders 198, Headquarters Hazelhurst Field, Long Island, N.Y., 16 August 1919.

12. Special Orders 236, Headquarters Hazelhurst Field, Long Island, N.Y., 3 October 1919.

13. Special Orders 170, Headquarters Hazelhurst Field, Long Island, N.Y., 15 July 1919, and Special Orders 218, Headquarters Hazelhurst Field, Long Island, N.Y., 12 September 1919.

14. Unidentified newspaper clipping, Kindley Personnel File.

15. Receipt No. 24, Coffeyville, Kans., Post of the American Legion, 21 July 1919, Kindley Personnel File.

16. K. M. Molson, "First International Air Race: August 1919, New York–Toronto," *American Aviation Historical Society Journal* 16, No. 4 (Winter 1971): 263.

17. *New York Times*, 24 August 1919, sec. 2, 1.

18. Molson, "First International Air Race," 263. The race prize money had been provided by a Canadian, John M. Bowman.

19. *New York Times*, 26 August 1919, 3.

20. Elliott Springs's blue aircraft was considered one of the fastest and one of the most powerful in the race. When he approached the Albany field, he had to circle for fifteen minutes before landing, and despite being warned off several times, he finally put his machine down.

21. *Knickerbocker Press*, Albany, N.Y., 26 August 1919, 1.

22. Ibid.

23. James J. Hudson, "Air Knight of the Ozarks: Captain Field E. Kindley," *American Aviation Historical Society Journal* 4, No. 4 (Winter 1959): 251.

24. *New York Times*, 26 August 1919, 3. Molson, "First International Air Race," 266, claims that Kindley broke a shock absorber on landing his S.E. 5, causing the aircraft to veer toward the crowd.

25. Telegram, Lt. Col. H. E. Hartney, Albany, N.Y., 9:18 P.M., to General Menoher, Air Service, Hazelhurst Field, Mineola, Long Island, N.Y., 25 August 1919, Kindley Personnel File.

26. *New York Times*, 26 August 1919, 3.

27. *New York Times*, 1 September 1919, 4.

28. *New York Times*, 29 August 1919, 8.

29. *New York Times*, 2 September 1919, 16.

30. War Department, Air Service, Washington, D.C., Personnel Orders No. 173, 2 October 1919, Kindley Personnel File.

31. Unidentified newspaper clipping, Kindley Personnel File.

32. Ibid.

33. Air Service Information Circular, "Report on First Transcontinental Reliability and Endurance Test," vol. 1, 5 February 1920.

34. Ibid. Also see *New York Times*, 19 October 1919, 1, 3; *New York Times*, 20 October 1919, 26.

35. Air Service Information Circular, "Report on First Transcontinental Reliability and Endurance Test," vol. 1, 5 February 1920.

36. Ibid.

37. Special Orders No. 230, Headquarters Mitchel Field, Long Island, N.Y., 22 November 1919, Kindley Personnel File.

38. Letter, George C. Kindley, Pili, Ambos Camarines, Philippine Islands, to Capt. Field E. Kindley, Hazelhurst Field, Mineola, Long Island, N.Y., 12 November 1919.

39. U.S. Congress, House of Representatives, Subcommittee on Aviation of the Committee on Military Affairs, Hearing, 66th Cong., 2d sess., 12 December 1919, 371. The discussion in the following paragraph draws on this source.

40. *New York Times,* 13 December 1919, 2. Only four aces were listed by name.

41. Letter, Capt. Field E. Kindley, Headquarters, Mitchel Field, Long Island, N.Y., to Hon. James A. Frear, House of Representatives, Washington, D.C., 24 December 1919.

42. Letter, Capt. Field E. Kindley, Headquarters Mitchel Field, Long Island, N.Y. to Maj. Maurice Connelly, American Flying Club, 11 East 38th Street, New York City, 20 December 1919.

43. Interview, Bruce Bentley by James J. Hudson, Coffeyville, Kans., 3 January 1958, Special Collections Division, University of Arkansas Libraries, Fayetteville.

44. Special Orders No. 10, Headquarters, 1st Wing, Kelly Field, South San Antonio, Tex., 15 January 1920, Kindley Personnel File.

45. Special Orders No. 8, Headquarters 1st Pursuit Group, Kelly Field, San Antonio, Tex., 13 January 1920, Kindley Personnel File.

Chapter 9: Fallen Aerial Warrior

1. Interview, Freeman Stokes Ballard by Jack Ballard, Gravette, Ark., 13 August 1966.

2. Bruce D. Callander, "The Return of Kelly Field," *Air Force Magazine,* July 2001, 46–47.

3. In Memoriam Statement for Field E. Kindley, Captain, A.S.A., 1 February 1920, Special Collections Division, University of Arkansas Libraries, Fayetteville.

4. Mimeographed letter, Capt. Clayton Bissell to 148th Aero Squadron Members, 8 February 1920, Kindley Personnel File. The description in the following paragraphs is based on this source.

5. Letter, USAF Maj. Gen. Harry A. Johnson, San Antonio, Tex., to Maj. Jack S. Ballard, Air Force Academy, Colorado, 28 December 1967. At the time, General Johnson was a flight commander and engineering officer of the 11th Bomb Squadron of the First Day Bombardment Group.

6. In Memoriam Statement for Field E. Kindley, Captain, A.S.A., 1 February 1920, Special Collections Division, University of Arkansas Libraries, Fayetteville.

7. *New York Times,* 2 February 1920, 13.

8. Western Union Telegram, War Department, Kelly Field, Tex., to Mr. Uther Kindley, Gravette, Ark., 1 February 1920, Special Collections Division, University of Arkansas Libraries, Fayetteville.

9. Letter, George C. Kindley, Pili, Ambos Camarines, Philippine Islands, to Uther Kindley Gravette, Ark., 8 February 1920, Special Collections Division, University of Arkansas Libraries, Fayetteville.

10. Captain Bissell, from Kane, Pa., and a graduate of Valparaiso University, would

become a major general in World War II and commander of the U.S. Tenth Air Force in the Far East. He contacted the adjutant general of the state of Arkansas to arrange for a firing squad and a band, and notified members of the 148th Aero Squadron.

11. *Gravette News Herald,* 13 February 1920, 1.

12. *Benton County Record,* Bentonville, Ark., 6 February 1920, 1. Also, *Gravette News Herald,* 6 February 1920 and 13 February 1920, 1.

13. Interview, Lillian Boggs and Freeman Stokes Ballard by Jack Ballard, Gravette, Ark., 14 August 1966.

14. The investigation was authorized in Special Orders No. 27, Headquarters, Kelly Field, South San Antonio, Tex., 2 February 1920.

15. Proceedings of Board Appointed to Investigate Death of Capt. Field N. [*sic*] Kindley A.S.A., 1 February 1920, Kelly Field, South San Antonio, Tex., 4 February 1920.

16. Ibid.

17. Letter, Capt. Clayton Bissell, Kelly Field, Tex., to Uther Kindley, Gravette, Ark., 8 February 1920, Special Collections Division, University of Arkansas Libraries, Fayetteville.

18. Letter, Kathryn Seibold, Fort Worth, Tex., to Uther Kindley, Gravette, Ark., 12 February 1920, Special Collections Division, University of Arkansas Libraries, Fayetteville. Mrs. Seibold also stated, "Captain Bissell wired me all that he could." She mentions that Captain Bissell and Field Kindley were with her husband, George, in France.

19. Letter, Capt. Clayton Bissell, Kelly Field, Tex., to Uther Kindley, Gravette, Ark., 14 February 1920, Special Collections Division, University of Arkansas Libraries, Fayetteville.

20. Letter, George C. Kindley, Naga, Ambos Camarines, Philippine Islands, to Uther Kindley, Gravette, Ark., 16 February 1920, Special Collections Division, University of Arkansas Libraries, Fayetteville.

21. Burke Davis, *War Bird: The Life and Times of Elliott White Springs* (Chapel Hill: University of North Carolina Press, 1987), 7.

Appendix B

1. "Sixteen New Fields 'Christened,'" *Air Corps News Letter,* 1 July 1941.
2. Ibid.
3. Ibid.
4. "25th Silver Anniversary Press Release—Kindley Air Force Base," Information Office, 1604th Air Base Group, Kindley AFB, Bermuda, March 1965 and February 1966.

Appendix C

1. Civic Improvement Club Minutes, Gravette, Ark., 20 April 1920.
2. Ibid., 25 May 1920.
3. Ibid., 1 June and 8 June 1920.

4. Warranty deeds between Minnie Covey and G. H. Buffington and between G. H. Buffington and Incorporated Town of Gravette, Ark., 16 June 1920.

5. Letter, Mary A. Meek, Long Beach, Calif., to Women's Civic Improvement Club, Gravette, Ark., 21 October 1920.

6. Letter, Coffeyville Post No. 20 of American Legion, Coffeyville, Kans., to Uther Kindley, Gravette, Ark., 29 January 1931, Special Collections Division, University of Arkansas Libraries, Fayetteville.

7. Letter, Charles D. Ise, Coffeyville, Kans., to Mollie Kindley, Gravette, Ark., 6 February 1931, Special Collections Division, University of Arkansas Libraries, Fayetteville.

8. Letter, Charles D. Ise, Coffeyville, Kans., to Mollie Kindley, Gravette, Ark., 14 February 1931, Special Collections Division, University of Arkansas Libraries, Fayetteville.

9. Letter, Charles D. Ise, Coffeyville, Kans., to Mollie Kindley, Gravette, Ark., 16 February 1931, Special Collections Division, University of Arkansas Libraries, Fayetteville.

Appendix D

1. British citation for the award of the Distinguished Flying Cross to Capt. Field E. Kindley, n.d., copy in files of Arkansas Air Museum, Drake Field, Fayetteville. At the time cited, Kindley was flying for the 148th Aero Squadron.

Bibliography

Anders, Curtis. *Fighting Airmen.* New York: Putnam, 1966.

Angelucci, Enzo. *The Rand McNally Encyclopedia of Military Aircraft 1914–1980.* New York: Military Press, 1983.

Arango, Javier. "Tommy Sopwith: Revolutionary Aircraft Designer." *Aviation History,* March 2001.

Archibald, Norman. *Heaven High, Hell Deep, 1917–1918.* New York: Albert & Charles Boni, 1935.

Army Times Editors. *Famous Fighters of World War I.* New York: Dodd, Mead, 1964.

Army War College. *The Signal Corps and the Air Service, 1917–1918.* Washington, D.C.: Government Printing Office, 1922.

Arnold, Henry H. *Global Mission.* New York: Harper & Brothers, 1949.

Baldwin, Hanson W. *World War I.* New York: Grove Press, 1962.

Ballard, Jack S. "Ace from the Ozarks." *Aerospace Historian* 16, No. 4 (Winter 1969).

Baring, Maurice. *Flying Corps Headquarters, 1914–1918.* London: William Blackwood & Sons, 1968.

Barker, Ralph. *The RAF at War.* Alexandria, Va.: Time-Life Books, 1981.

Barnett, Correlli. *The Sword Bearers: Supreme Command in the First World War.* New York: Signet Books, 1963.

Barrett, William E. "Elliott White Springs, the War Bird Who'll Never Die." *Cavalier,* March 1960.

Beaver, Daniel R. *Newton D. Baker and the American War Effort, 1917–1919.* Lincoln: University of Nebraska Press, 1966.

Benton County Heritage Committee. *History of Benton County, Arkansas.* Rogers, Ark.: Curtis Media Corp., 1991.

Berry, Henry. *Make the Kaiser Dance.* Garden City, N.Y.: Doubleday, 1978.

Biddle, Maj. Charles J. *Fighting Airmen: The Way of the Eagle.* Garden City, N.Y.: Doubleday, 1968.

Biddle, Tami. "A Learning in Real Time: The Development and Implementation of Air Power in the First World War." In *Air Power History: Turning Points from Kitty Hawk to Kosovo,* ed. Sebastian Cox and Peter Gray. Portland, Ore.: Frank Cass, 2002.

Bingham, Hiram. *An Explorer in the Air Service.* New Haven: Yale University Press, 1920.

Bishop, William A. *The Courage of the Early Morning.* New York: David McKay Co., 1966.

———. *Winged Peace.* New York: Viking Press, 1944.

———. *Winged Warfare.* New York: Arco Publishing, 1967.

Black, J. Dickson. *History of Benton County.* Little Rock, Ark.: International Graphics Industries, 1975.

Bowen, Ezra, et al. *Knights of the Air.* Alexandria, Va.: Time-Life Books, 1980.

Bowyer, Chaz. *The Age of the Biplane.* Englewood Cliffs, N.J.: Prentice-Hall, 1981.

———. *Airmen of World War I.* London: Arms & Armour Press, 1975.

Boyce, Col. J. Ward, ed. *American Fighter Aces Album.* Mesa, Ariz.: American Fighter Aces Association, 1996.

Boyle, Andrew. *Trenchard, Man of Vision.* London: Collins, 1962.

Boyne, Walter J. *Beyond the Wild Blue: A History of the U.S. Air Force, 1947–1997.* New York: St. Martin's Press, 1997. [Contains a chronology of aerospace power since 1903.]

———. *The Influence of Air Power upon History.* Gretna, La.: Pelican Publishing, 2003.

Bradshaw, Stanley O. *Flying Memories.* London: John Hamilton, 1935.

Brewer, Leighton. *Riders of the Sky.* New York: Houghton Mifflin, 1934.

Briand, Paul L. "A Fateful Tuesday, 1918: The Last Combat Flight of James Norman Hall." *Aerospace Historian* 11, No. 2 (April 1964).

Bright, Charles D. "Air Power in World War I, Sideshow or Decisive Factor?" *Aerospace Historian* 18, No. 2 (June 1971).

Briscoe, W. A., and H. R. Stanard. *Capt. Ball, V. C.* London: Herbert Jenkins, Ltd., 1938.

Brooks, John B. (as told to John Paul Hefferman). "How to Enter Flying Training (1915 Version)." *Aerospace Historian* 18, No. 3 (September 1971).

Brown, H. Hallock, and Arthur D. Dodds. *History of the 141st Aero Squadron in World War I.* N.p., 1968. Pamphlet, Lafayette Foundation Archives.

Bruce, John M. *British Aeroplanes, 1914–1918.* London: Putnam, 1957.

Bruno, Henry A. *Wings over America: The Inside Story of American Aviation.* New York: McBride, 1942.

Budiansky, Stephen. *Air Power: The Men, Machines, and Ideas That Revolutionized War from Kitty Hawk to the Gulf War II.* New York: Viking, 2004.

Burlingame, Roger. *General Billy Mitchell, Champion of Air Defense.* New York: McGraw-Hill, 1952.

Callander, Bruce D. "The Return of Kelly Field." *Air Force Magazine,* July 2001.

Callender, Gordon, Jr., and Gordon Callender, Sr., eds. *War in an Open Cockpit: The Wartime Letters of Captain Alvin Andrew Callender, R.A.F.* West Roxbury. Mass.: World War I Aero, 1978.

Campbell, Christopher. *Aces and Aircraft of World War I.* Poole, Dorset, U.K.: Blandford Press, Ltd., 1981.

Carisella, P. J., and James W. Ryan. *Who Killed the Red Baron?* Greenwich, Conn.: Fawcett Publications, 1969.

Casari, Robert B. *Encyclopedia of U.S. Military Aircraft: The WWI Production Program.* Chillecothe, Ohio: Casari, 1974.

———. *U.S. Military Aircraft 1908–1917.* Chillecothe, Ohio: Casari, 1973.

Chamier, John A. *Strategy and Air Strategy.* Washington, D.C.: U.S. Air Service, 1921. Pamphlet U-557.

Chandler, Charles D., and Frank P. Lahm. *How Our Army Got Wings.* New York: Ronald Press, 1943.

Chant, Christopher. *A Century of Triumph: A History of Aviation.* New York: Free Press, 2002.

Christy, Joe. *American Air Power: The First 75 Years.* Blue Ridge Summit, Pa.: Tab, 1982.

Christy, Joe, and Page Shamburger. *Aces and Planes of World War I.* New York: Sports Car Press, Ltd., 1968.

Clapp, Frederick Mortimer. *A History of the 17th Aero Squadron.* N.p., 1920. Pamphlet, Lafayette Foundation Archives.

Clark, Alan. *Aces High: The War in the Air over the Western Front.* New York: G. P. Putnam, 1973.

Clark, Don. *Wild Blue Yonder: An Air Epic.* Seattle: Superior Publishing, 1972.

Codman, Charles. *Contact.* Boston: Little, Brown, 1937.

Coffman, Edward M. *The War to End All Wars.* Madison: University of Wisconsin Press, 1986.

Colliers New Photographic History of the World War. New York: P. F. Collier & Son Publishers, 1919.

Collishaw, Raymond. *Air Command: A Fighter Pilot's Story.* London: William Kimber, 1973.

Congressional Record. Vol. 55, Part 1. 65th Cong., 1st sess., 2–24 April 1917.

Cooke, James J. *The U.S. Air Service in the Great War, 1917–1919.* Westport, Conn.: Praeger, 1996.

Coppens, Willy. *Flying in Flanders.* New York: Ace Books, 1971.

Cuneo, John R. *The Air Weapon, 1914–1916: Vol. II of Winged Mars.* Harrisburg, Pa.: Military Service Publishing, 1947.

———. *Winged Mars, Vol. 1: The German Air Weapon 1870–1914.* Harrisburg, Pa.: Military Service Publishing, 1942.

Dade, George C., and Frank Strand. *Picture History of Aviation on Long Island, 1908–1938.* Mineola, N.Y.: Dover Publications, 1989.

Daso, Dik Alan. *Hap Arnold and the Evolution of American Airpower.* Washington, D.C.: Smithsonian Press, 2000.

Davies, John. *The Legend of Hobey Baker.* Boston: Little, Brown, 1966.

Davis, Burke. *The Billy Mitchell Story.* Philadelphia: Chilton Book Company, 1969.

———. *War Bird: The Life and Times of Elliott White Springs.* Chapel Hill: University of North Carolina Press, 1987.

DeWeerd, Harvey A. *President Wilson Fights His War: World War I and the American Intervention.* New York: Macmillan, 1968.

Douglas, Sholto. *Combat and Command.* New York: Simon & Schuster, 1963.

Driggs, Laurence LaTourette. *Heroes of Aviation.* Boston: Little, Brown, 1936.

Duiven, Richard. "Royal Prussian Jagdgeschwader II." *Over the Front* 9, No. 3 (Fall 1994).

———. "Royal Prussian Jagdgeschwader II." *Over the Front* 9, No. 4 (Winter 1994).

———. "Royal Prussian Jagdgeschwader II." *Over the Front* 10, No. 1 (Spring 1995).

Dupre, Flint O. *Hap Arnold, Architect of American Air Power.* New York: Macmillan, 1972.

———. *The U.S. Air Force Biographical Dictionary.* New York: Franklin Watts, 1965.

Eaker, Ira C. "Air Chiefs Patrick and Fechet, As I Remember Them." *Aerospace Historian* 20, No. 2 (June 1973).

———. "'The Little Big One' or 'The Last of the First.'" *Aerospace Historian* 17, No. 4 (December 1970).

Eder, Jack R., ed. *Let's Go Where the Action Is! The Wartime Experience of Douglas Campbell.* Knightstown, Ind.: JaaRE Publishing, 1984.

Eisenhower, John S. D. *Yanks: The Epic Story of the American Army in World War I.* New York: Free Press, 2001.

Elliott, Stuart E. *Wooden Crates and Gallant Pilots.* Philadelphia: Dorrance & Co., 1974.

Ellis, John, and Michael Cox. *The World War I Databook.* London: Aurum Press, Ltd., 1993.

Emme, Eugene M., ed. *Two Hundred Years of Flight in America: A Bicentennial Survey.* San Diego: American Astronautical Society, 1977.

Falls, Cyril. *The Great War.* New York: Capricorn Books, 1959.

Feeny, William D. *In Their Honor.* New York: Duell, Sloan & Pearce, 1963.

Fitzsimons, Bernard. *Warplanes and Air Battles of World War I.* New York: Beekman House, 1973.

Flammer, Philip M. *The Vivid Air: The Lafayette Escadrille.* Athens: University of Georgia Press, 1981.

Fonck, Captain René. *Ace of Aces.* Garden City, N.Y.: Doubleday, 1967.

Foulois, Maj. Gen. Benjamin D. *From the Wright Brothers to the Astronauts: The Memoirs of Major General Benjamin D. Foulois.* New York: McGraw-Hill, 1968.

Franks, Norman. *Aircraft versus Aircraft: The Illustrated Story of Fighter Pilot Combat since 1914.* New York: Macmillan, 1986.

———. *American Aces of World War I.* Oxford: Osprey Publishing, Ltd., 2001.

———. *Dog-Fight: Aerial Tactics of the Aces of World War I.* London: Greenhill Books, 2003.

———. *Sopwith Camel Aces of World War I.* Oxford: Osprey Publishing, Ltd., 2003.

Franks, Norman L. R., Frank W. Bailey, and Russell Guest. *Above the Lines: The Aces and Fighter Units of the German Air Service.* London: Grub Street, 1993.

Fredericks, Pierce G. *The Great Adventure: America in the First World War.* New York: Ace Books, 1960.

Fredette, Lt. Col. Raymond H. "Luke: Watch for Burning Balloons." *Air Force Magazine,*September 1973.

———. *The Sky on Fire: The First Battle of Britain, 1917–1918.* New York: Harcourt Brace Jovanovich, 1966.

Funderburk, Thomas R. *The Early Birds of War: The Daring Pilots and Fighter Aeroplanes of World War I.* New York: Grosset & Dunlap, 1968.

———. *The Fighters: The Men and Machines of the First World War.* New York: Grosset & Dunlap, 1965.

Fussell, Paul. *The Great War and Modern Memory.* London: Oxford University Press, 1975.

Gamble, William B., ed. *History of Aeronautics.* New York: New York Public Library, 1938.

Gauvreau, E., and Lester Cohen. *Billy Mitchell.* New York: E. P. Dutton, 1942.

Gibbons, Floyd. *The Red Knight of Germany.* Garden City, N.Y.: Garden City Publishing, 1927.

Gibbs-Smith, Charles H. *Aviation: An Historical Survey from Its Origin to the End of World War II.* London: HMSO, 1985.

———. *A History of Flying.* New York: Praeger, 1954.

Gilbert, Martin. *Atlas of the First World War.* New York: Dorset Press, 1984.
———. *The First World War.* New York: Henry Holt, 1994.
Goldberg, Alfred, ed. *A History of the United States Air Force, 1907–1957.* Princeton: D. Van Nostrand, 1957.
Gordon, Arthur. *The American Heritage History of Flight.* New York: American Heritage, 1962.
Gorrell, Edgar S. *Individual Combat Records of American Pilots Serving with the RAF.* Vol. 13, Series B, and Vols. 1–20, Series E: *Squadron Histories Air Service.* Washington, D.C.: National Archives.
———. *The Measure of America's World War Aeronautical Effort.* Northfield, Vt.: Norwich University, 1940.
Grant, R. G. *Flight: 100 Years of Aviation.* New York: DK Publications, 2001.
Gray, Peter, and Owen Thetford. *German Aircraft of the First World War.* London: Putnam, 1962.
Green, William, and Gordon Swanborough, eds. *An Illustrated Anatomy of the World's Fighters: The Inside Story of Over 100 Classics in the Evolution of Fighter Aircraft.* St. Paul, Minn.: MBI Publishing, 2001.
Greenhous, Brereton. "Close Support Aircraft in World War I: The Counter Anti-Tank Role." *Aerospace Historian* 21, No. 2 (June 1974).
Grider, John MacGavock. *War Birds: Diary of an Unknown Aviator.* College Station: Texas A&M University Press, 1988.
Grinnell-Milne, Duncan. *Wind in the Wires.* Garden City, N.Y.: Doubleday, 1968.
Gudmundsson, Bruce I. *Stormtroop Tactics: Innovation in the German Army, 1914–1918.* New York: Praeger, 1989.
Gunston, Bill. *Fighters, 1914–1945.* New York: Crescent Books, 1978.
———. *World Encyclopedia of Aero Engines: All Major Aircraft Power Plants, from the Wright Brothers to the Present Day.* 4th ed. Newbury Park, Calif.: P. Stephens, Haynes North America, 1998.
Gurney, Gene. *Flying Aces of World War I.* New York: Scholastic Book Services, 1965.
Guttman, Jon. "148th Aero Squadron: The 148th Americans." In *Plumage of the Warbirds.* N.d. Pamphlet. Part 27 of a Series on Famous Squadrons, Their Aircraft and the Men WhoFlew Them. Aerospace Education Center Library, Little Rock, Ark.
Hall, James N. *High Adventure.* New York: Houghton Mifflin, 1918.
Hall, James N., and C. B. Nordhoff. *The Lafayette Flying Corps.* Vols. 1 & 2. New York: Houghton Mifflin, 1920.

Hall, Norman S. *The Balloon Buster.* New York: Bantam Books, 1966. Originally published Garden City, N.Y.: Doubleday, Doran, 1928.

Hallion, Richard P. *Rise of the Fighter Aircraft, 1914–1918.* Annapolis, Md.: Nautical & Aviation Publishing Company of America, 1984.

———. *Strike from the Sky: The History of Battlefield Air Attack, 1911–1945.* Washington, D.C.: Smithsonian Press, 1989.

———. *Taking Flight: Inventing the Aerial Age from Antiquity through the First World War.* Oxford: Oxford University Press, 2003.

Hamady, Theodore M. "Fighting Machines for the Air Service, AEF." *Air Power History,* Fall 2004.

Harris, John N. *Knights of the Air, Canadian Aces of WWI.* New York: St. Martin's Press, 1958.

Harris, Sherwood. "Coast to Coast in 12 Crashes." *American Heritage* 15 (October 1964).

Hartney, Harold E. *Up and At 'Em: War Memoirs of an American Ace.* Garden City, N.Y.: Doubleday, 1971.

Haulman, Dr. Daniel L., and Col. William C. Stancik, eds. *Aerial Victory Credits: World War I, World War II, Korea, and Vietnam.* Montgomery, Ala.: U.S. Air Force Historical Research Center, 1988.

Hegener, Henri. *Fokker—The Man and the Aircraft.* Los Angeles: Aero Publishers, 1961.

Higham, Robin. *Air Power: A Concise History.* New York: St. Martin's Press, 1972.

———. *100 Years of Air Power and Aviation.* College Station: Texas A&M University Press, 2003.

Holley, I. B., Jr. *Ideas and Weapons: Exploitation of the Aerial Weapon by the United States during World War I: A Study in the Technological Advance, Military Doctrine, and the Development of Weapons.* New Haven: Yale University Press, 1953.

Howard, Michael. *The First World War.* Oxford: Oxford University Press, 2002.

Hudson, James J. "The Air Knight of the Ozarks, Capt. Field E. Kindley." *American Aviation Historical Society Journal* 4, No. 4 (Winter 1959).

———. "Captain Field E. Kindley: Arkansas' Air Ace of the First World War." *Arkansas Historical Quarterly* 18, No. 2 (Summer 1959).

———. *Hostile Skies: A Combat History of the American Air Service in World War I.* Syracuse, N.Y.: Syracuse University Press, 1968.

———. *In Clouds of Glory: American Airmen Who Flew with the British during the Great War.* Fayetteville: University of Arkansas Press, 1990.

———. "Reed G. Landis: America's SE-5 Ace." *Aerospace Historian* 18, No. 4 (December 1971).

Huie, William B. *The Fight for Air Power.* New York: L. B. Fischer, 1942.

Hurley, Alfred F. *Billy Mitchell: Crusader for Air Power.* Bloomington: Indiana University Press, 1964.

Imrie, Alex. *Pictorial History of the German Air Service, 1914–1918.* Chicago: Henry Regnery, 1973.

Ingells, Douglas J. *They Tamed the Sky: The Triumph of American Aviation.* New York: D. Appleton-Century, 1947.

Irvin, Francis L. *"Spike": Francis L. "Spike" Irvin's War Diary.* Manhattan: Kansas State University/Aerospace Historian, 1974.

Ivie, Tom. "Kentucky's First Ace: The Story of Lt. Jesse Orin Creech." *Air Classics* 21, No. 5 (May 1986).

Jackson, Robert. *Fighter Pilots of World War I.* New York: St. Martin's Press, 1977.

Jacobs, Josephine Grider. *Marse John Goes to War: True Story of John MacGavock Grider, Lt., USAS, of No. 85 Squadron, RAF.* Memphis: Davis Printing, 1927.

Jane's Fighting Aircraft of World War I. London: Random House Group, Ltd., 2001. Originally published by Jane's Publishing Company, 1919.

Jefford, C. G. *RAF Squadrons: A Comprehensive Record of the Movement and Equipment of All RAF Squadrons and Their Antecedents since 1912.* United Kingdom: Airlife Publishing, 2001.

Johnson, Herbert A. *Wingless Eagle: U.S. Army Aviation through World War I.* Chapel Hill: University of North Carolina Press, 2001.

Johnson, J. E. *Full Circle: The Tactics of Air Fighting, 1914–1964.* New York: Ballantine, 1964.

Josephy, Alvin M., Jr., ed. *The American Heritage History of Flight.* New York: American Heritage, 1962.

Keegan, John. *The First World War.* New York: Alfred A. Knopf, 1999.

———. *An Illustrated History of the First World War.* New York: Alfred A. Knopf, 2001.

Keene, Jennifer D. *Doughboys, The Great War, and the Remaking of America.* Baltimore: Johns Hopkins University Press, 2001.

Kennedy, David M. *Over Here: The First World War and American Society.* Oxford: Oxford University Press, 1980.

Kennett, Lee. *The First Air War, 1914–1918.* New York: Free Press, 1991.

Kenney, Gen. George C. "A Flier's Journal." *American Heritage* 21, No. 1 (December 1969).

Kent, Zachary. *World War I: The War to End Wars.* Hillside, N.J.: Enslow Publishers, 1994.

Kilduff, Peter. *Richthofen: Beyond the Legend of the Red Baron.* New York: John Wiley & Sons, 1993.

King, Jere Clemens. *The First World War.* New York: Harper & Row, 1972.

Knight, Clayton. *Pilot's Luck.* Philadelphia: David McKay, 1929.

Kroll, H. D., ed. *Kelly Field in the Great War.* San Antonio: Santonio Printing, 1919.

Lahm, Col. Frank P. *The World War I Diary of Col. Frank P. Lahm: Air Service, A.E.F.* Maxwell AFB, Ala.: Historical Research Division, Air University, 1970.

Lavinia, Joe. *Von Richthofen and Brown.* New York: Award Books, 1971.

Lawson, Eric, and Jane Lawson. *The First Air Campaign, August 1914–November 1918.* Conshohocken, Pa.: Combined Books, 1996.

Lee, Arthur Gould. *No Parachute: A Fighter Pilot in World War I.* New York: Harper & Row, 1970.

Levine, Isaac D. *Mitchell, Pioneer of Air Power.* Cleveland: World Publishing, 1944.

Lewis, Cecil. *Sagittarius Rising.* Harrisburg, Pa.: Stackpole, 1963.

Lewis, Peter. *Squadron Histories, RFC, RNAS, RAF.* London: Putnam, 1959.

Lewis, W. David. *Eddie Rickenbacher: An American Hero in the Twentieth Century.* Baltimore: Johns Hopkins University Press, 2005.

Libby, Frederick. *Horses Don't Fly.* New York: Arcade Publishing, 2000.

Liddell Hart, Captain B. H. *The Real War, 1914–1918.* Boston: Little, Brown, 1930.

Lloyd, Nelson. *How We Went to War.* New York: Charles Scribner's Sons, 1919.

Longstreet, Stephen. *The Canvas Falcons: The Men and the Planes of World War I.* New York: Barnes & Noble Books, 1970.

Maitland, Lester J. *Knights of the Air.* Garden City, N.Y.: Doubleday, Doran, 1929.

Maitland, Norman. *The Royal Air Force in the World War.* New York: Doubleday, Doran, 1929.

Mannock, Edward "Mick." *Personal Diary of Mick Mannock.* London: Neville Spearman,1966.

Marshall, S. L. A. *World War I.* New York: American Heritage, 1964.

Mason, Francis K. *Aces of the Air.* New York: Mayflower Books, 1981.

Mason, Herbert Molloy, Jr. *High Flew the Falcons: The French Aces of World War I.* Philadelphia: J. B. Lippincott, 1965.

———. *The Lafayette Escadrille.* New York: Random House, 1964.

Maurer, Maurer, ed. *The U.S. Air Service in World War I.* 4 vols. Washington, D.C.: Office of Air Force History, 1978–79.

McCaffrey, Dan. *Billy Bishop: Canadian Hero.* Halifax, N.S., Canada: Formac Publishing, 1990.

McConnell, James R. *Flying for France.* New York: Grosset & Dunlap, 1916.

McCudden, Maj. James T. B. *Flying Fury: Five Years in the Royal Flying Corps.* Garden City, N.Y.: Doubleday, 1968.

McKee, Alexander. *The Friendless Sky: The Story of Air Combat in World War I.* New York: William Morrow, 1964.

Meijering, Piet Hein. *Signed with Their Honor: Air Chivalry during Two World Wars.* New York: Paragon House, 1988.

Meyer, Corky. "Flying the D. VII: A Fabulous Fokker Fighter." *Flight Journal* 8, No. 5 (October 2003).

Middlebrook, Martin. *The Kaiser's Battle.* London: Penguin Books, Ltd., 1978.

Milbank, Jeremiah, Jr. *The First Century of Flight in America: An Introductory Survey.* Princeton: Princeton University Press, 1943.

Miller, Roger G. *Billy Mitchell: The Stormy Petrel of the Air.* Washington, D.C.: Air Force History and Museums Program, 2004.

Millett, Alan R., and Peter Maslowski. *For the Common Defense: A Military History of the United States of America.* New York: Free Press, 1984.

Mitchell, Ruth. *My Brother Bill: A Biography of General Mitchell.* New York: Harcourt, Brace, 1953.

Mitchell, William. *Memoirs of World War I.* New York: Random House, 1960.

Molson, K. M. "First International Air Race: August 1919, New York–Toronto." *American Aviation Historical Society Journal* 16, No. 4 (Winter 1971).

Moore, William E., and James Crussell. *U.S. Official Pictures of the World War: Showing America's Participation, Selected from the Official Files of the War Department.* Washington, D.C.: Pictorial Bureau, War Department, 1920.

Morrow, John H., Jr. *The Great War in the Air: Military Aviation from 1909 to 1921.* Washington, D.C.: Smithsonian Press, 1992.

Morrow, John H., Jr., and Earl Rogers, eds. *A Yankee in the RAF: The World War I Letters of Captain Bogart Rogers.* Lawrence: University Press of Kansas, 1996.

Morse, Edwin W. *The Vanguard of American Volunteers.* New York: Charles Scribner's Sons, 1919.

Munson, Kenneth. *Fighters 1914–19.* New York: Macmillan, 1968.

Neumann, Maj. Georg Paul, ed. *The German Air Force in the Great War.* Translated by J. E. Gurdon. Portway, Bath, U.K.: Cedric Chivers, Ltd., 1969.

Niccoli, Riccardo. *Book of Flight: From the Flying Machines of Leonardo da Vinci to the Conquest of Space*. New York: Michael Friedman Publishing Group, 2002.

"1919 Manufacturers' Banquet: Recalling the Industry's Achievements in World War I." *Air Power History* 36 (Summer 1989).

Nordhoff, C. B., and James N. Hall. *Falcons of France*. Boston: Little, Brown, 1936.

Norman, Aaron. *The Great Air War*. New York: Macmillan, 1968.

Norris, Geoffrey A. *The Royal Flying Corps, A History*. London: Frederick Muller, Ltd., 1965.

148th Aero Squadron Bulletins. Lafayette FoundationArchives. [These bulletins were used by the 148th veterans to keep members informed in the postwar years.]

Parsons, Edwin C. *The Great Adventure*. Garden City, N.Y.: Doubleday, Doran, 1937.

———. *I Flew with the Lafayette Escadrille*. Indianapolis: E. C. Seale Co., 1963.

Paschall, Rod. *The Defeat of Imperial Germany, 1917–1918*. Chapel Hill, N.C.: Algonquin Books, 1989.

Patrick, Maj. Gen. Mason M. *The United States in the Air*. New York: Doubleday, Doran, 1928.

———. *United States Army in the World War 1917–1918: Reports of Commander-in-Chief, AEF, Staff Sections and Services*. Washington, D.C.: Historical Division, Department of the Army, U.S. Government Printing Office, 1948.

Pitt, Barrie. *1918: The Last Act*. New York: W. W. Norton, 1962.

Platt, Frank C. *Great Battles of World War I: In the Air*. New York: Weathervane Books, 1966.

Pudney, John. *The Camel Fighter*. London: Hamish Hamilton, Ltd., 1969.

Puglisi, William R. "Jagdstaffel 5." *Cross & Cockade Journal* 1, No. 3 (Autumn 1960).

Rawlings, John D. R. *The History of the Royal Air Force*. New York: Crescent Books, 1984.

Reynolds, Quentin. *They Fought for the Sky*. New York: Bantam Books, 1957.

Richthofen, Manfred Freiherr von. *The Red Baron*. Translated by Peter Kilduff. Garden City, N.Y.: Doubleday, 1969.

Rickenbacker, Capt. Eddie V. *Fighting the Flying Circus*. Garden City, N.Y.: Doubleday, 1965. Reprint, Chicago: R. R. Donnelley & Sons, 1997.

———. *Rickenbacker*. Englewood Cliffs, N.J.: Prentice-Hall, 1967.

Robertson, Bruce, ed. *Air Aces of the 1914–1918 War*. Los Angeles: Aero Publishers, 1962.

Robie, William. *For the Greatest Achievement: A History of the Aero Club of America and the National Aeronautics Association.* Washington, D.C.: Smithsonian Press,1993.

Robinson, Douglas. *Giants in the Sky.* Seattle: University of Washington Press, 1973.

Rochford, Leonard H. *I Chose the Sky.* London: William Kimber & Co., Ltd., 1977.

Roger, Don T. "1st Lieut. Raymond Watts: Another of the War Birds." *Cross & Cockade Journal* 5, No. 3 (Autumn 1964).

Roseberry, Cecil R. *The Challenging Skies: The Colorful Story of Aviation's Most Exciting Years, 1919–1939.* Garden City, N.Y.: Doubleday, 1966.

Rowe, Josiah P. *Letters from a World War I Aviator.* Boston: Sinclaire, 1986.

Saunders, Hilary St. George. *Per Ardua: The Rise of British Air Power, 1911–1939.* London: Oxford University Press, 1945.

Scamehorn, Howard L. *Balloons to Jets: A Century of Aeronautics in Illinois, 1855–1955.* Chicago: Henry Regnery, 1957.

Schurmacher, Emile C. *Richthofen, the Red Baron.* New York: Warner Paperback Library, 1970.

Sharp, John R. *The Aces, WW I.* Sioux Falls, Iowa: Privately printed, 1955.

Shea, William L., and Earl J. Hess. *Pea Ridge: Civil War Campaign in the West.* Chapel Hill: University of North Carolina Press, 1992.

Sherman, William C. *Air Warfare.* New York: Ronald Press, 1926.

Simkins, Peter. *Air Fighting 1914–18.* London: Imperial War Museum, 1978.

Sims, Edward H. *Fighter Tactics and Strategy, 1914–1970.* New York: Harper & Row, 1972.

Skelton, Marvin L. "Flight 'C,' 148th Aero Squadron, USAS." *Cross & Cockade Journal* 17, No. 3 (Autumn 1976).

Sky Fighters of World War I. Greenwich, Conn.: Fawcett Publishers, Inc., 1961.

Sloan, James J. "The 148th American." *American Aviation Historical Society Journal* 4, No. 4 (Winter 1959).

———. *Wings of Honor: American Airmen in World War I.* Atglen, Pa.: Schiffer, 1994.

Smith, Page. *America Enters the World: A People's History of the Progressive Era and World War I.* New York: McGraw-Hill, 1985.

Smithers, A. J. *Wonder Aces of the Air: The Flying Heroes of the Great War.* London: Gordon & Cremonesi, 1980.

Spaight, James M. *British Aeroplanes, 1914–1918.* London: Longman, 1925.

Spick, Mike. *The Ace Factor: Air Combat and the Role of Situational Awareness.* Shrewsbury, U.K.: Airlife Publishing, 1988.

Springs, Elliott W. *Above the Bright Blue Sky.* London: John Hamilton, 1935.

———. *Nocturne Militaire.* New York: George H. Doran, 1927.

Stallings, Lawrence. *The Doughboys.* New York: Harper & Row, 1963.

Stokesbury, James L. *A Short History of Air Power.* New York: William Morrow, 1986.

———. *A Short History of World War I.* New York: William Morrow, 1981.

Strachan, Hew. *The First World War.* New York: Viking Penguin, 2004.

Strachan, Hew, ed. *World War I: A History.* Oxford: Oxford University Press, 1998.

Sumner, Ian. *German Air Forces 1914–18.* Oxford: Osprey Publishing Ltd., 2005.

Sweetser, Arthur. *The American Air Service.* New York: D. Appleton, 1919.

Taylor, John W. R., and P. J. R. Moyes. *Pictorial History of the R.A.F.* New York: Arco Publishing, 1968.

Taylor, John W. R., and Kenneth Munson. *History of Aviation.* New York: Crown, 1972.

Taylor, William P. *Items by William P. Taylor.* Falls Church, Va.: Ajay Enterprises,1977.

Taylor, William P., and Francis L. Irvin. *History of the 148th Aero Squadron.* Lancaster, S.C.: Tri-County Publishers, 1957.

Thayer, Lucien H. *America's First Eagles.* San Jose, Calif.: Champlin Fighter Museum Press, 1983.

Thetford, Owen. *Aircraft of the Royal Air Force, 1918–58.* London: Putnam, 1957.

Thompson, Dorothy B. "An Arkansas War Bird." Unpublished manuscript, 2 December 1993.

Tichnor, Caroline, ed. *New England Aviators, 1914–1919.* New York: Houghton Mifflin, 1919.

Titler, Dale M. *The Day the Red Baron Died.* New York: Walker & Co., 1970.

Toland, John. *No Man's Land: 1918: The Last Year of the Great War.* Garden City, N.Y.: Doubleday, 1980.

Toliver, Col. Raymond F., and Trevor J. Constable. *Fighter Aces.* New York: Macmillan, 1965.

Torr, James D., ed. *World War I Primary Sources.* San Diego: Lucent Books, 2002.

Toulmin, Harry A. *Air Service, American Expeditionary Force, 1918.* New York: D. Van Nostrand, 1927.

Tretler, David A. *Opportunity Missed: Congressional Reorganization of the Army Air Service 1917–1920.* Wright Patterson AFB, Ohio: Air Force Institute of Technology, 1978.

Udet, Ernst. *Ace of the Iron Cross.* Garden City, N.Y.: Doubleday, 1970.

U.S. Air Force. "AF Aces 1918–1972." *Air Force Fact Sheet 73–7,* May 1973.

U.S. Air Service. "Report on First Transcontinental Reliability and Endurance Test." *Air Service Information Circular* 1, 5 February 1920. [Various Air Service *Circulars* were issued after World War I.]

U.S. Congress, House of Representatives. *Hearing.* Subcommittee on Aviation, Committee on Military Affairs. 66th Cong., 2d sess., 12 December 1919.

———. *Operations of the U.S. Air Service.* Hearings of the Select Committee of Inquiry, Parts 1–6. Washington, D.C.: Government Printing Office, 1926.

Villard, Henry S. *Contact! The Story of the Early Birds.* Washington, D.C.: Smithsonian Press, 1987.

Wagner, Ray. *America's Combat Planes.* Garden City, N.Y.: Hanover House, 1960.

Weigley, Russell F. *The American Way of War: A History of United States Military Strategy and Policy.* New York: Macmillan, 1973.

———. *History of the United States Army.* New York: Macmillan, 1967.

White, Robert P. *Mason Patrick and the Fight for Air Service Independence.* Washington, D.C.: Smithsonian Press, 2001.

Whitehouse, Arch. *Decisive Air Battles of the First World War.* New York: Duell, Sloan & Pearce, 1963.

———. *Heroes and Legends of World War I.* Garden City, N.Y.: Doubleday, 1964.

———. *Legion of the Lafayette.* Garden City, N.Y.: Doubleday, 1962.

———. *The Years of the Sky Kings.* Garden City, N.Y.: Doubleday, 1959.

Williams, T. Harry. *The History of American Wars: From Colonial Times to World War I.* New York: Alfred A. Knopf, 1981.

Winchester, Barry. *Beyond the Tumult.* New York: Charles Scribner's Sons, 1971.

Woodhouse, Jack. *The War in the Air, 1914–1918.* London: Almark Publishing, 1974.

Woodman, Harry. *Early Aircraft Armament: The Aeroplane and Its Gun up to 1918.* Washington, D.C.: Smithsonian Press, 1989.

Woolley, Charles, with Bill Crawford. *Echoes of Eagles: A Son's Search for His Father and the Legacy of America's First Fighter Pilots.* New York: Dutton, 2003.

Wukovits, John F. *World War I Flying Aces.* San Diego: Lucent Books, 2002.

Yeates, V. M. *Winged Victory.* London: Jonathan Cape, 1934; reprint, 1961.

Zabecki, David T. *Steel Wind: Colonel Georg Bruchmüller and the Birth of Modern Artillery.* Westport, Conn.: Praeger, 1994.

Zieger, Robert H. *America's Great War: World War I and the American Experience.* Lanham, Md.: Rowman & Littlefield, 2000.

Index

Numbers in *italics* refer to illustrations.

ISBN-13: 978-1-58544-554-7
ISBN-10: 1-58544-554-1
52995
9 781585 445547